T0407108

Dangerous Jokes

Dangerous Jokes

How Racism and Sexism Weaponize Humor

CLAIRE HORISK

OXFORD
UNIVERSITY PRESS

OXFORD
UNIVERSITY PRESS

Oxford University Press is a department of the University of Oxford. It furthers
the University's objective of excellence in research, scholarship, and education
by publishing worldwide. Oxford is a registered trade mark of Oxford University
Press in the UK and certain other countries.

Published in the United States of America by Oxford University Press
198 Madison Avenue, New York, NY 10016, United States of America.

© Oxford University Press 2024

Library of Congress Cataloging-in-Publication Data
Names: Horisk, Claire, author.
Title: Dangerous jokes : how racism and sexism weaponize humor /
Claire Horisk.
Description: New York : Oxford University Press, 2024. |
Includes bibliographical references and index.
Identifiers: LCCN 2023040840 (print) | LCCN 2023040841 (ebook) |
ISBN 9780197691496 (hardback) | ISBN 9780197691502 (epub)
Subjects: LCSH: Wit and humor—Psychological aspects. | Racism. | Sexism. |
Stereotypes (Social psychology)
Classification: LCC PN6149.P5 H675 2024 (print) | LCC PN6149.P5 (ebook) |
DDC 809.7—dc23/eng/20231001
LC record available at https://lccn.loc.gov/2023040840
LC ebook record available at https://lccn.loc.gov/2023040841

DOI: 10.1093/oso/9780197691496.001.0001

Printed by Integrated Books International, United States of America

For Ellen

Contents

Note to Readers

In the endnotes I assume the reader has background knowledge of my field, is familiar with specialized terminology, and cares about philosophy of language as it is practiced by academics. If you have no particular interest in contemporary philosophy of language, I encourage you to skip the notes; they will bore the socks off a general reader.

Preface

Introduction

In this preface, I will talk about the language I use in the book and some of the decisions I made about what to exclude. While the book is about demeaning language, I have done my level best to write it without belittling anyone in the process. Furthermore, in the hope of making the book accessible to a broader audience, I have tried to explain how derogatory jokes work without overly relying on the technical apparatus of my field, and my academic peers may find less detail and rigor than they would like.

Why this book about jokes contains so few jokes

You might expect a book about derogatory jokes to include jokes. But since my primary interest is in jokes that reinforce unjust social hierarchies, including examples raises ethical issues. More often than not, I talk about jokes rather than quoting them in their entirety.

Philosophers who work on slurs have also struggled with whether or not they should include examples. In general, philosophy of language and linguistics distinguish between using a word and mentioning it. Compare these sentences:

Dublin is the capital city of Ireland

and

'Dublin' has six letters.

The first sentence *uses* a word to name a city; the second *mentions* a word to talk about the word itself, rather than about the city. The single quotation marks in the second sentence indicate that the word is mentioned. If the use/mention distinction applies to slurs, then it might be acceptable to mention a slur to talk about it, at least sometimes, even if we should not use a slur to refer to or to describe a person (Hornsby 2001). Indeed, some philosophers go further; not only may we mention slurs, we should mention actual, present-day, slurs—not slurs from previous eras that are no longer in use, except in historical fiction—so that we do not overlook their raw power (Camp 2013). Others believe that slurs are unusual in that the insult somehow leaps out of quotation marks (Anderson and Lepore 2013); if this is correct, then the standard distinction between use and mention does not apply to slurs. Indeed, there are philosophers who avoid mentioning specific examples at all (e.g., Hedger 2012).

I mention demeaning jokes in this book, but I have kept the number of jokes that I mention in full to a minimum. We might worry that we cannot mention slurs without insult, but there's no reason to suppose we cannot mention jokes without insult. But while most of us already know the slurs that are discussed in scholarly work about slurs, if I quote, say, a transphobic joke in its entirety, I may be teaching the joke to someone who will use it as ammunition against transgender people. I could not avoid giving the entire text of at least a few dangerous jokes, because I needed to illustrate a point. I hope readers of this book learn why these jokes are harmful, and choose not to retell them.

Slurs and expletives in court transcripts

In the book, I discuss court cases where the plaintiffs sued for hostile environment harassment, and where derogatory humor was an element of the harassment. In these cases, the work environment often involved racist slurs as well. Examples like these raise a difficult question for scholars—should the slurs be given verbatim in quotations, or should the slurs be specified by giving the first letter only, allowing the reader to fill in for themselves? These words convey contempt and hatred; they are used to dehumanize people, and they form part of a deeply harmful network of oppression that has at times included enslavement and that is still a systematic wrong that shapes the society in which I live. As I have said, some people believe that there are slurs that are so offensive that they ought not appear even in quotations; they are not part of the news that is "fit to print." On the other hand, omitting slurs from court transcripts screens out an element of the racism that formed the experience of the plaintiffs, and if we wish to understand and combat racism, it might be better to report the horrible truth.

The legal opinions that are relevant to my argument fall on both sides of this question, with some courts eliding slurs, and others typing them out in full. I have chosen to elide racial slurs, even if they were written in full in primary sources. Where I am discussing the slur and its effects, but not quoting from another source, I have chosen to describe the word rather than to write it out. Some legal opinions elide both expletives and slurs, and these I quote verbatim. However, where I am discussing an expletive and not quoting from another source, I write it out in full. Expletives like 'fuck' and 'damn' have shock value, but treating them in the same way as slurs undermines an important distinction between expletives and slurs, namely that expletives do not encode contempt and hatred for other human beings.

Professional comedy

This book is focused on humor in conversation with other people, not on professional comedy of the sort to be found in comedy clubs and on television. I mention professional comedians, and their opinions about how humor works, but the arguments I give about humor in conversation do not directly apply to professional comedy. Comedy, like other professions, has its own purposes and norms. For example, professional comedians are performers, and the expectations of the audience differ from the expectations when two people are conversing. Often in academic books, authors exclude something from the scope of their project, saying that they will tackle it on another occasion. But truth be told, I do not know enough about professional comedy to say anything worthwhile about it, and I do not enjoy professional comedy enough to learn what I would need to know to give an opinion of any value. In this case, I leave it to someone else to tackle on another occasion.

The terms 'speaker' and 'hearer'

Many deaf and hard of hearing people conduct conversations without auditory information, using languages like American Sign Language or Brazilian Sign Language; these are rich, complete natural languages with grammars and vocabularies that are distinct from each other and from the oral languages that are used in the same geographical areas. With sign languages, the equivalent of hearing someone is seeing them talk, i.e., seeing them communicate with the movements of their hands, bodies, and faces. While sign languages and oral languages differ in the physical skills and sensory capacities that they employ, there is no reason to suppose that they differ in other ways—e.g., with regard to how meaning can be conveyed literally or non-literally.

In English, the term 'hearing' usually excludes people who do not use auditory processes for communication. The Deaf community in the United States uses the American Sign Language term 'hearing' to refer to people who use auditory capacities for linguistic communication, and American Sign Language has different signs for listening with the ears and listening with the eyes. However, I will follow the conventions of my field, where the terms 'hearers', 'listeners', and 'audiences' apply to people who are lipreading or attending to sign language as well as those using auditory processes. Similarly, I use 'speaker' to include people who are using sign language. I recognize that using 'speaker' and 'hearer' to cover both oral and signed language treats oral languages as the norm, and thus the conventions of my field raise concerns about ableism and inclusion.

Singular 'they'

As a writer, I was trained to avoid using 'they' as a singular pronoun, even though it was widely used in speech, and in my earlier work I used 'he or she' instead. But 'he or she' assumes that gender is binary, and thus does not include everyone. Consequently, standards for writers about singular 'they' have shifted, as they should (Baron 2018).

A note for philosophers and linguists

I am greatly indebted to philosophers and linguists who have written about humor, as well as many who have written about a host of other topics—pragmatics, ethics, action, and omission, to name a few. Their work has informed my thinking about the issues I discuss. But only some of these people are mentioned in this book. There are many others whose work has influenced me, but whose research is not directly discussed. If you are one of these people, please know that I feel your pain; I am bummed if I read a paper or book on a topic on which I have published something significant, and do not find myself cited. The difficulty is that the book is intended to be accessible, and indeed enjoyable, for general readers who have no background in philosophy or linguistics, and that audience is not interested in detailed discussions of the existing literature of the kind expected in dissertations and monographs. All the bits of this book that would have been boring for such an audience are included in a long document on my hard drive. My discussion of your work, I am afraid, is there too. I plan to publish at least some of this material elsewhere in scholarly venues.

One downside of writing for a broader audience is that my field is as abstruse as people think, and, I regret to say, it is often dull as well; just ask my dad, who has tried to read my journal articles, but finds them impenetrable. I tried to write this book in a way that is both fully comprehensible to non-philosophers and that meets the standards of my scholarly peers. This is a more or less impossible goal, however, and on the whole, I have favored accessibility over philosophical precision, argumentative detail, and scholarly completeness.

Acknowledgments

I have talked to many people about this book since I began working on it, and given how long ago that is, and the vagaries of memory, I am sure to forget to thank some of them for their insight and their time. Furthermore, given my wish to understand people's everyday experience of derogatory humor, I don't know everyone's name. There were, for example, several cab drivers and a cashier at a local supermarket. My memory allows me to thank specifically Luvell Anderson, Louise Antony, Brian Ball, Dean Bennett, Jordan Booker, Kenny Boyce, David Braun, Elisabeth Camp, Jonathan Cohen, Alex Czopp, Frankie Devlin, Mitchell Farris, M. Folescu, Thomas E. Ford, Sara Gable, Michael Glanzberg, Sandy Goldberg, Mitch Green, Peter Hanks, Sally Haslanger, Heather Hatton, Reina Hayaki, Marta Heckel, Vaida Juma, Ted Koditschek, Candace Korasick, Melody Kroll, Alison Lacarrubba, Manuel Leal, Sarah-Jane Leslie, Lauren Leydon-Hardy, Bill Lycan, Michael Lynch, Ofra Magidor, Ishani Maitra, Bruce McClure, Mary Kate McGowan, Matt McGrath, Bennett McNulty, Andrew Melnyk, Andrew Mills, Jeanette Porter, Alex Radulescu, Wayne Riggs, Kate Ritchie, Gillian Russell, Mandy Simons, Elizabeth Allyn Smith, Rob Stainton, Karen Stohr, Isidora Stojanovic, David Taylor, Leah Thomsen, Valerie Tiberius, Lynne Tirrell, Judith Tonhauser, Peter Vallentyne, Paul Weirich, Tim Williamson, Al Willsey, Steve Yablo, the graduate students in my seminars at the University of Missouri, and the undergraduates in Philosophy and Gender in Fall 2019 and in Philosophy of Language in Spring 2022. Thanks also to Alice Nyarko, who worked as a research assistant in the last stages of manuscript preparation. Some of these people read drafts and gave extensive comments; this book is better because of them. It has further benefited from anonymous reviewers for Oxford University Press. I also wish to thank the staff of the Campus Writing Program at the University of Missouri, especially Christy Goldsmith; and audiences at the University of Minnesota Twin Cities, the University of Connecticut, Northwestern University, Shan'xi University, and the ILCLI International Workshop on Semantics, Pragmatics, and Rhetoric in Donostia. Any remaining silly arguments, oversights, and mistakes are entirely my own.

The University of Missouri Research Council and the College of Arts and Sciences provided research leave for this project; the Center for Arts and Humanities and the Provost's Great Books Program provided teaching release. The Campus Writing Program hosted an overnight writing retreat at which I grappled with drafting the last chapter.

The University of Missouri System also provided a scholarship for the Faculty Success Program offered by the National Center for Faculty Development & Diversity. My small group members during the program— Sabrina Burmeister, Michaele Ferguson, and Lindsay Schoenbohm—have turned into my FSP Posse; they have been a writing support group, pep squad, and source of wisdom for four years and counting.

I also want to thank the people who have cared for my children while I worked. A room of one's own is necessary, but it's of no use without a nanny or an excellent daycare. I owe a particular debt to Celina Castleman and Heather Dowling, who were our nannies during the COVID-19 pandemic, and the staff at the Child Development Lab at the University of Missouri, especially Beth Geyer, Kristin Heim, Frank Geyer, Ariel Robinson, Erin Angst Baker, Susan Garton, Eva Morrow, Laura Hays, Julia Moore, Logan Ferguson, LeAnn Sapp, Jenrose Malloy, Kaylee Cramer, Kait Tillin, Kailyn Watts, and Britney Enochs, as well as the myriad of students, floaters, and substitutes who worked at CDL with my children.

I am grateful to my colleagues in the Philosophy Department at the University of Missouri. Robert Johnson, Peter Markie, Matt McGrath, Andrew Melnyk, Peter Vallentyne, and Paul Weirich deserve particular mention, for their encouragement, mentoring, and support as I grew from a recently minted PhD to the faculty member that I am now. Andrew once described departmental colleagues as a family without the bonds of blood and affection; but with some colleagues, bonds of affection are not out of the question.

Thank you also to Bill Child, Mike Martin, and Tim Williamson, who launched me on this philosophical journey when I was an undergraduate at the University of Oxford, and the faculty at the University of North Carolina at Chapel Hill, most notably my PhD advisor Louise Antony.

The friendships I made while a graduate student at the University of North Carolina continue to sustain me in so many ways. I particularly want to mention Andrew Mills, Wayne Riggs, and Valerie Tiberius, as well as my very dear friend Karen Stohr. My friend Wendy Nankas is no longer with us, and my life is poorer because of her absence.

My family of origin has provided much love and support throughout my life. My parents, Eileen and Frank Horisk, may have had some doubts about the wisdom of my trying to become a professional philosopher, but kept it to themselves; and along with my siblings, Una Bennett, Catherine Devlin, and Brian Horisk, they have been there for me in good times and bad. The family members who have become mine through marriage also deserve special mention, especially my sisters-in-law Anne Adams, Kathryn Cocroft, and Nancy Cocroft, and my nephew Abraham Adams. I honor the memory of my sister-in-law Clare Horisk.

Expressing the depths of love and gratitude I feel toward Rex Cocroft would take me well beyond the word limit for this entire book. He is not only my better half; I am a better person because of him. He continues to have great compassion for my nerves, which have been his constant companion for more than twenty years. He is the kindest, sweetest, funniest daddy that our children could have. This book has benefited from the endless conversations I have had with him about the issues, and his gifts as a writer have been invaluable. Undoubtedly, it would be a better book if I had given him a freer hand.

The contribution of my children, Ellen, Lydia, and Jesse, is less direct, but no less necessary; along with Rex, they are the foundation of my reason to live.

This book would be a monograph if it were not for a suggestion from my editor, Peter Ohlin, at Oxford University Press, that I write a crossover book instead. I had very little idea of what a crossover book was, or should be, and I appreciate Peter's support, guidance, and patience as I transformed my manuscript.

1

Why joking matters

Introduction

Troy Swinton took a job at a cardboard company in Woodinville, Washington, in 1996; he was the only African American among 140 employees. A supervisor in another department, Jon Fosdick, was a frequent visitor in the shipping department, where Swinton worked. A subsequent legal opinion reports that Fosdick "while there, would regularly tell racially offensive jokes in the presence of Swinton and others. . . . According to Swinton, Fosdick began telling such jokes soon after [Swinton] arrived at the company and continued 'whenever he felt like it, all the time'" (*Swinton v. Potomac Corporation* 2001).

Swinton needed the job, and the situation was delicate; his pregnant fiancée was Fosdick's niece, and she wanted Swinton to preserve family harmony. He put up with Fosdick's behavior for a while. But after about six months, he had had enough, and he quit in February 1997: "[H]e was 'fed up . . . with all the name-calling. I was angry. I was mad. I was upset. I was frustrated. I just couldn't take it no more. I had to get out of there'" (*Swinton v. Potomac Corporation* 2001). Swinton filed suit against the company, and at trial, the jury returned a verdict for Swinton and awarded compensatory damages for back pay and emotional distress, as well as one million dollars in punitive damages, an award that was upheld on appeal.

Federal courts in the United States are not alone in holding that jokes like the ones told by Fosdick cause real and significant harms. To take two examples, under British law, jokes can count as a form of harassment, and thus as discrimination under the Equality Act, and Australian law specifies that, in some circumstances, jokes and banter can amount to unlawful discrimination, sexual harassment, or racial hatred. But although the courts are in broad agreement, public opinion is divided.

Indeed, in sharp contrast with other forms of derogatory speech such as racial slurs and hate speech, there is open, and genuine, disagreement about whether there is anything wrong with telling derogatory jokes. Many people think that jokes, because they are *just jokes*, are beyond reproach. On the contrary, in this book I will argue that telling racist jokes and making racist jocular remarks is wrong, but that jokes do not work in the same way as racist statements, and that the distinctive properties of jokes allow them to do even more harm than racist statements. The same holds true for other demeaning jokes, such as jokes about sex and ethnicity. I will argue that jokes like this matter, even in casual conversations outside the workplace, where there is no possibility of legal action.

Jokes have unusual qualities that make them different from other kinds of derogatory speech. The differences are so striking that people often defend themselves when they say something racist or sexist by declaring that it was just a joke. For example, when the actor Roseanne Barr was accused of racism in 2018, in a tweet about Valerie Jarrett, President Obama's former advisor, her first line of defense was a further tweet, saying "It's a joke—." People who would not dream of making a racist *statement* may be comfortable making a racist *joke*. The comedian Trevor Noah, for example, himself born of mixed race in apartheid-era South Africa, is sensitive to issues concerning race but has made racist jokes, such as a joke about Australian Aborigine women told during a standup routine in 2013 (McGowan 2018). The idea that jokes do less harm than statements underlies the defense of sexist, racist, and ethnic jokes as "just jokes," or of the joker "as just joking around"; and defenses like Barr's often appear in apologies given by public figures who make such a joke.

Jokes are the last stronghold for discriminatory speech, which may explain why humor is one of the most widely experienced types of verbal discrimination. For example, a 2019 survey in Britain found that more than 50% of people from ethnic minorities had been subjected to racist comments made to sound like a joke (Ashe, Borkowska, and Nazroo 2019; Booth 2019). People use slurs, but they know it's offensive. They express stereotypes, but often preface them with 'I shouldn't say this . . .'. But people wouldn't defend racist or sexist or transphobic speech as a joke if they didn't think that there is something special and different about jokes, something that insulates jokes from criticism. I completely agree that jokes are different; but as I will argue in this book, the unusual properties of jokes make them particularly dangerous.

Jokes are funny peculiar

The defense offered by Barr and others—"It's just a joke"—begins with a foundation of truth; jokes have properties that other speech does not have.

One very salient difference is that many derogatory jokes do not explicitly express derogatory ideas.[1] The jokes told by Fosdick in Swinton's presence include the following:

> Why don't black people like aspirin? Because they're white, and they work.
> (*Swinton v. Potomac Corporation* 2001)

As speakers of the English language, and competent members of our cultural milieu, we can see that Fosdick's joke communicates a highly derogatory and dangerous stereotype about Black people—that they do not work. But how does it communicate that pernicious stereotype? It doesn't come right out and say it in so many words. In fact, it doesn't state any negative claims about the targeted group at all; there is nothing wrong with disliking aspirin, nor with disliking something because of its color and its efficacy.

Another salient quality of jokes is that there is no expectation that a person will tell the truth when telling a joke. Because of this quality, it is often supposed that we may say things jokingly that we may not say seriously. In *Pride and Prejudice*, when Elizabeth Bennet gives her beloved sister Jane the surprising news that she is engaged to Mr. Darcy, Jane says, "You are joking, Lizzy. This cannot be!—engaged to Mr. Darcy! No, no, you shall not deceive me." In Elizabeth's reply, she tells her, "I am in earnest. I speak nothing but the truth" (Austen 2006a, 413–14; first published 1813). A common thought, dressed up in technical language, is that jokes have a different communicative intent than statements or assertions. We might think, simplistically, that assertions are intended to communicate information, whereas jokes are intended to make us laugh. We are not meant to believe any statements that appear in the joke—we are not meant to believe, for example, that a chicken crossed the road, or that a man found a fly in his soup. The thought goes that since they are just jokes—mini-fictions told with humorous intent—there could be no real harm in them, or at least, there is less harm in a joke than in an explicit statement of the same stereotype.

The thought that jokes are somehow less harmful than assertions is extended from formulaic jokes—such as narratives with punchlines—to defenses of derogatory jocular remarks as "just jokes." Consider, for example, how the shock jock Don Imus defended his description of a women's basketball team as "nappy-headed ho's" on his radio show as "some idiot comment meant to be amusing" (Carr 2007a); and how the shock jock Howard Stern suggested that

Imus should have replied to his critics by saying, "[Fuck] you, it's a joke" (Faber 2007). Imus's comment—unlike the aspirin joke told by Fosdick—openly expressed a demeaning claim about these basketball players; so why might he and Stern think that categorizing this piece of misogynoir[2] as a joke makes it inoffensive, or at least, less offensive than a racist assertion?[3] Perhaps it is because as a general rule the literal content of a joke is not meant to be believed; perhaps it is because of the humorous intent; perhaps it is for some other reason.

People who think that derogatory joking is acceptable are sufficiently persuasive that others wonder if they may legitimately object. I began working on this book when a student told me that her peers were telling jokes about Asian women. My student had a genuine question for me—did the fact that her peers were joking mean that what they were doing was acceptable, and that she had no right to ask them to stop? By contrast, it is hard to imagine someone defending a comment by saying it was "just an epithet," or to imagine a student wondering if it was all right for other students to use racial slurs about her social kind; we have much greater moral clarity and certainty about slurs than we have about jokes.

The moral uncertainty we have about derogatory joking stems from our confusion about how jokes work from a communicative point of view. If we want to understand what is wrong with derogatory jokes and derogatory joking, we need to understand how derogatory jokes operate in conversation: How do racist jokes communicate derogatory ideas, and what makes joking so different from other kinds of speech? These are the central questions in this book. I answer them from the perspective of philosophy of language, my field, and of linguistics, a closely related field, while drawing on evidence from other disciplines. Philosophers of language and linguists specialize in the study of human communication, so their research can be harnessed to explain how a joke like Fosdick's communicates a harmful idea, and how jokes differ from serious speech. Once we know that, we will know more about how jokes work and about what they do. This is the first step on the path to understanding how humor supports unjust social hierarchies.

How philosophy can help

Philosophers of language and linguists have helped us understand how people communicate things that they do not explicitly say. An illustrative example: Suppose Sally asks Kate, "Are you going to the party?" and Kate replies, "I have to work" (Davis 2019). Kate's *words* mean she has to work. But Kate gets across more than this; she also communicates to Sally that she will not go to the party, even though the words 'I have to work' do not standardly mean that the speaker is not going to a party—in other circumstances, saying 'I have to work' is not a way to communicate that I will not be going to the party, and I would get no points on a French exam if I translated 'I have to work' as 'Je ne vais pas à la fête'. Since what Kate explicitly said communicates something entirely different, Sally's interpretation of Kate must rely on more than her knowledge of the vocabulary and grammar of English. Of course, Sally doesn't need any academic expertise to conclude that Kate won't go to the party. The contribution of philosophy of language and linguistics is to describe and explain how Kate communicated something she doesn't literally say, and what Sally uses to correctly interpret Kate. Furthermore, philosophy and linguistics explain what happens in this example in a systematic way, giving a theory that covers this example and many others. We don't need to get into the specifics of the explanation right now; the crucial point is that the disciplines of philosophy and linguistics can explain *how* we communicate more than we actually say.

Returning to Fosdick's joke, the words he used do not standardly mean that Black people do not work. Yet somehow, Fosdick got across the false and dangerous stereotype that Black people do not work. It is typical of derogatory jokes that the words used do not have the derogatory ideas they convey as their standard meaning. So, as with Kate and Sally, we cannot explain everything Fosdick communicated by focusing on vocabulary and grammar. We need to go beyond the literal meaning of Fosdick's words to explain what his joke communicated.

The study of how people communicate more than they say is known as pragmatics, and researchers who work in this area have identified different mechanisms that can be exploited to communicate unspoken content. In the example above, Kate used one of these mechanisms to communicate that she would not go to the party. But which of these pragmatic mechanisms of communication does the work in derogatory joking, and how? This question has not been fully addressed, and certainly not fully answered, by either philosophers or linguists.[4] When my student asked me whether it was all right to tell racist and ethnic jokes, I thought I would find an article for her to read that would answer her question; it would explain what derogatory jokes communicate and thus how, for example, Fosdick's joke communicates a pernicious stereotype about African Americans. If we understood exactly how Fosdick's joke communicates something it does not straightforwardly say, then we would be partway toward an explanation of why his joke demeaned Swinton and other African Americans and why he should not have told it. But to my surprise I learned that the article I wanted to give her did not exist, and I began to write on the topic myself.

Jokes versus joking remarks

In a book like this, a reader might expect a crystal-clear definition of what counts as a joke and what doesn't. But I am not going to try to give one; jokes form an unruly class, and any simple definition is certain to have exceptions. The concept of a joke is what Wittgenstein called a family resemblance concept; we should not expect to find precise criteria for what counts as a joke, but there are characteristic properties that are shared by some jokes, just as there may be characteristic traits of a family that are exhibited by some, but not all, members. I will assume that we have a rough and ready concept of what jokes are that will suffice for the purposes of this book.

Although I will not define what a joke is, I will distinguish between scripted jokes and jocular remarks. They communicate derogatory ideas in different ways, and I will talk about them separately in later chapters of the book. Both scripted (or formulaic) jokes and jocular (or joking) remarks are described as jokes in common parlance. But a canonical example of a scripted joke is a question with a punchline answer, like Fosdick's aspirin joke, or a fictional mini-narrative with a conclusion that is meant to be funny.[5] Jocular remarks, on the other hand, have the same grammatical form as assertions.[6] In brief, derogatory jokes need not explicitly express any negative ideas about an individual or group, whereas derogatory jocular remarks do explicitly express negative ideas about a derogated group or about members of that group— that is, the remark expresses negative ideas via the standard meanings of the words used.[7] What makes jocular remarks different from other derogatory assertions is the intent of the speaker. For example, Imus's comment about the Rutgers basketball team, "That's some nappy-headed ho's there," has the grammatical form of an assertion, even though the grammar is colloquial.

It employed terms—'nappy-headed' and 'ho'—whose standard meaning is negative, the former a derogatory description of African American hair and the latter a slur about women's sexuality.[8] The remark is an intersectional insult, expressing negative ideas about Black women via the standard meaning of the words used. If Imus's intent was humorous—as he insisted it was—then it was a derogatory jocular remark.

The ethics of joking and cultural limitations

Let's turn now to the main themes of the book. There are ethical considerations about joking that circulate in society, and that many of us endorse. I think we should take these pre-existing ethical ideas seriously, and I talk about them in detail in the early chapters of the book. I focus on the ideas that are commonplace in the cultures that are familiar to me; I grew up in Northern Ireland, spent my college years in England, and since then have lived in the United States. I have talked to people from other cultures about how derogatory jokes are used in their countries of origin and their communities, and they were all familiar with the same ethical concepts about jokes, although of course the typical targets of derogatory jokes vary widely. But it wouldn't be at all surprising if some cultures did not share the ethical ideas common in my milieu (Jiang, Li, and Hou 2019).

The ideas about the morality of derogatory jokes that circulate in the British Isles and North America are largely about who may tell derogatory jokes and when they may tell them. For example, many people think that the social identity of the joker is relevant to the moral appropriateness of telling a joke. In accordance with this guideline, we might think that I can permissibly tell a joke about Irish women, since I am one myself, but my male English colleague should not tell the same joke. The social identity of the audience is also often thought to be relevant to whether telling the joke is morally acceptable—e.g., we might think that my male English colleague might permissibly tell a joke about Irish women to another male non-Irish colleague, but should not do so in my presence. The behavior of the audience on hearing a derogatory joke is subject to moral evaluation as well. For instance, laughing at such a joke instead of maintaining a stony silence is thought to be morally questionable. Finally, listening to such a joke without raising any objection makes many people feel uneasy; they feel regret and perhaps pangs of conscience that they raised no objection. They think they "should have said something."

While I think we should take these cultural guidelines seriously, that's not to say that they are unassailable. In fact, as we will see, empirical work in social psychology suggests that most of these ethical ideas are a mishmash of truth and error. The communicative effects of jokes are not what most people think they are, and as a consequence, the ethical considerations about joking that circulate among us are not correct.

Jokes that cross the line

While joking may allow us more latitude in what we say, there are some joking remarks, and some jokes, that pretty much everyone thinks go too far. *Saturday Night Live* comedian Michael Che received widespread censure for a horrendous joke that was shared on his Instagram account, which Che says was hacked (Bella 2021). It concerned Olympic gymnast Simone Biles and Larry Nassar, who sexually abused Biles and other young gymnasts while working as the USA Gymnastics team doctor. But there are also circumstances in which derogatory jokes seem acceptable, even valuable— e.g., joking about a dictator might be important to the endurance of people living in a totalitarian state.

I don't have to tell you that one factor that distinguishes jokes that draw condemnation and jokes that do not is whether they 'punch up' or 'punch down'. In an interview with Larry King, standup comedian George Carlin says, "Comedy has traditionally picked on people in power, people who abuse their power." His fellow comedian Andrew Dice Clay is "unusual" because he doesn't do that—his "targets are underdogs . . . women and gays and immigrants" ("George Carlin Interview" n.d.). But can we explain Che's transgression as targeting an underdog? Biles is considered the best gymnast in the world, and her excellence arguably gives her more power than Che. However, the joke concerned Biles as a child who suffered sexual abuse, as well as Biles as an elite athlete. Children who are subjected to sexual abuse are also subjected to a network of oppressive forces. In addition, there is an intersectional aspect to public perception of sexual violence, with sexual violence against Black women being treated with less seriousness than sexual violence against

White women (see, e.g., Herndon 1990). The remark also exhibited what Kate Manne has christened himpathy—"the flow of sympathy away from female victims toward their male victimizers" (2017, 23). The remark, then, punched down at Biles as an abused child—a member of a seriously disadvantaged group—even though it does not punch down at Biles as an elite gymnast.

On my view, derogatory jokes (and joking remarks) fall into a special category when they target groups that suffer from unjust disadvantage. In general, to derogate is to lower someone. We might derogate someone by expressing a low opinion of them, lowering them in the honor or esteem of others; but, more seriously, we might derogate someone by detracting from their status, condition, rights, or authority. For example, I might lower an organizing guru in honor and esteem by revealing that he won't help his mother with her junk drawer, without lowering his condition or status, since his unkindness to his mother does not undermine his credentials as an organizer. On the other hand, one could lower someone in honor or esteem *and* lower them in status—perhaps I reveal that the organizing guru has a junk drawer himself, thus undermining his mystique. However, his success as an organizer and his possession of a junk drawer have nothing to do with social injustice. But if the organizing guru is African American, and I lower his status by invoking damaging stereotypes about his race, then I derogate him in an egregious way. The derogation reduces and limits him; I make him smaller; I belittle him. Later in the book, I will argue, roughly, that the line between acceptable and unacceptable derogatory jokes is set by whether the joke invokes ideas that reinforce and maintain systems of unjust disadvantage or discrimination, such as racism or anti-Semitism. I'm going to use the term 'belittling' for jokes that are derogatory in this unacceptable way. Obviously, that's not what a dictionary would say about what 'belittle' or 'belittling' means; I'm giving it a special meaning for my own purposes.

Derogatory jokes and implication

I will argue that derogatory jokes—that is, scripted or formulaic jokes—convey derogatory ideas or stereotypes by a type of implication. This type of implication relies on general practices and background knowledge. For example, if Fred says, 'There are two pears', he generally implies that there are *only* two, because customarily we don't say 'There are two__' if we think there are three or more. Similarly, if Greg says, 'There is a dog in the garden', he generally implies that the dog is not his dog, because customarily we don't say 'a dog' if we think it's our dog. I will argue that when someone tells a scripted derogatory joke, they customarily imply a derogatory idea or stereotype. I will say much more about how this kind of implication works, and why I think that's what's happening with derogatory jokes, in Chapter 5.

At first sight, this explanation of how derogatory jokes convey derogatory ideas may seem implausible; after all, there are derogatory jokes that are new to you, but you still know what they mean. But as you read the book, you will see why I think that it is the correct explanation. The fictional detective Sherlock Holmes tells his sidekick, "When you have eliminated the impossible, whatever remains, however improbable, must be the truth." The reasoning I will offer isn't as invincible as Holmes would like; the main alternative is not impossible. But I will argue that this is the best available explanation of the evidence.

Derogatory jocular remarks and intent

To identify the belittling content of a joking remark, like Imus's, we don't need to work out its implications—the meaning is right there on the surface. But we do need to know why it seems we can say at least some outrageous things as a joke.

While speakers are expected to say only true things when they are speaking seriously, they may say things that are false when they are joking. But people sometimes tell the truth—or what they perceive as the truth—as a joke; one of George Bernard Shaw's characters says, "My way of joking is to tell the truth. It's the funniest joke in the world" (1907, 38). In fact, there are two senses of the verb 'to joke'; both involve humorous intent, but one requires that you think what you say is false and the other does not. In the latter case, you might think it is true, you might think it is false, or you might not know. I will argue that some people exploit these multiple meanings of 'to joke' to cover their tracks when they want to say something they shouldn't say. They speak their truth, humorously; and then, if they are called on it, they claim that since it was a joke, it must have been false.

Humor and harm

Descartes argued that he was essentially a thinking being; but of course, people have feelings as well as thoughts, and as philosophers have explored racist and sexist language, they have come to see that our feelings are significant from an explanatory point of view.[9] A standard response to a derogatory joke you find offensive is to say, 'That's not funny'. But while the derogatory stereotype conveyed may be far from funny, what if the joke itself is funny? I will argue that funniness makes jokes especially effective for conveying and cementing prejudice. Humor affects our cognitive processes—we know this from empirical work—and makes the derogatory utterance insidious in specific ways. The humor can sneak a derogatory idea into our minds more subtly than a statement. Our amusement encourages us to uncritically absorb ideas that we might otherwise treat with caution. Derogatory humor, I will argue, introduces (or reminds us of) ideas about groups of people while simultaneously putting us in a state of amusement that affects our cognitive processes and thus how we greet those ideas.[10]

Guilty listeners

When it comes to assessing moral fault and blame with regard to racist language of any sort, it is obvious that we must evaluate the actions and intentions of the speaker. However, I will argue that conversational partners of the speaker have moral responsibilities as well. The discomfort that some people feel when they hear racist language is the intuitive spur for this unsettling thesis. What listeners feel is not just discomfort but the feeling that they have done something wrong.

Of course, a sense of guilt is not a certain sign of wrongdoing; guilty feelings are sometimes misplaced feelings. But I think there are circumstances where guilt about listening to belittling language is appropriate. In a case like this, one might think the wrong done is an omission; that is, we might think that what the listener has done wrong (if anything) is failing to challenge the speaker when she should have. But on the contrary, in this book I will argue that the wrong done is not an omission, but rather an action.

The philosopher Robert Stalnaker argues that conversations have what he calls common ground. His concept of the common ground is a modification of the everyday concept of the common ground. For him, the common ground is all the assumptions that are taken for granted for the purposes of the conversation; everyone in the conversation accepts them, and everyone believes everyone else accepts them. When Sally asks Kate if she is going to the party, it's common ground that there is a party that they might attend. When Kate says she has to work, it might become common ground that Kate won't go. But imagine Sally replies, "You have to work? I thought your shift was on Friday and the party is on Saturday," and Kate says, "Oh! I thought the party was on Friday!"; then whether or not Kate is going becomes an open question. It's going to take further discussion to settle whether Kate is going to the party, and thus whether it should be common ground that Kate won't go.

The concept of the common ground has value in explaining some otherwise puzzling things about what we should and should not say in a conversation. For example, if it's common ground that Sally and Kate have been invited to more than one party in the near future, Sally really shouldn't say 'Are you going to the party?' unless the common ground already contains information about which party is the topic of this conversation—rather, she should say something like 'Are you going to the party on Friday?' or 'Are you going to Juan's party?'

The common ground in a conversation is shared information, and in the context of a conversation what is in the common ground is negotiated not just by those who speak but by those who listen. Later in the book I will argue that a conversational partner who listens quietly to racist language performs an action—she accepts a racist idea into the common ground; a conversational partner who listens quietly to sexist language accepts a sexist idea into the common ground, and so on. She can make amends for this wrongdoing by challenging the speaker, thereby expelling the belittling idea from the common ground. Sometimes, a person is so powerless in a conversation that they have little choice but to accept belittling ideas, and in such a case, they are not blameworthy. But sometimes, people have the power to shift the common ground and don't use their power; those people may do wrong by accepting those belittling ideas into the common ground. I call this phenomenon listener culpability.

Since my argument relies on how conversations work, my conclusions about listener culpability do not apply to people who are listening to a standup comedian giving a performance, or watching a comedian on TV. In fact, very few of the arguments in the book can readily be extended to professional comedy. In a conversation, however, I will argue that there are different degrees of listener culpability. A listener can admit racist ideas into the common ground silently; this is the common reaction of a listener who is uncomfortable with the ideas but unwilling to challenge them. The number of people who are in the conversation may be relevant; some courts have found that the number of witnesses to verbal harassment increases its severity (Hughes 2002, 1471–72; *Smith v. Northwest Financial Acceptance, Inc.* 1997). But along with cases where a racist idea is admitted into the common ground against a listener's will, there are also cases where listeners welcome racist ideas into the common ground, e.g., by laughing, which is what Swinton's immediate supervisor at work did, or by telling another racist joke.

The enthusiasm with which a racist or sexist idea is accepted into the common ground, I will argue, has a bearing on the degree of wrongness of the behavior. For example, laughing at a belittling joke wholeheartedly is quite different, from a moral point of view, from laughing from nervousness or anxiety, or laughing unwillingly. Sometimes we cannot suppress laughter even when we should; perhaps you have been overtaken by the giggles at a somber event, like a funeral, for example. It's not a good thing. But it is not as bad as giggling at a somber event and making no attempt to control it.

Conclusion

To sum up this introductory chapter, here is an overview of the remainder of the book. Chapters 2 and 3 explore and challenge ideas about jokes that are found in both popular and academic writing, using evidence from social psychology and the law, as well as philosophy and linguistics. In Chapter 4, I explain why some derogatory jokes—like jokes about Barack Obama's dad jeans—are acceptable, and some—like jokes about his race—are not, even though there is a sense in which both 'punch up' at a powerful person. Chapters 5 through 7 develop my theory about how derogatory jokes and joking remarks communicate derogatory ideas, how humor makes us more receptive to derogatory ideas, and what difference it makes if we say something with joking intent. Chapters 8 through 11 turn from what jokers do to what listeners do—what happens when we listen to belittling jokes, what happens when we laugh at belittling jokes, and why is it especially complicated if the joker is your racist uncle at a holiday dinner? Chapter 12 returns to power dynamics, and talks about how belittling jokes can cement—or undermine—social hierarchies. The book ends with a brief practical guide, concerning how you can effectively respond to belittling jokes, and why sometimes you should.

2

The popular wisdom about jokes

Introduction

If your social circle is rarefied—e.g., if most of your friends work at universities—you may not have heard a derogatory joke about an ethnic or racial minority in a long time. But just as the hummingbirds that visit backyards in Tucson are familiar to Arizonans and unusual to Vermonters, these jokes are common in some segments of society and on the internet even if they seem like a dated phenomenon to you, something you haven't heard since childhood. The Trade Union Congress (TUC) commissioned a survey in 2016–17 of racism in the workplace in England. They found that "46% of respondents from a Black, Asian and Mixed heritage background, and 32% of non-White Other participants reported that they had been subjected to 'verbal abuse and racist jokes'" (Ashe, Borkowska, and Nazroo 2019, 7); the report also documents jokes experienced by Jewish, Irish, and Eastern European workers. In a collection of essays about covert misbehavior at work, sociologist Christie Boxer and social psychologist Thomas Ford hold that "[g]ender harassment in the form of sexist jokes and teasing is the most commonly experienced type of sexual harassment by women in the workplace" (2011, 178). If we want a theory of how derogatory jokes work, we need to do enough fieldwork to understand what these jokes are like, where they occur, and what people think of them.

This book is grounded in work by scientists, philosophers, and linguists, but I start by accumulating evidence about how derogatory jokes are perceived outside academia, particularly in Britain and North America. In this chapter, I identify three central claims that circulate in popular culture. These claims are about the ethics of derogatory jokes and the prudence of telling them. The first of the three is that there is nothing wrong with jokes; jokes, by their nature, are harmless fun. Sometimes people express this claim by saying they are "just jokes." I'll call this the Harmless Fun claim.

The second claim is that when someone should not have told a joke, her mistake was telling the joke to the wrong audience; furthermore, what makes the audience the wrong audience is its inability to appreciate the joke as it should be appreciated. If she had told the joke to the right audience, she would have done nothing imprudent, and certainly nothing improper. Sometimes people express this claim by saying that the listener has "no sense of humor" and should "lighten up." I'll call this the Wrong Audience claim. The Harmless Fun and Wrong Audience claims are closely related. Harmless Fun is a claim about the essential nature of jokes; it tells us that jokes, and joking, do no harm. But if jokes are incapable of causing harm, then how can we explain what has happened when people think that the joke-teller has done something wrong? Wrong Audience provides an explanation—the joker has not harmed anyone, but has caused offense in an overreactive audience. Some listeners pretend to be offended by jokes, even though they are not really offended; other listeners, who are genuinely offended, do not understand that jokes are harmless, and thus do not understand that the joke-teller is absolved of wrongdoing by the very nature of jokes.

The third claim, which I will call the Wrong Joker claim, is about who may tell derogatory jokes. It says that while perhaps one ought not tell a joke derogating a group to which you do not belong—at least, it is risky—it is all right to tell a joke derogating a group to which you do belong. Like Wrong Audience, Wrong Joker offers an explanation of why, despite the harmless nature of jokes, jokers sometimes appear to have put a foot wrong. It explains a different set of cases, however. According to Wrong Joker, on some occasions, the problem is not with the joke itself, nor with a misguided audience, but with the social identity of the joker.

Varieties of these three claims about the ethics and propriety of telling derogatory jokes are defended in scholarly literature as well as in popular wisdom, but in this chapter, I will draw on legal opinions and surveys about discrimination that document people's experience of derogatory jokes, as well as sources like the news and social media. It is essential to take the popular wisdom about jokes into account because a theory about how derogatory jokes convey and reinforce derogatory ideas and stereotypes is a theory about how people talk and think—what do people do with derogatory jokes, and how do they think derogatory jokes work?

Jokes and harm in popular wisdom

The Harmless Fun claim—the idea that a joke is a trivial, innocuous thing—is found in the legal case with which I began Chapter 1, *Swinton v. Potomac Corporation*. The lower court ruled against Potomac, and Potomac appealed; their appeal relied partly on Harmless Fun. However, both the appeal and Harmless Fun were denied by the Ninth Circuit Court of Appeals. Judge McKeown, who wrote the opinion for the Ninth Circuit, tells us: "Potomac asserts on appeal that, though 'tasteless, objectively offensive joking' occurred in its workplace, it was, at the end of the day, nothing more than 'joking,' and did not justify such a large punitive damages award. We reject this benign characterization of the evidence presented at trial" (*Swinton v. Potomac Corporation* 2001).

Humorous derogation has a distinctive role in the workplace. Barbara Plester, a social scientist who studies organizational humor, describes how some people see humor as a "protective cloak" (2016, 116). She discusses an example of a poster, depicting an episode of domestic violence, on the wall of a staff kitchen at a technology company in Australia. Workers there, men and women alike, told Plester it was "just a joke" (118). It is implicit in this defense that the poster would be a problem if it was not a joke, but since it is a joke, it is fine.

The section of the TUC report on anti-Semitism quotes a man who said, "I was on the receiving end of Jewish jokes that my work colleagues thought were just banter"; the report also quotes a White woman who works in transport who says she has witnessed "[g]enerally racist comments about others: blacks, Asians, Jews . . . Colleagues being offensive towards service users . . . especially Jews and Blacks. It's never direct, but 'jokes' and 'banter' though some of it does have a particularly nasty undertone" (Ashe, Borkowska, and Nazroo 2019, 49). In its recommendations, the report emphasizes that policy statements from employers to employees must be clear that "jokes" and "banter" count as forms of racism (107)—a warning that is necessary because humorous derogation is accorded a special status that is not shared by other kinds of derogation, like racial slurs and insults.

Perhaps because of the perception that jokes do no harm, racist humor may be more widespread than non-humorous expressions of racism. An article in *The Guardian*, reporting the results of a 2019 survey of racism in Britain,

includes a graphic which indicates that people from ethnic minorities witness racist comments made to sound like a joke more often than racism on
social media, more often than ranting or commenting negatively about im-
migration, and more often than racism in the press. "Looking at the types
of racial discrimination faced, the proportion saying they have experienced
someone making a racist comment in jest has risen to over half (55%) of
people from ethnic minorities" (Booth 2019).

Harm versus offense

Harmless Fun is widely held. But nevertheless, people often think that when
a derogatory joke is told, an apology is appropriate—perhaps even required.
If derogatory jokes are truly innocuous, as Harmless Fun claims, why should
someone ever have to apologize for telling such a joke? The second and third
claims of popular wisdom, Wrong Audience and Wrong Joker, provide an
explanation.

Harmless Fun is a blanket claim about jokes and joking; it doesn't have
any subtleties about the setting in which a joke is told. For example, it says
nothing about who is telling the joke, who else is there, or what else is going
on when the joke is told—is the joke-teller at a work meeting, in a pub with
friends, or attending a memorial service? Wrong Joker and its companion
Wrong Audience, however, concern themselves with the joke-teller and with
those present, and in doing so, they distinguish between the telling of a joke
on a particular occasion and telling that joke in general. Thus, they acknowledge that it might be fine to tell the very same joke in one context but not
in another. Furthermore, they (mostly) assume that when something goes
wrong in the telling of the joke, the problem is not that it caused harm; rather,
it caused offense.

Harm and offense do not always go hand in hand. Some harmful things
are inoffensive. People take offense partly because of cultural norms; so, for
example, encouraging women to feed their newborns with formula rather
than breast milk in Britain in the 1950s was arguably harmful, but not at
all offensive—it was accepted as the norm. More importantly for current
purposes, there are also offensive things that are harmless, such as a bad
smell (Feinberg 1985).

Both Wrong Joker and Wrong Audience rely on the idea that harmless things (jokes, in this case) can cause offense; so, the fact that someone

is offended does not mean that they were harmed. The *Cambridge English Dictionary* draws definitions from real-life sources, both spoken and written,[1] and it happens to use an example sentence about jokes in its definitions of both 'harmless' and 'offensive': "There were those who found the joke offensive, but Johnson insisted it was just a bit of harmless fun" ("Harmless" n.d.; "Offensive" n.d.). In this instance, Johnson insists that the joke was harmless fun despite the fact that some people were offended. Wrong Joker and Wrong Audience both exploit the difference between harm and offense to explain why people sometimes object to derogatory jokes, even if no harm has been done.

Audiences in popular wisdom

Wrong Audience tells us that when a person shouldn't have told a derogatory joke, her mistake was misjudging her audience, and in particular, how readily the audience would take offense. We can see Wrong Audience at work when joke-tellers apologize for telling derogatory jokes; it is common for them to apologize only for any offense caused, or to apologize only to those who were offended, as opposed to apologizing for telling the joke. For example, Jim Jones, who at the time was national security advisor for the Obama administration, told a joke about a Jewish shopkeeper and a Taliban fighter as a warm-up joke at the start of a speech; the joke involves anti-Semitic stereotypes surrounding money. Later, Jones said, "I wish that I had not made this off-the-cuff joke at the top of my remarks, and I apologize to anyone who was offended by it" (Calabresi 2010). If Jones's apology is for telling the joke, one might expect that he would apologize to everyone, not just to those who were offended by it. But he doesn't apologize to everyone; he apologizes *only* to those who were offended. Others apologize conditionally; they apologize *if* someone felt offense, which is the course taken by Liam Fox, then a Conservative member of the British Parliament and a member of the shadow cabinet. Fox told a joke about the Spice Girls that describes Mel B. as a "blackbird" and her three bandmates as "dogs." He did not apologize for telling the joke: "In repeating a widely circulated joke, I very much regret if anyone was offended. I naturally apologise if any offence was caused" (Hall 2000). Ann Winterton, who like Fox was a Conservative MP and member of the shadow cabinet at the time, also gave a conditional apology for a racist joke which treated British immigrants from Pakistan as numerous and without value: "I apologise unreservedly if anybody felt offended by my remarks" (Watt 2002). So, these three public figures do not apologize for telling the joke; they apologize for any offense that might have been caused.

These kinds of apologies are not restricted to jokes—they are of a type common in political apologies. All three apologies illustrate the idea that what went awry in the telling of the joke was that some members of the audience found it offensive; there is an unspoken suggestion that there would have been nothing wrong with telling the joke if the audience had not been offended. This idea is even more explicit elsewhere. For example, in a blog for the *Washington Post*, Alexandra Petri (2012) says:

> In politics, bad jokes were once a way of warming the room. They were how you broke the ice, established common ground. . . . The ability to make an off-color remark or quip and get away with it relied upon a precise calibration of the feeling in a particular room. . . . [These days there is] nowhere the bad-joke-makers can turn, no place of refuge where their remarks will be hidden from the ones who wouldn't get it.

Petri writes humorous op-eds for a living; much of what she says in her op-eds does not represent her own opinion, but lampoons someone else's position. But the tone of this blog post suggests that she is saying something she believes here. Petri expresses the idea that whether telling a joke is appropriate depends on the audience. She says that telling jokes is "an art" whose "habitat is threatened," because of the possibility that what you say might be recorded, and shared with an expanded audience on social media; this leaves no way to assess whether one's audience will appreciate the joke or not. She goes on to say that perhaps this is a good thing; but it makes the world "a bit duller too."

Wrong Audience is also evident in a discussion of Jones's Jewish shopkeeper joke by blogger Mark Kleiman.[2] Kleiman defends Jones, arguing that Jones's joke falls in a tradition of Yiddish humor about "Jews getting clever revenge on goyim who mistreat them," and he recounts another joke in the same tradition. Kleiman's joke is set in the 1940s and concerns a woman in the South of the United States, a Jewish army sergeant, and six African American soldiers. The joke is arguably intended to derogate only the woman, for her anti-Semitism and racism, but it also represents an African American corporal speaking in African American Vernacular English—a dialect also known as Black English and as Ebonics. Kleiman says he would choose his audience for this joke with care; "But though I'd be a little afraid—not very afraid, but a little—of offending black or Southern audiences, I know that one gets a big laugh from Jews" (Kleiman 2010).

If Wrong Audience is correct, what these public figures did wrong was telling the joke to the wrong audience. Presumably, then, it would have been all right to tell the jokes they told to a different audience. So, on this view, there is nothing wrong with telling derogatory jokes in itself. Thus, a potential problem for Harmless Fun is explained by Wrong Audience: Harmless Fun is correct—joking is essentially harmless—but sometimes jokers do not understand their audience and tell a joke to an audience who takes offense, and this is why, sometimes, a joker is expected to apologize for such a joke. Such a joker has done nothing harmful but has nevertheless caused offense.

But what is it that makes an audience the "wrong" audience; i.e., what has the joker failed to grasp about her audience? Kleiman suggests that the social identity of the audience is a central consideration; a Southern audience is not a good audience for a joke mocking the mores of the South in the Jim Crow era, and a Black audience is not a good audience for a joke in which a Black person is represented as speaking Black English. It is also commonly thought that there is an interactive effect between the social identity of the audience and the social identity of the joker, so, e.g., a non-Jewish person should not tell a Jewish joke to a Jewish audience; but I set this aside for now, returning to it in the section "Jokers in popular wisdom," which focuses on the social identity of the joker.

If people really think that it is all right to tell a derogatory joke if nobody in the derogated group is present, we might expect that people tailor their jokes to their company. Anecdotal evidence suggests they do. One respondent in the TUC survey, a White man working in transport, said:

> I have found that the worst racism I've heard was without the presence of any People of Colour. It is usually said by an outspoken racist then others bounce off him and make their remarks. It could be making jokes about women wearing veils while driving past in the van or something on the news and this being ammunition to start a rant about Muslims or immigration. (Ashe, Borkowska, and Nazroo 2019, 79)

Another respondent, a White man working in education, commented on "[i]nappropriate comments/racist jokes/ignorant attitudes said in presence of a group. In my opinion, the perpetrators have felt safe to do so because their 'audience' has been perceived to be White British and therefore not ex-pected to take offence" (Ashe, Borkowska, and Nazroo 2019, 79). So, these people observed more racist remarks and more racist jokes being told when the jokers thought nobody from the targeted group was present, and thus that nobody would be offended.[3]

Social identity, however, is not the only thing that distinguishes a Wrong audience from a Right audience; some people don't mind hearing jokes about their social group. A survey conducted in Britain for the Commission for Racial Equality (CRE) interviewed Irish people living in London and Birmingham; it notes a "mismatch between numbers of respondents describing the atmosphere at work as bad (20%) and those reporting anti-Irish jokes and comments (79%)" (Hickman and Walter 1997, 195). The re-port suggests that this is evidence of "widespread acceptance of anti-Irish racism as normal in Britain" (196). But perhaps it is also evidence that people see jokes in a different light. Although 70% of those who answered the question "Did you find these jokes/comments offensive or not?" found them at least somewhat offensive, a sizable minority, 30%, "said that they had no objection to jokes and comments about the Irish" (198). One of these respondents commented that it was "[j]ust in fun," and another, "I find them funny. I wouldn't take it as being horrible. Just somebody having a laugh at my expense" (198). One of the survey participants, a London police officer, distinguished between his reaction to jokes and his reaction to comments. In explaining his answer to the question about whether he found jokes and comments offensive, he said, "Jokes I wouldn't, but the comments I find ex-tremely offensive" (199).

If the social identity of the audience were the only factor that distinguished a Wrong audience from a Right audience, it would be easier for jokers to figure out what jokes they could prudently tell in present company—at least, if they knew or guessed the social identity of the audience members. Jim Jones—who told the Jewish shopkeeper joke—was speaking to a think tank focused on policy in the Middle East; he can't have believed that no-body Jewish was present, or that nobody Jewish would see the transcript of his remarks. So, if Jones was not mistaken about the social identity of the au-dience, what would Wrong Audience say went wrong?

Some sources express the idea that when an audience finds a joke trou-bling, it is the audience, not the teller of the joke, who has erred. In March 2012, Newt Gingrich, Rick Santorum, and Mitt Romney were seeking the

Republican presidential nomination. At a fundraiser with Michelle Obama in support of Barack Obama's second presidential campaign, the actor Robert De Niro told this joke: "Callista Gingrich. Karen Santorum. Ann Romney. Now do you really think our country is ready for a White First Lady?" (Maher 2012). Newt Gingrich described the joke as "utterly and totally inexcusable," and De Niro apologized. The comedian and talk show host Bill Maher, however, thought that there was no need to apologize, as we find in his *New York Times* opinion piece on the subject, with the headline "Please Stop Apologizing." Maher's op-ed has two themes. The first is that nobody was genuinely offended by this joke—those who protest this kind of joke "pretend to be outraged about nothing." He says:

> Let's have an amnesty—from the left and the right—on every *made-up, fake, totally insincere, playacted* hurt, insult, slight and affront. Let's make this Sunday the National Day of No Outrage. One day a year when you will not find some tiny thing someone did or said and *pretend* you can barely continue functioning until they apologize. (Maher 2012, emphasis added)

So according to Maher, what De Niro said was fine. The problem is not with the joke; it is wholly generated by the audience. In fact, the offense Gingrich claims to feel is trumped up, a claim also made by conservative commentator Ann Coulter (*Huffington Post* 2012). So, in this case, De Niro's error (if he was in error at all) was telling the joke to an audience who feigned offense.

The second theme is that when we feel real offense at what someone says, we shouldn't complain. "If [the amnesty on made-up offense] doesn't work," Maher has another solution:

> We need to learn to coexist, and it's actually pretty easy to do. For example, I find Rush Limbaugh [the host of a conservative talk radio show] obnoxious, but I've been able to coexist comfortably with him for 20 years by using this simple method: I never listen to his program. (Maher 2012)

The audience who is genuinely offended, then, is still the source of the problem—this time for continuing to listen, as opposed to ignoring the offender. The British journalist Douglas Murray shares Maher's opinion that people should learn to live with others who tell derogatory jokes, rather than asking the joker to change her behavior: "Being offended, and learning to deal with it, is part of being a grown-up in a grown-up society" (Murray 2010, 19).

This variant of Wrong Audience assumes that offense at harmless things is misplaced offense. If derogatory jokes are harmless fun, then an audience that objects to a joke has no substantial moral grounds for an objection. Consequently, audience members should suppress their offense; we should not make a mountain out of a molehill when we are offended by harmless things. Thus, this version of Wrong Audience explains why an apology for a derogatory joke is sometimes demanded even though telling jokes is harmless fun, and even when nobody in the audience belongs to the derogated group; in such cases, the audience does wrong, either by pretending to be offended, or by dealing with genuine feelings of offense in an inappropriate or immature manner.

However, this version of Wrong Audience overlooks the possibility that sometimes offense is appropriate and justified, even when the offending act harms nobody. For example, the philosopher Joel Feinberg distinguishes between what he calls offensive nuisances and profound offenses. An unwashed, drooling, farting, belching passenger on a bus is an offensive nuisance merely; but spying on women miners through a peephole in a bathroom wall is a profound offense (Feinberg 1985). Relatedly, the philosopher Renée Jorgensen Bolinger (2017) argues that some slurs morally warrant offense.[4] Unlike Feinberg and Bolinger, this version of Wrong Audience assumes that all offense is trivial.

Wrong Audience holds that there is nothing wrong with telling a derogatory joke when nobody is offended. However, some people also think there is nothing wrong with telling a derogatory joke when people *are* offended. As we saw, Bill Maher thinks that people should tolerate offense. The actor Rowan Atkinson is partially but perhaps not completely on Maher's side. Atkinson doesn't say that the audience is wrong to be offended, nor does he claim that the offense is imaginary. But like Maher, Atkinson does not think that people should be expected to apologize for making offensive jokes. In a letter to *The Times*, defending a remark made by Boris Johnson, who was then a Conservative MP and former member of the British cabinet and subsequently became the British prime minister, Atkinson (2018) said, "All jokes about religion cause offence, so it's pointless apologizing for them. You should really only apologize for a bad joke." In Atkinson's opinion, Johnson's joke about women wearing burkas was "pretty good," and thus required no apology.

Jokers in popular wisdom

Let's turn to the third claim from popular wisdom, Wrong Joker, which is that it is acceptable to tell jokes about one's own group, but not about someone else's group. For example, a journalist for the BBC comments that the British comedian Shazia Mirza "draws a distinction between joking about other cultures and joking about one's own"; Mirza said, "I make jokes about Pakistanis because I am Pakistani. I make jokes about Muslims because I am a Muslim. I would never make a joke about black people because I'm not black" (BBC News 2002). In the CRE survey of anti-Irish discrimination, a man who worked as a baker in Birmingham said he did not find all Irish jokes or comments offensive: "It depends on the context of the conversation. I feel hurt because they have that attitude. It's mostly the English. If I take part I talk about Irish comedians. It's only the Irish can laugh at ourselves" (Hickman and Walter 1997, 198). So, he and Mirza draw a similar distinction between laughing at one's own group and laughing at others.

The Wrong Joker claim surfaces elsewhere too. In a *New York Times* article about the publication of books of racial and ethnic jokes, Edwin McDowell quotes Jacqueline Wexler, who was then president of the National Conference of Jews and Christians: "I think it's the most wholesome thing in the world when ethnic groups laugh at themselves. But it's dangerous when someone else does it to you, because almost always there's an element of denigration" (McDowell 1983). A similar view is expressed later in the same article, although this time from a scholarly source:

> "Everybody else makes jokes about other people," said Dr. Martin Grotjahn, professor emeritus of psychiatry at the University of Southern California and the author of *Beyond Laughter*, a book on the symbolism of jokes. "But in all jokes there is a disguised aggression, and racial jokes could be an invitation to racial hatred."
>
> Dr. Grotjahn said that he would particularly advise against a non-Jew telling a joke about Jews or a white telling a joke about blacks. And one publisher said that he would issue a volume of black jokes only if the author were Richard Pryor, Bill Cosby, Eddie Murphy, or another well-known black (McDowell 1983).[5]

Thus, Grotjahn believes that while some jokes involve racial hatred, this aspect of jokes is undermined if the joke is told against a member of one's own group. Wexler believes it is "wholesome" to laugh at one's own group, but that laughing at other groups involves denigration. So, they both subscribe to Wrong Joker, but not to Harmless Fun—jokes may be harmful when told by the wrong joker.

While some people accept Wrong Joker and reject Harmless Fun, the two claims are not necessarily in conflict; someone could coherently endorse both of them. Like Wrong Audience, Wrong Joker proposes an explanation for an apparent exception to Harmless Fun—although jokes are harmless, people sometimes take offense to jokes told by a group outsider. But more must be said to fill out this explanation; why are jokes more offensive when told by an outsider? The greater offense could be explained by general social conventions about self- and other-deprecation; I may deprecate myself, but I ought not deprecate you, and by analogy, I may deprecate my people, but not your people. If this social convention is nothing more than an arbitrary convention of politeness, then a joke deprecating others may be offensive but not harmful. Understood in this way, Wrong Joker explains why people object to other people telling a joke deprecating their group, without compromising the generalization expressed by Harmless Fun.

However, conventions of politeness may be far from arbitrary. The philosopher Karen Stohr (2012), for example, argues that conventions of politeness are justified by moral principles and ideals, and are a means by which we express moral values such as respect for others. If she is correct, then there might be a genuine conflict between Harmless Fun and Wrong Joker: Perhaps deprecating others is impolite because it is a way of harming them.[6]

Regardless of whether social conventions about other-deprecation are grounded in moral considerations, there may be other ways in which Harmless Fun and Wrong Joker conflict. Wrong jokers offend people of another group. Not all offensive things are harmful—like bad smells—but we might argue that a person who deliberately causes offense to another person is harming them, at least a little. Perhaps Wrong Joker is meant to place a limitation on Harmless Fun, making it more plausible. The reasoning would go like this: Joke-telling is typically harmless fun, but telling jokes may be harmful if the joker sets out to offend a member of the deprecated group. This explanation, then, brings Wrong Audience into the mix. The possibility of offense is greater with particular audiences, and thus the potential harm is greater with particular audiences.

Interestingly, Wrong Joker may be more nuanced than it seems. One target of ethnic jokes thought that the rule "Don't tell a joke about someone else's group" was not respected for all groups. In the CRE survey of anti-Irish discrimination, one of the interviewees said: "It's a big thing about racism. No-one would dare tell a black joke to a black person. But no-one gives two shites about telling an Irish joke to an Irish person" (Hickman and Walter 1997, 192).

Why might this be? One possibility, raised by the CRE report, is that there is a conception that discrimination is experienced in Britain only on the basis of color, and thus that the Irish, who are considered White, are not perceived as subject to discrimination. So perhaps the Wrong Joker claim is more subtle than it appears. Perhaps the third claim isn't that we shouldn't tell a joke about someone else's group, but rather that we shouldn't tell a joke about a disadvantaged group unless the group is our own.

Further evidence that Wrong Joker may have additional subtleties comes from the comedian Shazia Mirza in a more recent article. She argues that where terrorism committed by Muslims is concerned, it is more difficult for her to joke about it than for White, non-Muslim comedians to joke about it. She has been criticized for a comedy show she wrote and performs, *The Kardashians Made Me Do It*, which is based on three British teenagers who ran away to join the terrorist group ISIS in 2015. In the article, which was published during Donald Trump's first presidential campaign, she says:

> [The backlash] made me realize that when media talking heads say "Why aren't Muslims speaking up?" they don't *really* want us to speak up. We ruin their tidy us-versus-them narrative. It's not that they don't want to hear jokes about ISIS, either. It's just that they want to hear them from comics like Louis C.K., Bill Burr, and Daniel Tosh. Safe white guys they can relate to and feel comfortable with. Even Donald Trump can get away with saying things like, "Obama was the founder of ISIS" under the guise of "sarcasm." I'm a brown Muslim woman who is suggesting other ways to look at these situations—maybe the real reason why young girls go off to marry ISIS fighters is less about religion and more about sex and rebellion—and I get accused of supporting terrorism. (Mirza 2016)

Although ISIS members are Muslim, and thus part of Mirza's group in one sense, only a minuscule percentage of Muslims are members of ISIS; so, there is an important sense in which jokes about ISIS are *not* jokes about Mirza's group. They are jokes about a very small subset of Mirza's group. This fact, however, does not explain why Louis C.K., who is not Muslim, would get away with making a joke about ISIS and Mirza would not.

Wexler said she thought that joking about one's own ethnic group is wholesome. Mirza takes this further, suggesting that her joking about ISIS is her contribution to combating terrorism. She ends the article, "Fortunately, freedom of speech . . . usually comes around to making room for new voices. This is especially true in comedy. . . . Now it's time for Muslims to be funny. Let us fight our own war on terror with laughter—it may work even better than the bombs" (Mirza 2016). So, for Mirza, joking about one's own group is not just socially acceptable; it can be socially beneficial.

Not everyone thinks that joking about one's own group is acceptable, as Wrong Joker claims. I have not found this view expressed in print, but in conversation, people often tell me that they think there is a significant inter-action between Wrong Joker and Wrong Audience.[7] Wrong Joker says we shouldn't tell jokes against other people's groups, but may tell them against our own. Wrong Audience says we shouldn't tell jokes to certain audiences, and on some versions of Wrong Audience, the wrong audience is one that contains members of the derogated group. Some people argue, however, that we may tell jokes against our own group only to audiences consisting of our own group. For example, a Jewish person may tell Jewish jokes when he is with his Jewish friends, and a gay woman may tell jokes about gay women to her gay women friends; but a Jewish person should not recount Jewish jokes in the presence of people who are not Jewish. These people believe, then, that we may tell derogatory jokes about our own group only to people of our group, and not to outsiders. The reasoning offered is that we should not provide ammunition against our group to others, or to encourage others to think that it is all right to express stereotypes about our own group because members of the group endorse those stereotypes themselves.

Is the popular wisdom consistent?

In the section "Audiences in popular wisdom," I argued that Harmless Fun and Wrong Audience are consistent; that is, given the assumption that someone can be offended by something harmless (or may pretend to be of-fended by something harmless), there is nothing logically amiss with holding both Harmless Fun and Wrong Audience. In the section "Jokers in popular wisdom," I argued that Harmless Fun and Wrong Joker are also consistent, given the assumption that other-deprecation can be harmless.[8] But what about the triad of views? Is it logically consistent to subscribe to Harmless Fun, Wrong Audience, *and* Wrong Joker?

I think the triad is logically consistent, and in fact, that both Wrong Audience and Wrong Joker can be used to bolster the case for Harmless Fun. Suppose Harmless Fun is true; then derogatory jokes cause no harm. Yet sometimes telling a derogatory joke is misguided, and people object. Why are there objections to a harmless practice? The advocate of Harmless Fun might argue that a person can make a mistake in telling a derogatory joke to the wrong audience, causing either real or imaginary offense; or they can make a mistake in telling a joke that derogates a group to which they do not belong, risking real or imaginary offense. In both cases, however, the advocate of Harmless Fun might insist that the mistake is one of prudence. Assuming that causing offense is not harmful in itself, in these cases, tellers of derogatory jokes cross a social boundary but not a moral boundary.

Conclusion

The popular claims about jokes that I have explored in this chapter give us evidence about how jokes are used, and about what people think about the ethics and etiquette of telling derogatory jokes. But are Harmless Fun, Wrong Audience, and Wrong Joker, correct? In Chapter 3, I will evaluate these three popular claims, and their scholarly equivalents. As we shall see, there are reasons to doubt all three of them.

3

Is the popular wisdom supported
by science?

Introduction

The ideas about jokes that I explored in Chapter 2—Harmless Fun, Wrong Audience, and Wrong Joker—are familiar, and widely held. Furthermore, they are not restricted to popular culture; they are echoed in work by philosophers and linguists. But are they true? There has been empirical work evaluating these claims, particularly in social psychology, but also in political science and communication studies. Using this work, I will argue in this chapter that none of the three is wholly true; derogatory jokes are not harmless fun, they can cause harm even when the audience does not take offense, and while telling a joke derogating one's own group is more socially acceptable than telling a joke derogating someone else's group, it is also more dangerous.

All three of the popular claims about derogatory jokes have been considered, and sometimes adopted, in the scholarly literature. For example, the philosopher Ted Cohen countenances Harmless Fun: While there are jokes he dislikes, he thinks that one cannot show that a joke is bad: "If I were to offer some resounding moral condemnation of this joke, no doubt I would have to invoke some 'moral theory,' and then show that an implication of the theory is that this joke is Bad. I will not do that. . . . I think it can't be done" (Cohen 2001, 81).

So, Cohen is a principled agnostic about Harmless Fun, because he believes there is no way to show that it is false. He grants that people may find some jokes upsetting, but he does not think their upset shows there is anything wrong with the jokes. The linguist Salvatore Attardo (1993, 1994) defends a version of Wrong Audience. On his view, jokes may imply derogatory ideas, but *only* when the audience takes the joke seriously, not when the audience takes the joke as a joke. Attardo also defends a version of Wrong Joker, pointing out that, for example, an Italian will respond differently to an Italian joke told by another Italian than to the same joke told by a non-Italian.[1]

Perhaps derogatory jokes, in the abstract, cannot be shown to be good or bad. But that's beside the point. The crucial issue is whether *telling* some jokes is bad, and as we shall see, there is compelling evidence showing that telling derogatory jokes is, at least sometimes, bad.

How can jokes be assessed in moral terms?

In Ted Cohen's book *Jokes: Philosophical Thoughts on Joking Matters*, he gives the same advice as the talk show host Bill Maher about the best approach to take with people whose jokes you dislike: "You can avoid people who tell jokes you hate" (2001, 83). Cohen allows that you may ask people to stop exposing you to jokes you dislike, "or at least insist that they not tell them to you or when you are present" (83). But he does not think that we should discourage people from telling such jokes on other occasions. This suggests that Cohen supports Wrong Audience; there is nothing wrong with telling a derogatory joke to a willing and appreciative audience.

It's fair to assume that when Cohen proposed his remedies—avoid the offending joker or ask them to stop—he was thinking of casual social interactions, rather than of people like Troy Swinton. Cohen's solutions were not readily available to Swinton. Since Swinton's life was entwined with Fosdick's at work and at home, the only way to steer clear of Fosdick was to quit his job and to avoid his fiancée's family. Furthermore, Swinton testified under oath that he did not ask Fosdick to stop telling the jokes "because he knew that Fosdick regularly carried a .22 caliber pistol in his back pocket" (*Swinton v. Potomac Corporation* 2001). Like Swinton, Gerald Moore, an African American who worked at a welding company, eventually quit his job to avoid further racial jokes and slurs, despite the fact that doing so left him worse off financially. Moore also had his reasons for not asking the joker to stop. The opinion from the Court of Appeals says that Moore told his supervisor that there were other employees using "race words"—behavior that the supervisor had witnessed—but says Moore was " 'afraid' to identify specific people because he was the only black on the [shop] floor and had no one to turn to if he complained about white employees" (*Moore v. Kuka Welding Systems* 1999).

Although Cohen's strategy of avoidance would not be of help in a hostile work environment, he is much more sympathetic to those offended by jokes than the popular sources I discussed in Chapter 2. Cohen says:

> When an obnoxious portrayal is in a joke, it is likely to be upsetting in a special regard. Jokes are humorous, amusing, fun. It is ponderous and obtuse to object to the fun. The offended person who takes issue with a joke finds himself doubly assaulted, first by the offensive portrayal in the joke, and then again by the implicit accusation that he is humorless. (2001, 83)

However, in accord with some popular sources, Cohen thinks that an offended person should not deny that the joke is funny.

Cohen also defends a version of Wrong Joker. He cites as an example a joke that his wife learned from a Chicago policeman; the joke is about a Chicago policeman who murders his wife to get a job with the Secret Service. Cohen says:

> I do know that the dynamics of joking—including the intimacy sought and achieved, the relief gained from unpleasantness, and the moral dimensions of all this—depend absolutely upon who tells the joke and who hears it. Do you think this story *says* something about Chicago cops? If it does, it may well not be the same thing said when cops tell the joke to one another as it is when civilians tell the joke, and it is yet different when cops and civilians exchange this joke. (2001, 85–86)

Although Cohen here expresses the view that the moral dimensions of a joke may depend on the teller and the audience—and thus acknowledges that there are moral dimensions to joke-telling—he nevertheless believes that it is not possible to show that jokes are, as he puts it, bad. Why is this?

Cohen considers two strategies that one might use to try to show that telling derogatory jokes is morally bad. The first strategy comes from virtue theory, which proposes that to assess if something is right or wrong, you should consider what an ideal observer or possessor of practical wisdom would do or think. Such a person has all the virtues—courage, compassion, honesty, integrity, and so on—in perfect balance. If a truly virtuous person would not steal a piece of pie, then you should not steal a piece of pie; if a truly virtuous person would help a stranger in distress, then you should help a stranger in distress. Virtue theory began with Aristotle, but it is by no means out of date; living philosophers continue to develop and defend it. On Cohen's view, however, virtue theory gives no guidance regarding derogatory jokes; he thinks we do not know whether a paragon like the possessor of practical wisdom "would disapprove of these jokes, whether he would tell them or laugh at them, and how he would feel about anyone who tells them" (2001, 81).

Cohen's second strategy comes from a broadly consequentialist approach. Consequentialism judges whether an action is right or wrong by the consequences of the action, rather than by the motivations of the person. The version of consequentialism that is most familiar outside professional philosophy is utilitarianism, which dates to the British philosophers Jeremy Bentham and John Stuart Mill, and judges whether an action is right or wrong by how much happiness it produces. Not all consequentialists assess the outcome of actions in terms of happiness, however.

Cohen says that the way to apply consequentialism to jokes is to show that "traffic in these jokes produces genuine harm to someone, or at least that it reduces the moral character of those who traffic in them. It seems to me preposterous to suppose that anyone could show that either of these consequences obtains" (2001, 81). He also says:

It is possible that the existence of such jokes and commerce in them are symptoms of pernicious attitudes and beliefs, and perhaps the jokes even are causes of this perniciousness. If that were true, then of course that would be the basis of a moral objection to the jokes. I do not know that this is true, and I do not know that it is false. And neither does anyone else know about this, nor does anyone have any idea how to discover whether it is true. (2001, 79)

Cohen, then, is not committed to Harmless Fun; but if he is right, Harmless Fun cannot be proven to be true or false. However, as we will see, we ought not share Cohen's pessimism about the possibility of showing that jokes are causes of pernicious attitudes or of genuine harm, or his confidence that nobody knows how to find out.

Are belittling jokes harmless fun?

Unlike Cohen, I think we have at least some idea of how a fully virtuous person would consider derogatory jokes; for example, there is quite a bit of evidence that there are correlations between enjoying derogatory jokes and possessing pernicious attitudes, and while there may be plenty we do not know about what it is to be truly virtuous, we can be confident that a fully virtuous person would not have unjustified negative beliefs about races, ethnicities, genders, and so on.[2] Furthermore, virtue theory and consequentialism aren't the only moral theories; a third main contender derives from Kant, who holds, among other things, that everyone should be treated as an end in themselves. In the interests of brevity, however, I am going to focus on Cohen's consequentialist strategy in this chapter, even though much of the argument of my book is non-consequentialist.

To convince someone like Cohen that there is a moral objection to derogatory jokes on consequentialist grounds, showing that derogatory jokes and negative outcomes are associated with each other is not enough. In the classic example, ice-cream sales rise and fall in parallel with the number of shark attacks on swimmers, but more ice-cream sales do not cause more shark attacks. Rather, the two are correlated; in warm weather, more people buy ice cream and more people swim in places where there are sharks. So, even though we would like to prevent shark attacks, there is no consequentialist reason to crack down on the ice-cream trade. Similarly, if derogatory joking and pernicious attitudes and beliefs are merely correlated, rather than causally connected, there would be no consequentialist objection to derogatory joking. For this reason, I will focus on the effects of derogatory joking in this section, saying relatively little about correlations between derogatory jokes and people's attitudes; I will talk about those correlations in more detail in Chapter 9, in the section "What kind of person is amused by derogatory jokes?"

Cohen allows that there would be a consequentialist objection to jokes if jokes were causes of pernicious attitudes and beliefs, or if jokes were symptoms of pernicious attitudes and beliefs, or if jokes cause genuine harm (2001, 79). So let's consider whether there is a moral objection to jokes in any of these three ways. If there is, we will want to reject the first claim of popular culture, Harmless Fun.

First, can derogatory jokes cause pernicious attitudes and beliefs? The work of social psychologist Thomas E. Ford and his collaborators shows that they can. Ford (2000), for example, assessed whether exposure to sexist humor affects one's perception of sexist events. The subjects in the experiment were evaluated for hostile sexism, i.e., sexism "rooted in antagonism and feelings of indignation toward women," as opposed to benevolent sexism, "rooted in subjectively positive attitudes toward women in traditional sex-typed roles such as wives, mothers, and romantic love objects" (2000, 1096). Some weeks later, the subjects were given either sexist jokes or sexist statements to read, and then asked to evaluate a written vignette in which a male supervisor patronizes a young woman at work; specifically, they were asked to rate how offensive they found the described behavior. For both men and women who were high in hostile sexism, those who read sexist jokes were more tolerant of the sexist vignette than those who read sexist statements. There was no significant difference in tolerance for those who were low in hostile sexism.

People who are high in hostile sexism have pernicious beliefs and attitudes toward women already; in this study, those attitudes are not caused by exposure to sexist jokes. But this study does suggest that, for people who have hostile sexist beliefs, hearing sexist jokes affects attitudes toward and beliefs about sexist events, and perceiving a sexist event as acceptable is pernicious. An interesting aspect of this study, of course, is that sexist jokes were *more* effective than sexist statements in eliciting tolerance of the sexist vignette; this gives the lie to the popular idea that jokes, by their nature, do no harm.

Ford et al. (2014) conducted a similar experiment regarding anti-Muslim discrimination; again, they found that those exposed to Muslim jokes as opposed to non-humorous anti-Muslim statements were more tolerant of an anti-Muslim vignette. As with the earlier study of sexism, the effect was present in a group that already had higher ratings of prejudice against Muslims, but not in a group that were not highly prejudiced against Muslims.

In this and other work, Ford and his colleagues give no evidence that suggests that derogatory jokes induce prejudice in people who were not already prejudiced. Rather, Ford and his colleagues argue that the role of humor is that it releases pre-existing prejudice. Derogatory jokes make the environment seem more tolerant of prejudice, so people are more likely to allow their prejudices to inform their beliefs and more likely to express prejudice openly than they would in other circumstances. This is a hypothesis, not an empirical finding, but if it is correct, then perhaps there is an alternative explanation of the greater tolerance of sexism and of anti-Muslim discrimination; perhaps the prejudiced beliefs of those affected are not changed by the jokes, but rather are more freely expressed. However, even if the hypothesis is correct, and the jokes in these experiments did not cause new pernicious beliefs about Muslims or women, the jokes caused other pernicious beliefs, about the environment and about how discriminatory attitudes will be viewed in that environment; for example, the subjects came to believe that this was an environment in which sexism/anti-Muslim discrimination will be tolerated, and thus need not be suppressed.

Turning to Cohen's second criterion, are appreciating and telling derogatory jokes symptoms of pernicious attitudes and beliefs? Whether we can provide an answer to this question depends on what is meant by 'symptom', which has at least two meanings—first, a symptom may be something that is caused by an underlying condition, and second, a symptom may be a clue as to whether a person has an underlying condition. As you recall, on the consequentialist strategy, it is causation that matters, not correlation. So, what really matters for the consequentialist strategy is whether appreciating and telling derogatory jokes is a symptom of pernicious attitudes and beliefs in the first sense—i.e., that a penchant for derogatory jokes is caused by having pernicious attitudes and beliefs. To the best of my knowledge, there is no evidence either for or against this claim. So, we can't draw a moral conclusion about derogatory joke-telling from Cohen's second consequentialist concern.

However, it is worth mentioning that appreciating and telling derogatory jokes is a symptom of pernicious attitudes and beliefs in the second sense—i.e., it is a clue that a person possesses such beliefs. For example, in a study conducted in Canada, Hodson, Rush, and MacInnis (2010) found that people who favor a society in which there is a social hierarchy—for example, who believe that some groups are and should be superior to others— were more likely to agree with statements like "Jokes are simply fun," "Society needs to lighten up about jokes and humor generally," "Sometimes people need to relax and realize that a joke is just a joke," and "People get too easily offended by jokes"—that is, they were more likely to endorse Harmless Fun and Wrong Audience.[3] Those who favored a social hierarchy were also more likely to enjoy jokes about a lower-status out-group—Mexicans—than people who didn't favor a social hierarchy, although there was no relationship between fondness for a social hierarchy and enjoyment of jokes about a high-status out-group—citizens of the United States. (Of course, the very same people who support a social hierarchy are not likely to think that their beliefs and attitudes about social hierarchy are pernicious.) Focusing on a specific form of social hierarchy—the hierarchy which places men above women— Thomas and Esses (2004) found that men who were high in hostile sexism reported themselves as more likely to tell sexist jokes. There is also substantial evidence that there is a correlation between having negative beliefs about women and appreciation of sexist humor—I will return to this topic in the section "What kind of person is amused by derogatory jokes?" in Chapter 9.

Finally, let's consider Cohen's third reason for consequentialist concern about jokes—can they cause genuine harm? Legal cases document harm done by racist jokes. We have met two of these cases already. Troy Swinton suffered "personal distress and indignity," to the extent that he sought the help of a therapist (*Swinton v. Potomac Corporation* 2001). The Sixth Circuit found that the emotional distress experienced by Gerald Moore counts as an injury. Moore

> testified that he was injured because he was "angry" and "upset" about the jokes and slurs and that he "just couldn't take it any more." Plaintiff also complained to his supervisors and started looking for a new job. Accepting plaintiff's narration of the facts as true, this evidence sufficiently demonstrates the requisite injury to support compensatory damages. (*Moore v. Kuka Welding Systems* 1999)

For both Swinton and Moore, the harassment at work involved an exceptionally offensive racist slur, as well as jokes. And the jokes and slurs were repeated, not isolated. Even so, both the Sixth Circuit and the Ninth Circuit found that jokes were at least in part the cause of emotional distress.

Can jokes alone—i.e., without slurs—cause harm? In a study conducted by Ford et al. (2008), male undergraduates were told that they would complete two different studies in the same session. First, they were shown videos of comedy skits. They were told that they were rating the skits for funniness in preparation for a study to be conducted the following semester. Half were shown five neutral comedy skits, and the other half were shown one neutral and four sexist comedy skits. For the second study, they were asked to complete a survey which they were told would help the student government determine student opinion about cutting the budgets for registered student organizations at their campus; thus, they were led to believe that their decisions would have real-world consequences. Five organizations were listed: Jewish Cultural Collective, Safe Arrival for Everyone, National Student Council of Women, Study Abroad Learning Program, and Michigan Black Student Union. Those who were high in hostile sexism recommended more substantial budget cuts for the National Student Council of Women if they had first seen sexist comedy skits than if they had first seen neutral comedy skits. Curiously, they also recommended more substantial budget cuts for the Michigan Black Student Union. Let's assume, for the sake of argument, that such cuts are harmful. Then jokes may cause harm; in this study, sexist jokes encouraged men with negative beliefs about women to be less supportive of organizations for women and for Black students. Ford et al. (2014) conducted a similar experiment, but this time with antigay jokes versus neutral jokes or antiracist jokes. They saw a similar effect; participants who were high in prejudice against gay people proposed greater cuts for the Gay and Lesbian Student Association, described as "committed to serving and protecting the political and social advancement of homosexual people" (190), if they had read antigay jokes than if they had read neutral jokes or antiracist jokes.

Ford and his collaborators believe that sexist humor makes it seem as though prejudice is the local norm, and this encourages the expression of sexist behavior that otherwise would be repressed. For those who saw the sexist humor, hostile sexism was positively related to a perceived norm that others in the testing group approved of cutting funds to the women's organization. Ford et al. do not offer a detailed explanation of how seeing sexist humor releases prejudice against Black students; however, they note an earlier study by Glick and Fiske (1996), showing that people high in hostile sexism tend to hold negative attitudes to both women and African Americans.

Additional work by Ford's lab group suggests that derogatory humor has this effect only for some targeted groups. The effect is apparent with humor about women, gay people, and Muslims, for example, but not for humor about racists or terrorists. Ford and his collaborators argue that the groups for whom the effect is evident are groups for whom "[b]latant prejudice and discrimination ... [has] been largely replaced by ambivalence" (2014, 180); there was, but is no longer, a societal consensus that prejudice against these groups is justified. Increasingly, there are societal norms requiring that members of these groups be treated fairly, thus encouraging people to keep any prejudice they feel under wraps. For groups like these, then, groups of "shifting acceptability," contextual factors may influence the expression of prejudice against them, with derogatory humor being one of these factors. In contrast, if prejudice against the group is considered justified, and where there is high societal consensus that the group—such as terrorists and racists—should be subject to restrictions, exposure to derogatory humor in Ford's experiments has no effect on people's decisions about how well members of these groups should be treated. Unlike prejudice against women or gay people, prejudice against groups like terrorists is contextually stable.

To summarize, then, derogatory jokes about some groups—although not about other groups—encourage pernicious attitudes and beliefs and they cause genuine harm. So, the popular view that jokes are harmless fun is misguided. Furthermore, Cohen is wrong to think that there is no way to show that jokes can be assessed in moral terms; there is a way.

Assessing Wrong Audience and Wrong Joker

As we saw in the previous section, derogatory jokes seem to have different effects in different audiences—Ford and his co-authors, for example, found effects in audiences high in hostile sexism but not in audiences low in hostile sexism. So, we might think this experimental work shows that there is an element of truth in the Wrong Audience claim expressed in popular culture, that when a joker makes a mistake in telling a joke, the mistake is telling it to the wrong audience. However, as the thesis is expressed in popular culture, the 'right' audience is an audience that does not take offense at the joke, either because nobody in the audience is a member of the derogated group, or because everyone in the audience understands the essentially harmless nature of jokes—i.e., embraces Harmless Fun.

Wrong Audience isn't completely mistaken. The idea that the 'right' audience should not contain members of the derogated group has some empirical support. First, people who are a member of the derogated group are less likely to be amused by the joke (Ferguson and Ford 2008); see also "What kind of person is amused by derogatory jokes?" in Chapter 9. Second, Ford et al. (2020) explore the effects of derogatory humor on members of the derogated group. The derogated groups were liberals, conservatives, and women. For all three groups, derogatory humor had a negative effect, increasing concerns that they would be treated as less valuable and that they would be discriminated against by others. They saw themselves as less qualified, less competent, and less motivated; they were more likely to say they were scared, anxious, or uncomfortable; and they felt more socially excluded, like outsiders. The apparent teller of the derogatory jokes in these experiments was a person in authority—someone from Human Resources for liberals and conservatives, and a teaching assistant for women. So as Ford et al. point out, we do not know if the same effect occurs within a peer group. Nevertheless, the study shows that Wrong Audience gets something right—telling a derogatory joke where a member of the derogatory group is in the audience isn't a good idea.[4] Some proponents of Wrong Audience like to think it's not a good idea because the victims are immature or oversensitive, but that's not so; rather, it's not a good idea because it is damaging to members of those groups in various ways.

What about the other part of Wrong Audience—the idea that the 'right' audience is an audience that considers jokes harmless fun? We have enough evidence to see that it is unlikely that jokes are harmless when told to an audience who welcomes the joke; we know from Ford's work that jokes encourage pernicious beliefs, attitudes, and actions in audiences who are high in hostile sexism, and we also know that people who are high in hostile sexism tend to find sexist jokes funnier, and enjoy them more, than people who are low in hostile sexism (Greenwood and Isbell 2002; Thomas and Esses 2004).[5] Putting these two findings together, we might speculate that sexist jokes do substantial harm when told to an audience who enjoys them and finds them funny. Although to the best of my knowledge, there is no study that directly assesses whether appreciation of the joke is positively correlated with an increase in pernicious attitudes, beliefs, or actions,[6] from what we do know it seems unlikely that the 'right' audience for a derogatory joke, the audience that robs it of harm, is the audience that enjoys the joke.

In fact, there is evidence that an audience who treats the joke critically is more likely to disarm some of the pernicious effects of jokes on their beliefs and actions. In a second experiment, Ford (2000) assessed tolerance for a sexist event (as before, depicted in a written vignette) by students who had read sexist jokes and those who had read neutral jokes. Their tolerance was evaluated by their responses to the questions "How offensive is the behavior described in this situation?" and "How critical are you of the behavior described in this situation?" Half the subjects were given instructions to "read the jokes on a serious level and think about the content of each joke or the underlying message that is implied by the joke" (1099–100); the other half were given no explicit instructions about how to read the jokes. Ford found that, even for subjects who were high in hostile sexism, those who were given instructions to read the jokes critically were *not* more tolerant of the sexist event than those who had read neutral jokes. As before, those who were given no specific instructions and read sexist jokes were more tolerant of the sexist event than those who had read neutral jokes.

In a third experiment, Ford aimed to induce a critical mindset toward the sexist jokes by a means more likely to be present in social settings. In previous work, Ford et al. (1999) found that people who are high in hostile sexism, but not those low in hostile sexism, find sexist jokes more offensive when they are told by a man or by someone whose gender is not revealed. This meshes with the popular view, Wrong Joker, that derogatory jokes are more socially acceptable when told by a member of the derogated group than by someone who is not a member of that group. Ford speculates that a critical mindset may be induced, then, if a sexist joke is told by a man. So for the third experiment, Ford (2000) compared tolerance of the sexist vignette among participants who read sexist jokes told by men, told by women, and where the gender of the teller was not revealed. Participants high in hostile sexism who read jokes told by men were not more tolerant of the events depicted in the sexist vignette than those who read neutral jokes; but participants high in hostile sexism who read jokes told by women, or by people whose gender was not revealed, were more tolerant of the events depicted in the sexist vignette than those who read neutral jokes. This result is surprising; it flies in the face of the popular wisdom that there is nothing wrong with telling a joke derogating one's own group, since in this case jokes that derogate the teller's own group increased tolerance of sexism.

So, what does the popular wisdom get right about audiences and jokers? It is right that the harm done by a derogatory joke depends, at least to some extent, on the audience. But it is not right that a joke-teller has done nothing wrong if the audience takes no offense. Derogatory jokes have fewer harmful effects on the subsequent beliefs and attitudes of audiences who are critical of the joke; an audience who takes offense is, in some ways, a 'better' audience for a derogatory joke than an audience who takes the joke lightly. Furthermore, the popular wisdom is right that whether a joke is viewed as acceptable depends on the identity of the teller. But it is probably not right about *how* the identity of the teller affects the harm done to beliefs and attitudes by the joke. Popular wisdom supposes that it is all right for a woman to tell a joke derogating women, for example; but if Ford (2000) is correct, in fact jokes may be more harmful when told by a member of the derogated group than by someone who is not a member of the derogated group. So, the publisher who would issue a book of jokes derogating African Americans only if the author was Black would be doing what is socially acceptable; but such a book might in fact do more to encourage pernicious attitudes and beliefs than the same book with a White author.

Conclusion

Wrong Audience and Wrong Joker contain a smattering of truth, but not much; and Harmless Fun is misguided. But that doesn't mean that these three claims of popular wisdom should be dismissed completely. If we want to explain how people communicate ideas with jokes, we need to take their concept of what they are doing seriously—at the very least, we should be able to explain why they think jokes work that way, even if they are wrong. As I develop my explanation of how derogatory jokes communicate derogatory ideas, a benchmark for success is that it explains both why people embrace the mistaken views of popular wisdom, and what scientists have revealed about how jokes really work.

4

Crossing a line

Introduction

People like me—you know, people who don't wholeheartedly embrace Harmless Fun—are sometimes perceived as humorless killjoys. You might be surprised to learn that I love to laugh, and I love to make people laugh with joking remarks—although scripted jokes aren't my cup of tea. And yes, I have offended people with what I thought was a funny remark, but that for them, cut too close to the bone. Furthermore, I think it's clear that there are times that disparaging humor has genuine value. There are studies of the function of derogatory jokes in politically oppressive systems, where jokes may be made about dictators, armies, or the state police.[1] An argument can be made that in contexts like this, derogatory jokes told by the powerless against the powerful are an important social tool in combating oppression, or at least in helping the human spirit survive oppression. Mel Watkins, who was the first African American to be appointed as editor at the *New York Times Sunday Book Review*, argues that in the United States, "[b]lack humor most often satirizes the demeaning views of non-blacks, celebrates the unique aspects of black community life, or focuses on outwitting the oppressor" (1999, 29). So, I do not advocate a prohibition on derogatory joking—rather, there are times and places where derogatory joking is morally permissible and perhaps even valuable.

What is the difference, then, between derogatory jokes that are definitely morally unacceptable, and derogatory jokes that are acceptable—perhaps even good? Is it just that acceptable derogatory jokes "punch up" and unacceptable derogatory jokes "punch down"? In my opinion, the idea that you may punch up but not down is on the right track, but needs more nuance. In this chapter, I argue that what matters is the connection between the message conveyed by the joke and unjust disadvantage. Before I develop that idea, however, let's return to what I think distinguishes a derogatory joke from a derogatory joking remark. It's important to separate these two kinds of derogatory humor, because they communicate derogatory ideas by different mechanisms.

How derogatory jokes and joking remarks differ

In the section "Jokes versus joking remarks" in Chapter 1, I distinguished between scripted (or formulaic) jokes, on the one hand, and jocular (or joking) remarks, on the other. Scripted jokes are the kind of joke with a mini-narrative and a conclusion that is meant to be funny, or the kind with a question and a punchline—so "A man in a restaurant says, 'Waiter, what is this fly doing in my soup?' The waiter replies, 'Sir, it looks like the breaststroke'" is a scripted joke, as are knock-knock jokes. Obviously, joke-tellers may not follow a script exactly—we might deviate in wording, for example, or in the order in which we tell elements of the narrative. Jocular (or joking) remarks, on the other hand, have the form of an assertion; saying "It's a beautiful day!" while in the eye of a hurricane is a joking remark.

There are lots of innocuous jokes and joking remarks. What makes a joke or joking remark derogatory is that it expresses negative ideas or stereotypes about an individual or a social group. A *derogatory remark* has the form of an assertion[2] and explicitly expresses negative ideas or stereotypes about an individual or about a social group via the standard meanings of the words used and the grammatical structure of the remark.[3] What makes it a derogatory *jocular* remark is the humorous intent—or feigned humorous intent—of the speaker. Don Imus's remark about the Rutgers basketball team is an example. A *derogatory joke*—like the aspirin joke Jon Fosdick told in Troy Swinton's presence—conveys negative ideas or stereotypes about an individual or about a social group, but it need not have the form of an assertion; further-more, often jokes do not explicitly express negative ideas or stereotypes via the standard meanings of the words used and the grammatical structure of the sentences in the joke. With derogatory jocular remarks, the negativity is openly expressed, and the reason for thinking it is an acceptable thing to say is the joker's humorous intent. With derogatory jokes, in addition to the teller's humorous intent, there is a second reason for thinking that what the joker said is acceptable—the negativity is implied by the joke and inferred by the listener.

Although derogatory jokes and derogatory remarks are different, and work in different ways, there isn't a bright line separating the two. Some

derogatory jokes contain words whose standard meaning is derogatory—
some of Fosdick's employed racial slurs (*Swinton v. Potomac Corporation*
2001)—and while derogatory jocular remarks must explicitly express a negative idea or stereotype, some may imply additional negative material without
explicitly expressing it. Furthermore, some scripted jokes have the grammatical form of assertions; e.g., "This year's annual prize for Polish medicine
went to a surgeon in Krakow who performed the world's first appendix trans-
plant" (Cohen 2001, 77). It qualifies as a derogatory joke, not as a derogatory
jocular remark, because it does not explicitly express a negative idea about
Polish people, or an individual who is Polish, or surgeons in Krakow: There
is nothing negative about winning a prize for medicine. The hearer must understand more than the standard meaning of the words to interpret the negativity; e.g., the hearer must have background knowledge about the historical
assumption that the appendix is superfluous.

Derogating, disparaging, and belittling

I will use the word 'derogatory' as a general term, covering any joke or joking
remark that conveys negative stereotypes or ideas about an individual or social group. As I've said, I will argue that some derogatory jokes and joking
remarks are morally unacceptable, because they communicate stereotypes
and ideas that support or maintain unjust disadvantage. I'm going to use the
word 'belittling' to describe jokes that have this special role in shoring up
unjust disadvantage. But there are also derogatory jokes and joking remarks
that do not support or maintain unjust disadvantage; I will say that these
jokes are merely disparaging, not belittling. You might reasonably think that
saying something disparages someone but does not belittle them is nonsen-
sical, since the contemporary meanings of 'disparage' and 'belittle' overlap.
Indeed, a thesaurus might suggest that the words are synonyms. However,
I am going to use them as technical terms, diverging from their contemporary usage.

The *Oxford English Dictionary* inspires my choices about how to use these
words for the purposes of this book. It emphasizes different aspects of the way
in which someone is lowered or reduced in its definitions of 'disparage' and
'belittle'. The definition of 'disparage' focuses on lowering someone in people's
opinions and beliefs. To disparage someone is to discredit or dishonor them;
to bring reproach upon them; to lower them in honor or esteem; "to speak

of or treat slightingly; . . . to undervalue; to vilify" ("Disparage, v." n.d.). Like disparaging, belittling involves lowering in opinion and belief, since to belittle someone is to dismiss their importance or depreciate them; but unlike disparaging, to belittle someone can also be to reduce them in size or to make them small ("Belittle, v." n.d.). So, disparaging something involves treating it, and encouraging others to perceive it, as diminished. Belittling something, in addition, may actually diminish it, shrinking it in status or power.

One can lower someone in people's opinions without reducing their status or power. For example, I might detract from my dean's standing in opinion by spreading vicious rumors that he picks his nose when he thinks nobody is looking, and have no effect on his power—he remains the dean, with the same rights, privileges, and authority as before. On the other hand, one could lower someone in opinion *and* reduce their status or power. Suppose the rumors say he has no respect for faculty and staff, so they undermine the dean as an authority figure; then he is reduced in power as well as in people's perceptions.

I still wouldn't say that the dean was belittled, however, and here I am leaving the dictionary far behind. Whether a joke counts as solely disparaging or as both disparaging and belittling depends on details about the stereotypes or other damaging ideas conveyed by the joke and about the role of those stereotypes or ideas in supporting or maintaining unjust disadvantage. The falling fortunes of the dean have nothing to do with unjust disadvantage, and so I do not consider him to be belittled. I will explain.

Let's begin with the aspirin joke told in Troy Swinton's presence. It conveys a pernicious stereotype about African Americans—that they are lazy and do not work—that plays a larger role in the oppression of African Americans. The false idea that African Americans are lazy has a long history in undermining their group, despite the fact that throughout that history African Americans have worked extremely long hours in physically demanding jobs for little—or in the times of slavery, no—pay. It is an idea that supports the mistaken view that African Americans bring their relative poverty on themselves by their characters and actions, as opposed to their economic circumstances being the consequence of a complex network of forces that have, for example, resulted in their having little inherited wealth, in their living in neighborhoods with low property values and underfunded schools, and in limiting their access to college education and to professions that have higher wages. I would argue that the aspirin joke is a belittling joke because the stereotype that it conveys has a role in (falsely) justifying and maintaining a network of oppressive forces, and oppression is unjust disadvantage taken to an extreme. Thus, the joke has a role in lowering power and status.

But not all derogatory jokes convey stereotypes that have roles like this. Consider this joke:

> An Irishman and an Englishman walk into a bakery.
>
> The Englishman steals 3 buns and puts them into his pockets and leaves. He says to the Irishman, "That took great skill and guile to steal those buns. The owner didn't even see me."
>
> The Irishman replied, "That's just simple thievery, I'll show you how to do it the honest way and get the same results." The Irishman then proceeded to call out the owner of the bakery and says, "Sir, I want to show you a magic trick." The owner was intrigued so he came over to see the magic trick.
>
> The Irishman asked him for a bun and then he proceeded to eat it. He asked 2 more times and after eating them again the owner says, "Okay my friend, where's the magic trick?"
>
> The Irishman then said, "Look in the Englishman's pockets." (Jokes of the Day n.d.)[4]

There is no common stereotype that the English are casual thieves, or that they are dishonest. There is also no stereotype that the Irish are clever—quite the reverse. In a typical ethnic joke about the English and the Irish, the Englishman is above reproach, and the Irishman is cast as a dupe or as stupid. Certainly, there is an idea in circulation that the Irish resent the English, but that is not an idea that plays a significant role in the historical oppression of the Irish. If the idea played a role in their oppression, it was a minor role. This joke, then, is derogatory—the Englishman is a dishonest stooge, and the Irishman tricks both him and the owner of the bakery. But it isn't belittling, because the stereotypes that it conveys do not have a role in justifying and maintaining unjust disadvantage.

Now imagine that same joke with the roles reversed—the Irishman steals the buns, the Englishman cleverly gets given buns and then turns the Irishman in. Would that joke belittle the Irish? While the Irish may, in some places, still be subject to discriminatory attitudes and practices, they are, arguably, no longer an oppressed group. They are well-integrated in society as a whole and are economically successful. However, they have been an oppressed group in the recent past, who have been denied political and economic independence, who have been deprived of civil rights, and who have had their native language suppressed and almost wiped out. The economic legacy of this oppression was documented in mainland Britain as recently as the 1990s (Hickman and Walter 1997). The idea that Irish people are stupid and dishonest played a role in that historical oppression. So, even though the stereotypes the joke conveys with the roles reversed does not justify and maintain a network of unjust disadvantage now, the fact that these stereotypes have contributed to the justification and maintenance of oppressive forces, and the fact that such jokes are still told in an exclusionary way (Moore et al. 2012; Ashe, Borkowska, and Nazroo 2019), puts this revised joke on the wrong side of the line between merely disparaging versus belittling as well as disparaging. This belittling joke, however, is of less concern than the aspirin joke, because although the discrimination supported by the stereotype is in living memory, it is not a current injustice.

The most clear-cut cases of belittling jokes are those where the conveyed stereotypes or ideas play a role or have played a role in an oppressive system. While there are competing theories about what constitutes oppression, there is general agreement that oppression privileges one group over another; that oppression is often built into policies and institutions and thus is systemic; that oppression may be unintentional, i.e., oppressive social structures may be inadvertently discriminatory; and that most cases of oppression disadvantage people in multiple, interlocking ways, limiting members of the oppressed group.[5] Paradigm examples of oppressed groups include Black people, people with disabilities, and women. But one might reasonably think that there are groups that suffer from unjust disadvantage but are not oppressed. For example, people who are below average height suffer disadvantages, including earning less than tall people (Judge and Cable 2004); but even though this discrepancy seems unjust, one might hesitate to say that short people are oppressed.[6] Let's assume, for the sake of argument, that short people are unjustly disadvantaged, but that they are not oppressed—whereas Black people are unjustly disadvantaged, and are oppressed. Nevertheless, derogatory jokes about short people can communicate stereotypes that play a role in unjust disadvantage; so, jokes about short people may be belittling—no pun intended—because, depending on their content, they support and maintain unjust disadvantage.

Finally, let's consider an example about a named individual like Hillary Clinton. We might joke about her alleged coziness with big business, or we might make jokes about her as a woman. Overall, Clinton is a powerful figure, and although her relationships with Wall Street hurt her in the opinion of

Democratic voters in the 2016 election, the idea that she is overly friendly with business interests does not form part of a network of forces that unjustly disadvantages her or women in general. So, I would argue, jokes about her business interests are disparaging but not belittling. However, she is subject to larger forces that continue to make women an unjustly disadvantaged group. Thus, jokes about her gender may be belittling. Similarly, jokes about Donald Trump's tax returns may be disparaging but not belittling, whereas jokes about his weight may be belittling; and jokes about Joe Biden's bromance with Barack Obama may be merely disparaging, whereas jokes about his age may be belittling. So even though Clinton, Trump, and Biden are powerful figures, and thus may seem fair game for punching up, some jokes about them are off-limits.

Moral concern about (merely) disparaging humor

Thus far in this chapter, I have drawn two distinctions, between disparaging and belittling, and between jokes and jocular remarks. To summarize, a *derogatory joke* is a joke that conveys negative ideas or stereotypes about an individual or about a social group; a *belittling joke* is a derogatory joke where the conveyed ideas or stereotypes support or have supported unjust disadvantage. *Disparaging* jokes are derogatory jokes that do not belittle. Joking remarks, unlike scripted jokes, communicate information by the standard meanings of the words used, along with the grammatical structure of the remark. A *derogatory jocular remark*, then, is a jocular remark that conveys negative ideas or stereotypes about an individual or about a social group; a *belittling jocular remark* is a derogatory jocular remark where the conveyed negative ideas or stereotypes play or have played a role in supporting unjust disadvantage. At the risk of stating the obvious, *disparaging jocular remarks* are derogatory jocular remarks that do not belittle.

My main concern in this book is belittling jokes, particularly those that support and maintain oppressive systems. But belittling jokes are not the only morally concerning derogatory jokes. The jokes told about liberals and conservatives (who are not unjustly disadvantaged groups, whatever they might think) in Ford et al. (2020) are examples—as we saw in the section "Assessing Wrong Audience and Wrong Joker" in Chapter 3, the joke-telling undermined their self-confidence, their assessment of their qualifications, and their feelings of inclusion.

There also may be moral concerns about telling a disparaging joke if the telling involves undeserved mockery of the target, or if it causes unwarranted social discomfort, or if it discourages otherwise desirable courses of action. Suppose my friend mocks my household campaign to use less plastic, and that her joke conveys negative ideas or stereotypes about the group of people who want to limit their use of plastic; i.e., it is a derogatory but not a belittling joke, since there are no unjust disadvantages for people who want to use less plastic. Let's also suppose that reducing my use of plastic has at least minimal environmental benefits. If her mockery comes in the context of a friendship that involves substantial social support and approbation, it may cause no harm. I may be willing to laugh at myself, and for her to laugh at me, over my wish to reduce my relatively small contribution to the huge ocean vortex of plastic; I may be unmoved by her teasing, and continue an environmentally desirable course of action. On the other hand, it may be morally questionable of her to tell a similar joke in a context in which I am a nervous newcomer to a social group in which she is already comfortable, and in which my concern with the global environment will emphasize my differences from, rather than my commonalities with, other members of that group; or if her mockery leads me to abandon otherwise beneficial practices like taking my own bags to the supermarket. So, a derogatory but not belittling joke may have moral weight.

There are certainly circumstances in which telling derogatory jokes is morally permissible—e.g., it might be morally permissible to tell a joke derogating a dictator—as long as it does not belittle a disadvantaged group. So, if the dictator was a member of an unjustly disadvantaged indigenous group in a formerly colonized country, yet rose to power, it still would be belittling to joke about his origins or his accent—because such jokes convey stereotypes and ideas that support and maintain unjust disadvantage for others. But it would be permissible to joke about other traits of the dictator or his family. A joke about Imelda Marcos's shoes, for example, raises no concerns. Furthermore, derogatory jokes about other aspects of the dictator can have social benefits that make them not only permissible, but beneficial. Lowering him in public opinion, as disparaging jokes do, is all to the good. But wouldn't lowering him in status or power—e.g., ending his dictatorship— be good too? Yes, it would. As I have defined belittling jokes, however, they convey negative stereotypes or ideas that support or have supported unjust disadvantage. Ending his dictatorship would be a disadvantage to him, but it would not be unjust. Lowering him in power or status, however, while *also* lowering other members of his indigenous group, would be belittling people who suffer from unjust disadvantage.

I have argued that we should beware of jokes that support and maintain (or have supported and maintained) unjust disadvantage—so we should not tell derogatory jokes that communicate harmful stereotypes about African Americans, or the disabled, or the short of stature. But what about jokes derogating White people, non-disabled people, or tall people? By my reckoning, these jokes are not belittling—they do not communicate ideas that support unjust disadvantage, because these groups are not unjustly disadvantaged, and never have been; rather, they are unjustly privileged. So, my suggestion that we should not tell belittling jokes allows telling derogatory jokes about these groups. It should be clear by now, however, that I do think one can tell a derogatory joke that is not belittling but that nevertheless is of moral concern—perhaps the circumstances are such that emphasizing difference, and fostering feelings of social exclusion, should be avoided. Telling such a joke could be just plain mean, even if it isn't belittling.

Why, then, is it obnoxious to tell tall people jokes about their height? Is it only the circumstances that matter? No doubt there are many reasons they don't like it. There are some disadvantages that accrue if you are very tall—discomfort in airplane seats and lecture halls, for example, and unwanted attention. Another reason that you might take into account is that they have heard them all before. These jokes are not belittling, but they are tiresome.

Jokes that do not derogate

In this book I focus on derogatory jokes, but that's not to say there are no moral considerations governing the telling of jokes that are not derogatory. There are other ways in which jokes can be insensitive or unkind. There may be topics that are not suitable for joking, or social situations in which we ought not joke, or people with whom we should not joke. These are interesting issues, and worth considering; but I won't consider them in this book.

Where do jokes that convey positive ideas and stereotypes fit in my scheme? There are positive stereotypes that play a role in systems of unjust disadvantage. For example, stereotypes about the dominant group—e.g., that they are smart or hard-working—may help maintain the group's dominance. Thus, there may be jokes that are neither disparaging nor belittling but that convey stereotypes that play or have played a role in creating or maintaining unjust disadvantage. We should not continue to propagate these stereotypes, because they support unjust disadvantage for the group that has a subordinate position with respect to the targeted group. It follows that telling them may also be morally questionable.

Conclusion

In this chapter, I have distinguished between the disparaging and the belittling, and between jokes and jocular remarks. I have argued that what makes a joke or remark belittling is that it communicates stereotypes and ideas that support and maintain, or have supported and maintained, unjust disadvantage. I have also said that joking remarks communicate stereotypes and ideas through the standard meanings of the words used and the grammatical structure of the remark. But I haven't said anything about how scripted jokes communicate stereotypes and ideas. Obviously, this is a crucial issue. If they don't communicate stereotypes and ideas through the standard meanings of the words used and their grammatical structure, how do they communicate anything at all? I answer this question in the next chapter.

There's more to say about joking remarks too—we don't know yet how joking intent works—and I will come back to this topic in Chapter 7.

5

How do jokes communicate ideas?

Introduction

Common sense suggests that jokes convey stereotypes like the (false) stereotype that Irish people are lazy and drunken; and the empirical work I discussed in Chapter 3 confirms that such jokes communicate or reinforce derogatory ideas somehow—they must, since they affect how people think and act. But scripted derogatory jokes, unlike derogatory joking remarks, often do not convey derogatory ideas through the standard meanings of the words used. So how do they convey derogatory ideas?

In this chapter, I argue that scripted jokes communicate stereotypes and ideas by a kind of implication. It is a kind of implication we are all familiar with. Words for numbers, like 'two' and 'three', and the indefinite articles 'a' and 'an' provide classic examples: 'There are two apples' normally implies that there are only two apples; 'There's a dog in the garden' normally implies that it's an unfamiliar dog. These implications are not part of the literal meaning of 'two' or 'a'. If they were elements of literal meaning, a person who immediately revealed that there were more than two apples, or that it was a familiar dog, would contradict themselves. But these implications can be coherently denied; a person could say 'There are two apples; actually, there are five, but I need only two for this recipe', or 'There's a dog in the garden. It's Mr. Wheezy—that beagle mix from down the road'.

These kinds of implication have a fancy-pants name—they are called generalized conversational implicatures. But I will explain in plain English, so don't let the name put you off. They are called implicatures, rather than implications, because the philosopher H. P. Grice, who coined the term, wanted to distinguish them from other kinds of implication. For example, 'There are two apples' also implies that there are apples, but it would be self-contradictory to say, 'There are two apples, but there aren't any'. So, we have a reason to think 'There are two apples' implies there are *only* two apples in a different way than it implies that there are apples. The implicatures are described as *generalized* because they are implications of what a person says that are relatively constant from situation to situation. A person who says 'There are two___' normally implicates 'There are no more than two___'; it's a routine implication, rather than an implication caused by special details about this conversation. And they are called generalized *conversational* implicatures because Grice thought these implications exist because of rules and practices people follow in conversation; I will say more about this in the next section, "What are generalized implicatures?" The technical name 'generalized conversational implicature' is useful in philosophy and linguistics, but even people who work in those fields admit it's a mouthful, and use an acronym to talk about them. So, in this book, I will call them generalized implicatures.

To show that derogatory jokes have derogatory ideas and stereotypes as generalized implicatures, the first thing to establish is that jokes are sometimes told in order to communicate an idea for serious purposes. Let's start with an example of a joke that is not derogatory, told on the book jacket of a passionate guide to punctuation:

A panda walks into a café. He orders a sandwich, eats it, then draws a gun and fires two shots into the air. "Why?" asks the confused waiter, as the panda makes towards the exit. The panda produces a badly punctuated wildlife manual and tosses it over his shoulder. "I'm a panda," he says at the door. "Look it up." The waiter turns to the relevant entry, and sure enough, finds an explanation. "Panda. Large black-and-white bear-like mammal, native to China. Eats, shoots and leaves." (Truss 2003)

The last sentence of this joke provides the book with its title, *Eats, Shoots & Leaves*. On the book jacket, the joke is followed by the words: "So, punctuation really does matter, even if it is only occasionally a matter of life and death." This is not a non sequitur, but it does not follow from anything that the joke literally says, so it must follow from an idea that is conveyed by telling the joke. My explanation is that it follows from an idea that is generally implicated by telling the joke, that punctuation changes meaning. From the panda example, we know that jokes are sometimes told to communicate an idea; lecturers, pastors, and public speakers employ this strategy too.

The panda joke on the book jacket provides an example showing that jokes *can* be told because the joker intends to communicate an idea. But—to state the obvious—it would be foolhardy to argue that jokes are *always* told with the intent to communicate an idea. The panda joke, for example, might be told in a different context, where the joker's main intention is to amuse, say, to assuage boredom on a long car trip. On a car trip, telling the joke would still communicate that changes in punctuation cause changes in meaning. The teller does not choose the joke for that reason, however; she chooses it because she thinks her audience will find it funny. Similarly, tellers of derogatory jokes don't always intend to communicate derogatory ideas; sometimes, their primary intent is to amuse. But even in those circumstances, derogatory jokes have derogatory ideas as generalized implicatures, and so they communicate derogatory ideas even when that is not the teller's central goal. To understand why, we need to know more about what generalized implicatures are and how they work, and that is the topic of the next section, "What are generalized implicatures?" The explanation is going to take some time, but bear with me—we will get back to talking about jokes.

What are generalized implicatures?

A generalized implicature is a method of conveying information without explicitly saying it. People—including you—employ generalized implicature frequently, even though the term is not familiar outside philosophy and linguistics. In ordinary English, we use the term 'imply' to cover this phenomenon—as in, 'He implied there were only two apples'. I've given the example of words for numbers and the indefinite articles 'a' and 'an'; other examples are words that imprecisely describe a proportion, like 'some'— 'Some people love anchovies' generally implies that not everyone loves anchovies—and words like 'thinks'—'Alice thinks she left her keys at the office' generally implies that Alice doesn't know that she left her keys at the office.

In all these examples of generalized implicatures, the speaker can deny the implicature. So, someone could say, 'Some people love anchovies. In fact, everyone does'; or 'Alice thinks she left her keys at the office, in fact, she knows she did'. This kind of deniability has a technical name, cancelability. Alternatively, someone could go on to say what is generally implicated, without its seeming redundant. So, someone could say, 'Some people love anchovies. Some don't, though'. Or they could say, 'Alice thinks she left her keys at the office, but she doesn't know that she left them there'. This phenomenon also has a technical name, reinforceability. These properties of implicatures—cancelability and reinforceability—are part of the evidence that the implicatures aren't part of the literal meaning of what is said. By contrast, it is weird to try to cancel literal meaning—e.g., 'Alice thinks she left her keys at the office, in fact, she doesn't think she left her keys at the office'. It is also weird to reinforce literal meaning—e.g., 'Alice thinks she left her keys at the office, in fact, she thinks she left her keys at the office'—unless we are aiming for rhetorical effect.

While generalized implicatures—as the name suggests—are usually present, sometimes they are absent because of the specifics of the situation. Consider one of Grice's examples of a generalized implicature, "I broke a finger" (1989, 38). On most occasions, this implicates that the finger is one's own—so that you broke your own finger is a generalized implicature of 'I broke a finger'. But suppose a mobster is reporting back to the boss about an extortion attempt. "How did it go?" the boss asks. The mobster replies, "I broke a finger." In this conversation, the generalized implicature is overridden by the circumstances, and the mobster implies that the finger in question belonged to the victim.

It's important to note that while a generalized implicature may be one of the things a speaker is keen to communicate, it doesn't have to be the main thing they intend to communicate, and as cancelability shows, they might not have intended to communicate the implicature at all. Their main intent may be to communicate exactly what they said—e.g., that some people love anchovies, or that Alice thinks she left her keys at the office. Furthermore, a speaker might use a generalized implicature when they want to implicate something non-general as well. Let me illustrate. Suppose Alexandra and Betty are at a party, and Betty says, 'Some of the guests are already leaving'. What Betty implies depends on what has already happened in the conversation.

Consider this conversation about the time:

Alexandra: What time is it?
Betty: Some of the guests are already leaving.

Here, Betty implies that it must be late. But the generalized implicature that not all the guests are already leaving is present too.

Now consider this conversation, about John's whereabouts:

Alexandra: Where's John?
Betty: Some of the guests are already leaving.

Here, the same generalized implicature is present, but Betty also implies that perhaps John has already left (examples adapted from Levinson 1995, 92).

Betty's main implications in these two examples are also implicatures, even though they are not generalized implicatures. They are what Grice called particularized conversational implicatures. Explaining how they work requires a little more background knowledge.

Grice conceived of conversation as a form of rational behavior. When people behave rationally, they act in a way that helps them achieve their goals; for example, if my goal is to put dinner on the table, it would be rational of me to cook or order takeout, whereas it would be irrational of me to spend the available time shopping online instead. Often people work together to achieve shared goals; to get dinner on the table, perhaps I will take care of the kids and my husband will cook. Grice argues that we talk with other people because we have a purpose, and what we say contributes to that purpose, just as what we do contributes to a purpose when we behave rationally in other ways. Because talking is a form of rational behavior, Grice proposes that it is governed by a Cooperative Principle. In essence, the Principle instructs a speaker to say what is needed, when it is needed, for the conversation to reach mutually accepted goals. If the purpose of the conversation is to agree on what we will have for dinner, suitable conversational contributions would include seeking and giving information about what food is available in the fridge or pantry, or can be acquired in an appropriate time frame; what everyone likes to eat; what is reasonably healthy for us to eat; what we have time to cook; and so on. So, if my spouse asks, 'What do we have in the fridge?', the Cooperative Principle dictates against my listing inedible objects, like shelves and refrigerated medications. What is needed, at that point of the conversation, to reach our shared goal of putting dinner on the table is information about the things in the fridge that we might eat for dinner.

Implicatures arise because of the Cooperative Principle. Returning to Betty and Alexandra, Betty is supposed to say what is needed, when it is needed in the conversation. If Alexandra asks what time it is, then what is needed from Betty at that moment is information about the time; so, assuming Betty is cooperating, she intends to communicate something about the time by saying 'Some of the guests are already leaving'. A natural conclusion for Alexandra is that Betty doesn't know exactly what time it is, but that she takes the fact that some of the guests are already leaving to be relevant to Alexandra's question. So, Betty implicates that it must be late, because of the current purposes of this conversation. On the other hand, if Alexandra asks where John is, then what is needed from Betty at that moment is information about John's whereabouts; so, assuming Betty is cooperating, she intends to communicate something about where John is by saying 'Some of the guests are already leaving'. In this case, the natural conclusion for Alexandra is that Betty doesn't know where John is, but she takes the fact that some of the guests are already leaving to be relevant to Alexandra's question. Thus, Betty implicates that John might be leaving. (You may also recall an example from the introduction—Sally asks Kate, 'Are you going to the party?' and Kate replies, 'I have to work'. Since what is needed after Sally's question is information about whether Kate is going to the party, and Kate volunteers at that juncture of the conversation that she has to work, she implicates she won't be going to the party—it clashes with her work schedule.)

To summarize what I've said about generalized implicatures: Unlike particularized implicatures, generalized implicatures are not a product of the specifics of a conversation. They are routinely present with some words and phrases, and while sometimes they are the main thing the speaker wants to communicate, sometimes the main thing the speaker wants to communicate is something entirely different—think of Betty and Alexandra. Generalized implicatures are reinforceable—the speaker can go on to make the point explicitly; and they are cancelable—the speaker can coherently deny the generalized implicature. Finally, there are circumstances where a generalized implicature is absent because of specifics of the conversation—recall the mobster's check-in with his boss.

I promised that once I had described how generalized implicatures work, I would return to the topic of jokes, and now is the time. The remainder of the chapter gives some reasons for thinking that derogatory jokes communicate derogatory ideas by generalized implicature. I will start with asking whether the derogatory ideas conveyed by derogatory jokes act like other examples of generalized implicature—do they have the same properties of reinforceability and cancelability? I add some circumstantial evidence in favor of the theory that implicature is at work in derogatory joking, by pointing to other instances where people use implicature to communicate things they don't want to say straight out. Then, I show that the theory that derogatory jokes convey derogatory ideas by generalized implicature can explain the evidence we accumulated from popular wisdom and from science about Wrong Audience and Wrong Joker. At the end of the chapter, I'll talk about a few worries you might have about my theory.

To be quite clear, the argument in this chapter is not conclusive. My reason for thinking that this is the right explanation of how derogatory jokes work is that it is the best explanation. I'll talk about the main alternative explanation, and its failings, in "Telling derogatory jokes and presupposition" in Chapter 9.

Reinforcement and cancelation

If derogatory jokes have derogatory ideas as generalized implicatures, then the derogatory ideas that they convey should behave like other generalized implicatures—i.e., they should be reinforceable and cancelable. Let's start with reinforceability. Think of this joke:

> How many philosophers does it take to change a light bulb? It depends on
> how you define 'change'. (adapted from Bigelow n.d., quoted in Miller)

A person could tell that joke and go on to say, 'Philosophers can't answer a simple question without defining their terms', thus making the message of the joke explicit.

The conveyed derogatory idea should also be cancelable. Imagine the joke-teller is challenged—someone says, "Do you mean philosophers can't answer simple questions without defining their terms?" The joke-teller could, quite convincingly, say, "Oh, no, of course I don't mean that. They can answer simple questions without defining their terms."

It also would be quite natural for the joke-teller to then say, 'It's just a joke'—thus claiming that the generalized implicature is not the point he meant to convey. He might even claim that he didn't intend to communicate the implicature at all—all he wanted to do was to amuse. Similarly, when Betty answers Alexandra's question about John, she implicates that not everyone is already leaving, but if Alexandra goes on to ask if she means that not everyone is already leaving, Betty could coherently say 'Oh—I didn't mean that not everyone is already leaving—I just meant that John might be leaving'.

A joker who says he didn't mean to convey a derogatory claim by the joke might be telling the truth—perhaps he didn't think it through, or perhaps Harmless Fun has convinced him that jokes don't really communicate derogatory ideas. But as we all know, the joker might be lying—he really did mean to derogate with the joke, but now denies it.[1]

Using implicature to mislead and insinuate

Conversational implicature—particularized or generalized—is a desirable form of communication for someone who wishes to get something across without explicitly saying it; implicatures always leave room for the communicator to deny that the implication was intended. There are at least two cases where people use conversational implicature to communicate things that they do not wish to state openly; if I am correct, derogatory jokes are a third case.

The first case is when we use a conversational implicature so that we can deceive or mislead without—strictly speaking—lying. In 1998, the journalist Jim Lehrer interviewed then President Bill Clinton about rumors that he had had an affair with Monica Lewinsky. Lehrer asked, "You had no sexual relationship with this young woman?" and Clinton replied: "There is not a sexual relationship; that is accurate" (Federal News Service 1998a). When Clinton later testified to the Grand Jury about this and similar present-tense claims denying a relationship with Lewinsky, Clinton said:

[T]hat was well beyond any point of improper contact between me and Ms. Lewinsky. So that anyone generally speaking in the present tense, saying there is not an improper relationship, would be telling the truth if that person said there was not, in the present tense; the present tense encompassing many months. That's what I meant by that. (Federal News Service 1998b)

In the interview with Lehrer, Clinton chose the present tense deliberately, leaving open the possibility of self-defense on the grounds that he did not lie, since he was not currently having a sexual relationship with her. But what he conversationally implicated, and what he wanted people to believe, was that he had *never* had a sexual relationship with her, and that was false. Clinton's self-serving explanation relies on what someone usually means when they use the present tense; he does not acknowledge that since he was answering a question that Lehrer posed in the past tense, his reply had a particularized implicature—that he had never had a sexual relationship with Lewinsky.

The second case is insinuation. The philosopher Elisabeth Camp defines 'insinuation' as "the communication of beliefs, requests, and other attitudes 'off-record,' so that the speaker's main communicative point remains unstated" (2018, 42). She offers one of Grice's canonical examples of a particularized implicature as an "elegant illustration of insinuation." In this example, Professor Adams is asked to write a letter of recommendation for his student Mr. Xavier, who is applying for a job teaching philosophy; and the letter says just "Mr. Xavier's command of English is excellent, and his attendance at tutorials has been regular" (example adapted from Grice 1989, 33; Camp 2018, 42). The letter does not say what is needed given the purpose of a letter of recommendation. So, Professor Adams must believe that Mr. Xavier is no good at philosophy, and should not be hired, but he does not want to come right out and say so. He says something entirely innocuous instead, implying—by particularized implicature—that Mr. Xavier is no good at philosophy. In cases of insinuation, the speaker designs what they say so that its explicit content is innocuous, and the controversial or objectionable point is implicit.

There are at least two other cases, then, in which conversational implicature is used as a means to get across something that we do not wish to state openly—misleading and insinuating. Stating or asserting a disparaging or belittling claim leaves the speaker open to censure. Conversationally implicating it, with a joke or with another statement, allows the speaker to deny, disingenuously, that she meant to communicate the implication. Since implicature is a mechanism that is used, in non-humorous cases, to convey something that we do not wish to state, its use in derogatory jokes for the same purpose would be unsurprising.

Explaining Wrong Audience

As I characterized it, Wrong Audience is the popular claim that when there is something wrong with telling a derogating joke, it is because it is told to the wrong audience: Some wrong audiences belong to the derogated group, while others either pretend to be offended or really are offended, but should get over it, since jokes are harmless fun (see "Introduction" and "Audiences in popular wisdom" in Chapter 2). But we saw that evidence from social psychology does not support the Wrong Audience claim (see "Assessing Wrong Audience and Wrong Joker" in Chapter 3); rather, the evidence suggests that belittling jokes have more harmful effects on attitudes and beliefs when told to receptive audiences than to audiences who object (Ford 2000). However, both the popular wisdom and science suggest that the effects of derogatory jokes are different for different audiences. If derogatory jokes generally implicate derogatory ideas, how can we explain both the popular wisdom and the competing evidence from science?

One route for explaining the popular wisdom is to say that the derogatory ideas that are generally implicated by jokes are present in some circumstances but not in others—just as 'I broke a finger' usually implicates it is your own finger, but does not have that implication when the mobster says it. For example, we might argue that if I tell a joke about gay men to an audience who think it is funny, and who feel no discomfort with the joke, the derogatory implicature is absent.[2] But this explanation does not fit well with the evidence from social psychology; if the derogatory implicature is absent where the joke is welcome, why would anti-gay jokes affect the future actions of people who are higher in anti-gay prejudice (Ford et al. 2014)? So, I don't think this is the correct explanation. Rather, I think the derogatory claim communicated by the joke is present, even for an appreciative audience. Furthermore, an unappreciative audience—the audience who takes offense or objects—can identify the communicated derogatory claim too; if they could not identify it, why would they object? So rather than arguing that the implicature is present in one case, but not in the other, I think we would be better off arguing that the same implicature is present with both audiences, and that something else explains the difference between Right and Wrong audiences.

Arguing that the derogatory claims conveyed by derogatory jokes are generalized implicatures explains why derogatory jokes have effects in both Right and Wrong audiences. Generalized implicatures are nearly always present, even though they can be overridden in some circumstances. So why do derogatory jokes have different effects in different audiences, and what explains people's commitment to Wrong Audience? My answer is that people think that derogatory generalized implicatures are acceptable in some circumstances but not acceptable in others.

In Chapter 4, I distinguished between jokes that belittle and jokes that merely disparage—the former support unjust disadvantage, whereas the latter do not; e.g., a joke about Donald Trump's weight is belittling, whereas a joke about his tax returns is disparaging (see "Derogating, disparaging, and belittling"). Let's start with disparaging jokes.

With jokes that disparage but do not belittle, my sympathies lie, to some extent, with popular wisdom. Disparaging jokes generally implicate disparaging claims. But while there are many circumstances in which you shouldn't disparage someone—say, it will embarrass a child, or discourage someone from trying something new, or the disparaged person is your employee— there are other circumstances where disparaging someone is not a bad thing. So, the fact that a disparaging claim is conveyed isn't necessarily a reason to avoid the disparaging joke. This isn't to say that you must suck it up if someone disparages you, or that you are immature if you dislike it—disparaging jokes can be a form of bullying. But, with regard to some traits, the ability to laugh at oneself can be a good thing. For example, you should feel free to make jokes about how much knitting yarn and quilting fabric I have stashed in my closet. But you should lay off if, say, I am meeting my husband's extended family for the first time—not because that would make the joke belittling, but because it would be unkind and unwelcoming.

But what about belittling jokes? Suppose that both Right and Wrong audiences recognize that belittling jokes normally imply belittling claims (of course, they need not be familiar with the concept of a generalized implicature—it is enough that they can identify the conveyed claim). The difference between Right and Wrong audiences is in their reaction to the implicated claim. The Wrong audience identifies the conveyed claim and finds it obnoxious because of, e.g., its role in present-day or historical un- just disadvantage. But what about the Right audience? Right audiences are not all the same. Some Right audiences may fail to understand that the implicated claim supports unjust disadvantage; e.g., they may not believe that the belittled group is or was subject to unjust disadvantage, or they may understand that the implicated claim supports disadvantage but they do not think the disadvantage is unjust—perhaps some members of Fosdick's au- dience at the cardboard company where Swinton worked fall in this group. These Right audiences mistakenly think that the jokes are merely dispar- aging. Other Right audiences might understand that the implicated claim usually supports unjust disadvantage, but mistakenly believe that since it is entered into this conversation in a humorous way, it doesn't support unjust disadvantage in this case—these people are in the grips of Harmless Fun. A third kind of Right audience may understand that the claim supports un- just disadvantage, and understand that it does so even under the guise of humor, and they just don't care—perhaps they favor the group in question being unjustly disadvantaged. This is the most malevolent kind of Right audience.

Explaining Wrong Joker

The popular wisdom is that one ought not tell a derogatory joke about someone else's group, but one may tell a derogatory joke about one's own group; i.e., the social identity of the joker matters to the morality, or at least to the prudence, of joke-telling. Suppose that derogatory jokes have generalized implicatures. How could it be that telling a joke about one's own group is acceptable, but that it is not acceptable to tell a similar joke about another group? There are a couple of options one might consider in answering this question. One option is to argue that there are different implicatures in the case where the speaker belongs to the derogated group than there are where the speaker does not belong to the derogated group; when a speaker tells a derogatory joke about her own group, she does not implicate a derogatory idea, whereas when a speaker tells a derogatory joke about someone else's group, she does implicate a derogatory idea.[3] However, I do not think that is the best explanation of Wrong Joker.

Recall that audiences seem to be more likely to be receptive to negative ideas when the joker is a member of the derogated group than when she is not (Ford 2000)—see "Assessing Wrong Audience and Wrong Joker" in Chapter 3. If the joker did not implicate a derogatory idea when telling a derogatory joke about her own group, that would explain the popular wisdom about Wrong Joker, but not the related evidence-based claim. To accord with the evidence-based claim, it would be better to argue that the same generalized implicature is present in both cases, but while it is commonly perceived as innocuous when implicated by a member of the derogated group, in fact it is more dangerous.[4]

In my opinion, what explains the popular wisdom is the general principle that it is socially acceptable to deprecate oneself, but it is not socially acceptable to deprecate others. This principle extends to one's group—it is socially acceptable to deprecate one's own group but it is not socially acceptable to deprecate someone else's group. This is why the identity of the joker matters; etiquette tells us I may express negative things about myself and my group, but I may not express negative things about others. Humor-specific etiquette also tells us that I may laugh at myself and my own group, but I may not laugh at others and their groups. (Think of the statement 'I'm laughing with you, not laughing at you'.) Furthermore, borrowing from Ford, when the speaker crosses the social boundary of laughing at others, what is expressed is subjected to more critical scrutiny than when she does not cross that boundary. So, when a speaker tells a derogatory joke about her own group, she has not crossed a social boundary and thus the implicature is more likely to be taken on board than when a speaker tells a derogatory joke about someone else's group. Crossing this social boundary alerts the listener's critical faculties. The popular wisdom that a speaker may tell a joke about her own group but not about another's group, then, rests on a general principle about the social acceptability of self-deprecation.

Troubleshooting: 'Missing' implicatures

So far, we have not run into any obstacles for my thesis that derogatory jokes have derogatory ideas as generalized implicatures; the ideas that derogatory jokes convey are reinforceable and cancelable, as we would expect, and we can explain both Wrong Audience and Wrong Joker. Furthermore, circumstantial evidence is on my side, since we use implicature to mislead and to insinuate. But wait, you might think—what about the mobster? In that case, I said that the generalized implicature—that the mobster broke his own finger—was overridden by circumstances. So, if derogatory jokes have derogatory ideas as generalized implicatures, shouldn't there be cases where we can tell a derogatory joke but the derogatory claim is overridden? And in such cases, wouldn't a restricted version of Harmless Fun be correct; i.e., wouldn't it be true that at least sometimes, there is nothing wrong with telling derogatory jokes?

To answer this question, we need to think more about why generalized implicatures sometimes seem to be missing. Grice noted that implicatures may be in short supply in relatively uncooperative conversations, like a cross-examination in a courtroom (1989, 369–70). Suppose that the color of the apples at the scene of a crime is relevant to establishing guilt, and the witness says, 'Some of the apples were red'; it would be advisable for the lawyer to ask whether there were some apples that were not red, i.e., to check whether the witness is committed to the generalized implicature. Here, the witness might have chosen to say that some of the apples were red because it is in her interest for the court to believe that there were non-red apples too, but she doesn't want to lie under oath; she wishes to tell the truth, but not the whole truth. Similarly, if teenage siblings are bickering about sharing apples, and one of them says, 'There are two apples', it might be necessary to ask explicitly if there are no more than two apples. We attribute conversational implicatures to others only on the assumption that the conversationalists are cooperating, and where there is reason to doubt that they are cooperating, we also have reason to wonder about which implicatures they will espouse and which they will deny.

With the courtroom and the teenagers, we don't know if the speaker will openly commit to the implicature, so we have to ask. The implicature is present in the sense that it crosses the audience's mind, and an audience who is not exercising due caution may take the implicated idea on board as a fact, concluding that there were non-red apples in the courtroom, and that there are only two apples with the teenagers. So, if we choose to say the implicature is absent or missing in uncooperative conversations, what we mean is that we don't know whether the speaker will openly commit to the implicature—and we wouldn't be in the least surprised if they were not willing to openly state what they implicated. In both examples, the speaker wants us to believe the implicature, but doesn't want to be openly committed to it.

Similarly, with derogatory jokes, there are cases where we don't know if the speaker will openly commit to the derogatory implicature. But that doesn't mean that the speaker did not communicate the implicature; it also doesn't mean that the speaker didn't intend to communicate the implicature. It just means we can't be sure that the speaker will openly express the implicature.

Unlike a witness in a courtroom, the mobster is cooperative. The generalized implicature that the broken finger is his own is not in effect because of the particulars of the conversation. He is responding to a question about how the extortion attempt went, and thus it is more cooperative for him to describe the extortion attempt than to detail his injuries. In this example, there is a particularized implicature that replaces the usual generalized implicature that it is his finger—i.e., the broken finger belongs to the victim, not, say, a stranger who happened by during the extortion attempt. So, the generalized implicature is not present because the mobster was trying to communicate something else—in this case, something quite different from what is usually implicated by 'I broke a finger'. When Grice first introduces the concept of a generalized implicature, he says, "Sometimes one can say that the use of a certain form of words in an utterance would normally (in the absence of special circumstances) carry such-and-such an implicature or type of implicature" (1989, 37). So, as Grice thought of generalized implicatures, they are the default interpretation. The mobster's case is one where there are special circumstances that override the default. Note, however, that even in this circumstance, the boss might wonder if the normal implicature is still in place—'Wait, your finger or his finger?'; or he might say, 'Never mind about your finger, did you get the money?'

What would count as special circumstances in the case of derogatory jokes? To parallel the example of the mobster, there would have to be something about the prior conversation that made it clear that the joker did not mean the joke to communicate what it usually communicates; and there would have to be something else that the joker wanted to communicate instead. So, although many jokers would like to believe that when they tell a derogatory joke to be funny they divorce themselves from the derogatory implication, that would not parallel the mobster example, because there isn't something else that the joker was trying to communicate instead. (Trying to communicate that the joker is funny doesn't count, because there are lots of ways to be funny—there is no reason to choose this particular joke, one that normally communicates a derogatory idea, if the only goal is to entertain.)

Everyone I have talked to about derogatory jokes—and there are quite a few—thinks that derogatory jokes can be told ironically; e.g., a woman can tell a joke that would normally derogate women in circumstances where it is perfectly clear that she is airing an unwarranted prejudice, or expressing her exasperation with a stereotype. Perhaps this is a case where there is something else the woman wishes to communicate.

Troubleshooting: Unconvincing cancelations

I said that the derogatory claims conveyed by derogatory jokes are cancelable, just as they should be if they are generalized implicatures. But you might wonder if that's true—even if a joker denies the derogatory claim associated with the joke, isn't the denial rather unconvincing? So, is it really cancelable? Technically speaking, it is cancelable, but there are unconvincing cancelations.[5] Grice gives the following example, in which he is reporting about a student's progress at an end-of-term meeting with his colleagues:

> All I say is 'Jones has beautiful handwriting and his English is grammatical.' . . . I (the speaker) could certainly be said to have implied that Jones is hopeless. . . . The implication is cancellable. . . . [I]f I add 'I do not of course mean to imply that he is no good at philosophy' my whole utterance is intelligible and linguistically impeccable, even though it may be extraordinary tutorial behavior; and I can no longer be said to have implied that he was no

good, even *though perhaps that is what my colleagues might conclude to be the case if I had nothing else to say.* (1961, 130, my emphasis)[6]

In the case as described, the implication can be canceled; but his colleagues might conclude that Jones is no good at philosophy *even if* the imaginary Grice cancels it as an implicature. If Grice adds no further explanation or comment, the cancelation is unconvincing.

Similarly, someone who tells a derogatory joke might deny a derogatory claim conveyed by the joke. The denial may be unconvincing. But that does not mean that the claim is uncancelable.[7]

Conclusion

The argument in this chapter supports my thesis that derogatory jokes convey derogatory claims by generalized implicature. I established (with the panda joke) that there are some clear-cut cases where jokes are used to communicate ideas. I showed that the derogatory claims conveyed by derogatory jokes have the properties of generalized implicatures—they are reinforceable and cancelable. I pointed to some circumstantial evidence that there are other cases (misleading and insinuating) where implicature does the dirty work of communicating a claim without saying it outright. I also argued that the thesis explains the evidence about derogatory jokes from popular wisdom and from science. But all that is not enough to establish my thesis that derogatory jokes convey derogatory claims by generalized implicature.

To see why I think generalized implicature is at work in derogatory joking, I regret to say, you will have to read on. My argument for this thesis is what is called 'an argument to the best explanation'. People use arguments to the best explanation all the time. For example, I recently concluded that the kids who lived half a mile away in our rural neighborhood must have moved; my evidence was that we hadn't seen the school bus in a while, and that they didn't stop by to trick-or-treat, even though we are a very reliable source of Halloween candy. The absence of the school bus could have been explained if the family had started homeschooling during the pandemic, but homeschooling wouldn't explain their failure to come to our house on Halloween; the best explanation was that the kids didn't live there anymore. And sure enough, a neighbor confirmed that the house had been sold. Arguments to the best explanation are also a mainstay of science; scientists support theories by showing that they explain the evidence better than any other available theory. To do so, of course, it's important to consider whether those other theories are any better. Fortunately, in the case of derogatory jokes, there is really only one viable competitor. I'll talk about it in Chapter 9; see "Telling derogatory jokes and presupposition." Before we get to that, I will say more about how my theory works. Next up, in Chapter 6, we turn to the topic of why humorous derogation is particularly insidious.

6

Humor and hostility

Introduction

Joking is an indirect and sometimes long-winded way of communicating a derogatory idea; but indirect communication can be highly effective. The most direct way of communicating an idea is not always the best way, and gifted speakers might choose to communicate something indirectly for rhetorical reasons. Jesus told parables; there is wisdom in Aesop's fables; novelists, poets, and playwrights share insights through creative writing. In this chapter, I will argue that there are aspects of human cognition that give humor additional power, so it is far from true that we can say whatever we like if it is framed as a joke. We know from empirical work that a derogatory joke can have more impact than a non-humorous derogatory statement, having a more significant effect on the beliefs and actions of, for example, people high in hostile sexism (see "Are belittling jokes harmless fun?" in Chapter 3). There may be multiple factors that explain why humor has this extra oomph, but in this chapter, I am going to focus on humor's effect on critical thinking.

In work that won a Nobel Prize in economics, Daniel Kahneman and his collaborator Amos Tversky argue that human beings employ two cognitive processes (see, e.g., Tversky and Kahneman 1983; Kahneman 2011). One of these is highly intuitive and provides seemingly instantaneous judgments; this fast method is known as System 1. The slow method, System 2, involves more effort, along with conscious thought and reasoning. Work on dual-process systems of cognition indicates that being in a good mood invites us to rely on the speedy System 1 as opposed to the more ponderous System 2. But System 1, in addition to being fast and intuitive, is prone to error. This, I will suggest, helps derogatory ideas that are expressed in humor bypass our critical defenses, as well as affecting how conversations develop. I begin by saying more about how System 1 and System 2 are thought to work; then I'll turn to the effect of mood on our cognitive processes.

Dual-process theories of cognition

There are many theories, that, like Kahneman's, propose that there are dual processes of cognition. If you see a quilt on a bed, System 1 will tell you if the quilt is too big or too small. But if you are calculating how many log cabin blocks you need to make a quilt that will cover the bed, you will use System 2—considering the dimensions of the blocks and the dimensions of the bed, adjusting for seam allowances, and planning a layout of the blocks; perhaps you will consult books, draw a diagram, and plan on graph paper. Practice and expertise can change whether you need System 1 or System 2 for a task; a very experienced quilter may be able to say how many blocks of a given size are needed for a quilt with no explicit calculations.

System 1 is fast because it relies on heuristics and generalizations. But this also makes it prone to mistakes and cognitive biases. While an expert relying on System 1 can be very reliable—the canonical example is of a chess grandmaster taking a glance at a game in progress and knowing how many moves are needed to checkmate—even experts can mess up when using System 1. Tversky and Kahneman (1983) asked a group of physicians to evaluate the probability that a patient who had a pulmonary embolism following a surgery would have various symptoms. The doctors rated it more probable that the patient would experience shortness of breath *and* partial paralysis than that she would experience partial paralysis. But that can't be correct, since any experience of both symptoms is also an experience of one of the symptoms—similarly, it cannot be more likely that I have a fever *and* a sore throat than that I have a fever. Tversky and Kahneman also asked a group of professional forecasters, many of whom were employed as analysts, to estimate the probability that there would be "a complete suspension of diplomatic relations between the USA and the Soviet Union, sometime in 1983" (307); others were asked to estimate the probability that there would be "a Russian invasion of Poland, and a complete suspension of diplomatic relations between the USA and the Soviet Union, sometime in 1983" (307). The latter event—invasion plus suspension—was rated as more probable than the former event—suspension alone. But any invasion-plus-suspension is also a suspension of diplomatic relations, and so invasion-plus-suspension cannot be more probable than suspension by itself.

Tversky and Kahneman propose that the forecasters were misled because the invasion story introduces a plausible scenario in which suspension of diplomatic relations would be probable. They argue that the doctors were misled because shortness of breath is a typical symptom of pulmonary embolism, whereas partial paralysis is not. Both professional forecasters and physicians have training in probability and statistics, and recognize that these are errors when they are pointed out, so Tversky and Kahneman argue that these errors are generated by System 1. Tversky and Kahneman revealed the error in a discussion group with some of the doctors who participated in the study; they report, "Most participants appeared surprised and dismayed to have made an elementary error of reasoning" (1983, 302). Subsequent research has shown that there are many factors that encourage the use of one of the two cognitive systems rather than the other; for our purposes, the most significant of these is the thinker's mood.[1]

How a good mood affects cognitive processing

On the dual-process model endorsed by Kahneman, System 2 monitors System 1, checking for errors and intervening when needed, substituting a slower, more deliberative process to evaluate information more carefully. Factors that restrict our ability to avoid intuitive errors include time pressure and multi-tasking. What matters most for understanding the role of humor in propagating and reinforcing discrimination, though, is that being in a good mood encourages the use of System 1 and makes it less likely that System 2 will intervene and correct course. For example, Isen, Nygren, and Ashby (1988) found that subjects in a better mood—because they had been given a small bag of candy—made choices that deviated further from rational ideals than the control group; Bless et al. (1996) showed happy or sad video clips to induce a happy or sad mood, and found that the happy participants relied more on general knowledge in recalling events in a story than those in a sad mood. To generalize, a good mood encourages the use of System 1, and thus encourages more errors because of System 1's reliance on heuristics and stereotypes, and its susceptibility to cognitive biases.

Let's make a not very rash assumption: Being amused by a joke is one way of being in a good mood. Then we might expect that people who are amused by a joke would be less critical as they absorb its message, and more prone to subsequent errors of judgment, than those who have not. To the best of my knowledge, nobody has tested whether jokes, specifically, encourage the use of System 1 at the expense of System 2. But evidence collected by the Ford lab is concordant with the hypothesis that amusement about a joke would encourage use of System 1. As you recall, subjects high in hostile sexism were more likely to have sexist attitudes and to exhibit sexist behaviors after hearing a sexist joke than hearing a sexist statement; but the effect was dissipated if they were told to read the jokes critically—i.e., told to kick in System 2 (see "Are belittling jokes harmless fun?" in Chapter 3). To make a second not very rash assumption: Being offended by a joke is one way of being in a bad mood. Then we might expect that those who are offended would be more critical, and less subject to errors of judgment, than those who are amused. This is an oversimplification, but when we ask someone who is offended by a joke to lighten up, we ask them to set aside System 2 and relax into using the error-prone System 1.

If humor, to some extent, diminishes our use of System 2, and thus diminishes our use of rationality, it does so regardless of whether the content of the humor is derogatory or not. So even though lecturers often use humor to draw in an audience, in doing so we may be discouraging one of the things we most want from our students—critical thought about what we say. When the content of the humor is derogatory, there is no reason to suppose that humor dims rationality only about the people or group of people we derogate; the effects of a good mood on cognition are global. In Isen, Nygren, and Ashby (1988), for example, a good mood was induced by giving a small amount of candy, but the irrational behavior was exhibited in gambles about the course credit students would earn for participating in the experiment. In Bless et al. (1996), mood was induced either by watching a video clip or by describing a happy or sad event in the subjects' lives in vivid detail; but greater reliance on System 1 in the happy subjects was exhibited in recall of stories that were unrelated to the method of mood induction—stories about going out to dinner, riding on a tram, or making a phone call from a public telephone.

One effect of derogatory humor might be that listeners are more open to, and less critical of, the negative stereotypes that are conveyed by the humor; but we might expect them to make other, unrelated, errors of rationality as well. An unexplained piece of data from Ford et al. (2008) is suggestive: Subjects who were high in hostile sexism and exposed to sexist comedy skits, as opposed to non-sexist skits, proposed more budget cuts for the Michigan Black Student Union as well as for the National Student Council of Women, even though the humor did not communicate negative stereotypes about Black people (see "Are belittling jokes harmless fun?" in Chapter 3). Ford et al.'s discussion points to a finding of Glick and Fiske (1996), that people who are high in hostile sexism tend to be prejudiced against both women and African Americans. Perhaps, for these people, sexist humor encourages greater reliance on the stereotypes they hold, and discourages their better selves from countering those stereotypes with more conscious considerations along with knowledge about racist discrimination and its effects.

Troubleshooting: Why is neutral humor harmless?

If humor, in general, encourages System 1 to take over at the expense of System 2, why doesn't neutral humor have the same effects on sexist behavior and attitudes as sexist humor? In a review of literature about affect and cognition, Gasper and Spencer (2019) say that "numerous studies indicate that people in happy moods are more likely to rely on stereotypes to make judgments than those in neutral or sad moods" (723). But human beings are aware of many stereotypes and cognitive shortcuts, and circumstances might determine *which* of these stereotypes are more available. Furthermore, some people may have worked to reduce their dependence on a widespread stereotype because they believe it to be false and unfair, whereas others remain reliant on that very same stereotype. In addition, some recent studies challenge the idea that happiness promotes System 1 reasoning, per se, and argue that happiness promotes whatever processing strategies are readily available, reducing the likelihood that people will employ less accessible methods of reasoning; on this view, happy moods promote use of System 1 because System 1 is in general more accessible than System 2. So perhaps neutral humor encourages System 1 processing, with its use of generalizations, stereotypes, and heuristics as opposed to careful, considered, reasoning, whereas sexist humor encourages reliance on System 1 *and* makes sexist stereotypes particularly salient among the many cultural stereotypes that float around in our minds.

How might humor influence cognitive processing?

We know that being in a good mood invites System 1 processing, and it's reasonable to suppose that being amused is one way of being in a good mood. But is there anything specific about humor, as opposed to other good moods, that explains why it encourages System 1 processing and discourages System 2 processing?

Dannagal Young, a communications professor, proposes that humor affects both our motivations and our abilities to critically examine the messages conveyed by jokes (2008). With regard to motivation, we like feeling good, and we feel good when we are amused. In general, we are motivated to continue feeling good, and are disinclined to do things that would make us feel less good; this is a fact about the reward system in the human brain. So we are less motivated to find fault with the message of a humorous remark, and to express it, because doing so would bring negative feelings along with it.

With regard to our abilities to critically examine jokes, Young argues that humor introduces greater cognitive load than serious speech—a listener has to interpret the humorous remark, recognize incongruity, draw on background knowledge about stereotypes, and so on. This load decreases the availability of processing power for other things, including being critical about what is conveyed by the humor. This idea is consonant with the work of Ford, who argues that humor discourages a critical mindset—although he does not discuss possible mechanisms (2000); see "Assessing Wrong Audience and Wrong Joker" in Chapter 3. It is also consonant with what is known about the effect of multi-tasking on the use of System 1 versus System 2 cognitive processing—if I am preoccupied with one demanding cognitive task, I am more likely to rely on the heuristics and shortcuts of System 1, than the slower, deliberative processes of System 2. So, expressing an idea humorously reduces the likelihood that the listener will expend cognitive effort on evaluating the idea expressed.

Young's thesis about how humor affects cognitive processing could be bolstered or undermined by functional magnetic resonance imaging (fMRI), since fMRI measures the activation of parts of the brain, and neuroscientists know something about what parts of the brain are associated with different cognitive processes. And indeed, there is fMRI evidence that humor activates areas of the brain involved in the reward system, including the nucleus accumbens, which is also activated with many other forms of reward, including food, sex, and cocaine (Mobbs et al. 2003). The fact that humor activates the reward system is consistent with Young's thesis that we are motivated to maintain the good mood promoted by joking, and disinclined to dispel our mood by engaging critically with the content of the joke.

What about Young's second thesis, that the greater cognitive load imposed by interpreting humor reduces the availability of cognitive resources for other tasks, and thus makes us more reliant on the heuristics and cognitive shortcuts of System 1? There's certainly reason to suppose that humor takes additional processing—since we need to do the cognitive work needed to "get" the joke. But there is also additional cognitive load imposed by the social conflict and hostility involved in disparaging humor. A team of neuroscientists in France and Italy conducted fMRI studies of people's brains processing disparaging jokes as opposed to non-humorous, but socially inappropriate, statements (Bartolo et al. 2021). They found that both humorous and non-humorous disparagement activated areas of the brain associated with empathy, with representing the mental states of others, and with processing of socially inappropriate content. Humorous disparagement, in addition, activated areas of the brain associated with detection, comprehension, and appreciation of humor. So humorous disparagement couples the cognitive load imposed by humor with the cognitive load imposed by social conflict—and we might conclude that disparaging jokes take more cognitive processing than neutral jokes because of the need to identify and process social conflict, and that disparaging jokes take more processing resources than non-humorous disparagement because of the need to interpret the humor and to interpret the motivations of the joker.

The evidence that disparaging jokes require us to process social conflict is boosted by the findings of a team led by Yu-Chen Chan, a psychologist. Chan and her colleagues used fMRI to study people processing what they call hostile jokes; unlike the derogatory jokes that are the focus of this book, hostile jokes are not aimed at social groups, but are a kind of humor "in which a target is humiliated, insulted, embarrassed, or physically hurt" (2016, 2). Chan et al. found that people who were listening to (or reading) hostile jokes as opposed to straight-faced hostility with similar content showed greater activity in areas of the brain that are associated with the processing of social aggression.

The subjects in Chan's study were native Mandarin speakers, and the research was conducted in Taiwan, so the cultural mores surrounding insult and social standing are different than they are in many parts of the United States, and we cannot assume that people born and raised in another culture would perceive the threat and significance of hostile humor in the same way. But these fMRI results are certainly consistent with Young's thesis that disparaging jokes take more processing power than non-jokes, and thus may introduce multi-tasking that limits our ability to critically assess the ideas introduced by the jokes. It's notable, however, that Young suggested that the additional processing power was needed to understand the humor, whereas Chan et al.'s work indicates that hostility expressed in jokes takes processing power beyond that needed to process non-hostile jokes; it was not just humor, but social conflict embodied in humor, that increased activation in the dorsal medial prefrontal cortex. It is also notable that the subjects in Chan et al. were in an fMRI machine; so, they were processing social conflict in the absence of a real interaction between others.

Expressing something as a joke, then, encourages listeners to be more accepting and less argumentative; it exploits facts about the reward system in the human brain, and facts about our cognitive processing, to allow its message to pass unchallenged into our minds. There's no reason to think that jokers understand this mechanism, of course, or explicitly intend to get the mechanism to kick in. But human beings spend a lot of time talking, so we have a lot of evidence to draw upon; we have seen what tends to happen when we use humor. So even though a joker may not understand that he is reducing the argumentative power of his listeners, he may know—at least implicitly—that his listeners are much less likely to argue back if he expresses something humorously.

How amusement affects the common ground

I have argued that humor may steer us toward System 1 processing and away from System 2 processing. Obviously, our cognitive processing will affect our beliefs about and our actions toward other people. But when we are engaged in conversation, we also have beliefs about the conversation itself, and participating in a conversation involves a series of actions, both verbal and nonverbal. In this section, I explore how humor may affect our cognition about the shared assumptions that underlie a conversation, and that change as the conversation continues.

You are familiar with the ordinary concept of common ground—shared interests or beliefs, that serve as a basis for discussion. The philosopher Robert Stalnaker has adapted that concept to help explain how conversations typically develop over time (2002). In Stalnaker's technical sense, the common ground in a group of people is the assumptions that the members of the group share and that they assume they all share. The common ground constrains how a conversation proceeds because it affects what the participants should and should not say. For example, generally participants in a conversation should not assert what is already in the common ground—since everyone already takes that for granted. So, assuming other people in the conversation do not know how many siblings I have, it is perfectly appropriate to say "I have three siblings. Their names are Una, Catherine, and Brian"; but it would be a little weird to say "My siblings' names are Una, Catherine, and Brian. I have three siblings." In the former case, the common ground first gains the information about the number of my siblings—three—and second gains information about their names. In the latter case, the common ground gains the information that I have three siblings when I list three names. This explains why it is odd to go on to specify the number of siblings—that information is already in the common ground.

The everyday concept of the common ground generally involves belief. In Stalnaker's technical sense, however, while some of the assumptions in the common ground may be shared beliefs, others are merely accepted for the purposes of the conversation. There can be something in the common ground that nobody believes, but that we accept for the sake of discussion. For example, if someone says, "Suppose you have enough money to take a private trip into space; would you go?," the common ground then contains the assumption that you have enough money to take a private trip into space. There also can be something in the common ground that some believe and others do not; all that matters is that it is treated as a shared assumption for this conversation. For example, if Suzanna says she would give the money to Doctors without Borders, some of us might believe that she would, and others might not; but it becomes common ground if none of us challenges her. In addition to what is added during the conversation, the common ground usually includes shared background that is taken for granted but that nobody has mentioned in this conversation—e.g., it might include as background that taking a private trip into space is very expensive.

In Stalnaker's terminology, the contents of the common ground are presupposed by the people who are conversing, and the shared assumptions are presuppositions. Stalnaker, like Grice, conceives of a conversation as a rational, cooperative effort, and rationality has a high standard for the common ground. For example, in an ideal conversation what is added to the common ground must be consistent with what is already there, or what is already there must be adjusted so that the new idea can be added without creating an inconsistency. An assertion is a proposal to add something new to the common ground. Unless someone rejects the proposal, everyone should add the new assertion to what they presuppose. Furthermore, something that was previously presupposed may need to be rejected, because it is incompatible with the newly acquired assumption. The future course of the conversation is affected because the addition of this assertion may rule out future assertions that contradict it, or that are redundant because of it. Implicatures also add information to the common ground, and as with assertions, the common ground may need to be adjusted to accommodate an implicature.

An ideal conversation has a carefully honed common ground, rationally constructed and adjusted by those who are involved in the conversation. But what about when things are non-ideal? As we learn from Tversky and Kahneman, along with a host of others, we are prone to mistakes when using the cognitive processes of System 1. So, the ideal conversation—from a rational point of view—would be conducted with System 2 in charge of our cognitive processing, since System 2 is much more likely to identify and correct logical mishaps in the common ground than System 1. We also learn that we are more likely to use System 1 when we are in a good mood. So, if we are amused by a joke, and thus in a better mood, the conversation may drift from the ideal; humor may loosen up our cognitive processing, encouraging the use of stereotypes and heuristics, and making it more likely that we will accept inadequately supported claims and make the mistakes of reasoning that are associated with System 1.

If we are talking to each other for sheer enjoyment, and the topics are of little import, there is little or nothing to worry about if System 1 is in charge. But if the topic is a weighty one, a humorous conversation might be imprudent, and even harmful, because it might encourage irrational thought; some things, as the cliché tells us, are no laughing matter. So, what if the joke that amuses us introduces or reinforces a harmful stereotype about an unjustly disadvantaged group? In such a case, allowing System 1 to steer our cognitive processing without the oversight of System 2 allows us to rely on that harmful stereotype rather than on realistic, rational assessments. A conversation that includes belittling jokes, then, may encourage unreliable, intuitive thought processes that allow the common ground—and thus our own thoughts—to include belittling ideas and stereotypes that might otherwise be rejected by the slower, more conscious, cognitive processes of System 2. At some level, of course, we may recognize that the derogatory ideas we are entertaining are false, and if asked about them directly, we might reject them. The common ground, as you recall, must be accepted for the purposes of the conversation but does not have to be believed. Unfortunately for us, though, what is in the common ground of this conversation might stick with us, worming its way into our future judgments and decisions. And indeed, Ford has shown that for some people, on some topics, exposure to belittling jokes does affect future behavior (Ford et al. 2008, 2014); for details, see "Are belittling jokes harmless fun?" in Chapter 3.

Dual cognitive processes and the Wrong Audience

One element of the popular wisdom about derogatory jokes is that some audiences do not understand that derogatory jokes are harmless fun. In popular wisdom, these Wrong audiences are overly punctilious; they have mislaid their sense of humor (or never had one), and should lighten up (see "Introduction" and "Audiences in popular wisdom" in Chapter 2). Research, however, suggests that an audience who takes a joke lightly may, in some circumstances, be adversely affected by the joke, although this effect can be disarmed by asking the audience to approach the joke "on a serious level" and to consider the "underlying message that is implied by the joke" (Ford 2000, 1099–100); see "How a good mood affects cognitive processing." Furthermore, research shows that being in a good mood encourages reliance on the heuristics and stereotypes of System 1, rather than on the careful, considered reasoning of System 2. We might argue, then, that so-called Wrong audiences evade the misleading effects of humor, kicking in System 2—with all its cognitive caution.

Popular wisdom also tells us that there are appropriate audiences for a joke. One aspect of the Wrong Audience claim concerns the social identity of the members of the audience. But the attitudes of audience members toward derogatory jokes are more important in determining which audiences are Right audiences, because sometimes attitudes override social identity (see "Are belittling jokes harmless fun?" in Chapter 3 and "What kind of person is amused by derogatory jokes?" in Chapter 9). According to popular wisdom, Right audiences understand that jokes are harmless fun. Right audiences are mature and don't take offense to something that is harmless; furthermore, they do not pretend to be offended for political convenience. All in all, the Right audience takes jokes lightly. But contrary to popular wisdom, the light-hearted mood of the Right audience presents cognitive dangers, since they are more likely to use System 1—that is, to rely on heuristics, stereotypes, and cognitive shortcuts that lead to error.

Conclusion

It is often thought that jokes are above reproach—or at least, that jokes are less worrisome than serious statements that convey the same message. This thought explains why people defend themselves by saying "It was just a joke." But the empirical work done by social psychologists suggests otherwise— jokes can have a greater effect than serious statements on beliefs and actions. Of course, there may be multiple mechanisms that make derogatory jokes more powerful than serious derogatory statements. But the argument of this chapter suggests one possible mechanism—jokes encourage a good mood, and a good mood discourages the use of the critical thinking of System 2, and encourages the use of the expedient, but less reliable, System 1.

For obvious reasons, psychologists and neuroscientists use scripted jokes, rather than unscripted joking remarks, in their experiments. In Chapters 5 and 6, I have focused on explaining how scripted jokes work—how they imply derogatory ideas, and how humor discourages critical thinking. But the telling of scripted jokes is only one kind of derogatory humor. There are also derogatory joking remarks—as I defined them, these are remarks that ex- plicitly express negative ideas or stereotypes about an individual or about a social group via the standard meanings of the words used and the grammat- ical structure of the remark (see "How derogatory jokes and joking remarks differ" in Chapter 4). What makes them 'jokes' is the intentions—or at least the declared intentions—of the speaker. If the remarks are funny, they will, like scripted jokes, steer our thought processes in the direction of System 1 and away from System 2.

Since derogatory jocular remarks explicitly express negative ideas, we don't need to identify a special pragmatic mechanism that allows them to convey those ideas, as we did with scripted jokes. But we do need to explain why we are allowed more leeway in what we say jokingly than what we say seriously; and to do that, we need to consider what the difference is between saying something jokingly and saying something seriously. I turn to this question in the next chapter.

7

Joking remarks and joking intentions

Introduction

The day after Joe Biden was inaugurated as president of the United States, there was a White House press briefing about the COVID-19 pandemic with Anthony Fauci, director of the National Institute of Allergy and Infectious Diseases. One reporter asked a question that began: "You've joked a couple times today already about the difference that you feel in being kind of the spokesperson for this issue in this administration versus the previous one. . . . Can you talk a little bit about how you feel kind of released from what you had been doing for the last year?" And here is how Fauci began his answer: "Yeah, but you said I was joking about it. I was very serious—(laughs)—about it. I wasn't joking" (Psaki 2021). On the other hand, Don Imus—a radio shock jock—said he was joking when he described the members of the Rutgers women's basketball team as "nappy-headed ho's," combining an overtly racist description of Black hair with the racist and sexist stereotype that Black women are sexually available (Carr 2007b). We might doubt that Don Imus was telling the truth when he said he was joking, but let's set that issue aside. In this chapter, I address a more fundamental question: What is the difference between joking and being serious that Fauci and Imus are getting at?

Two definitions of 'joking'

Neither Fauci nor Imus told a scripted joke in these incidents. Rather, they made jocular remarks. To remind you, a typical example of a scripted joke is a mini-narrative with a punchline, whereas a jocular remark has the grammatical form of an assertion (see "How derogatory jokes and joking remarks differ" in Chapter 4). At the White House press conference, there were several comments that the journalist suggested were made jokingly and that Fauci classified as serious. These included "But, you know, one of the new things in this administration is: If you don't have the answer, don't guess; just say you don't know the answer" and that he "got in trouble sometimes" during the previous administration, because he had based everything he said on science and evidence (Psaki 2021). Fauci's remarks implied negative stereotypes about Trump's administration, but they were not derogatory remarks by my (admittedly narrow) definition, because they did not explicitly express negative ideas or stereotypes via the standard meanings of the words used and the grammatical structure of the remark—rather, the negativity was implicated. Imus's remark was a derogatory jocular remark—i.e., if said seriously, the standard meanings of the words along with the grammatical structure of the remark explicitly express negative ideas or stereotypes.

As you know, dictionaries rarely give only one meaning for a word, but rather two or more. The verb 'to joke' has at least two meanings. One is, roughly, to say something that is not true, but with the intent to amuse rather than the intent to mislead; the other is to say something—that can be true or false—in a way that is intended to be funny.[1] While the former requires that what is said is false, the latter allows for the possibility that one might say something true in a funny way. Jane Austen's Emma is talking about joking in the first sense when she tells her father, "Mr. Knightley loves to find fault with me you know—in a joke—it is all a joke." Emma knows that Mr. Knightley's catalog of her flaws is both well-placed and meant in all seriousness. But if she can persuade her father to believe that Mr. Knightley intends to amuse by saying something that is not true, her father will not "suspect such a circumstance as her not being thought perfect by every body" (Austen 2005, 9; first published 1816). In Austen's Sense and Sensibility, however, when Elinor muses that "even Sir John's joking intelligence must have had some weight" in stoking Lucy Steele's suspicions about Elinor's relationship with Edward Ferrars, Elinor is thinking of joking in the second sense (Austen 2006b, 162; first published 1811). Sir John is said to like joking about what he thinks may be a romance between Elinor and Edward particularly because it is "more conjectural" than the open romance involving Elinor's sister Marianne and the dashing Mr. Willoughby (144). Sir John, then, does not know if what he says is true or false; perhaps he hopes it is true. But whatever Sir John thinks about the facts, Elinor believes that Lucy gleaned some information from his joking remarks.

The idea that one can speak the truth while joking is an old one, at least as old as The Canterbury Tales ("The Monk's Prologue," line 1964). More recently it appears in the aphorism "Many a true word is spoken in jest," which the Cambridge English Dictionary tells us is "said about humorous remarks that contain serious or true statements" ("Many a True Word Is Spoken in Jest" n.d.). While truths-in-jest can be accidental, sometimes we deliberately say something true in a joking way. Fauci was joking in the truth-in-jest sense. When he said he wasn't joking, he didn't mean that he did not intend to amuse. Rather, he meant that he was not joking in the saying-something-false sense: He did not intend what he communicated to be false. When Imus said he *was* joking, he meant he was joking in the saying-something-false sense, not that he was joking in the truth-in-jest sense. The saying-something-false sense is what people are getting at when they say they were "just joking," or respond to a surprising or outrageous claim with "You must be joking."[2]

Jocular remarks and the warranty of truth

Jocular remarks, as I have defined them, have the same grammatical form as a statement or assertion, but differ from other statements and assertions because of the speaker's intent to be funny; there are also joking questions, joking exclamations, and so on, but I won't consider them in this book. I have argued that if a speaker succeeds in being funny, listeners relax their cognitive guard, allowing intuitive System 1 processing to work unfettered by fastidious System 2 processing (see "How a good mood affects cognitive processing" in Chapter 6). But whether or not the speaker succeeds in being funny, their intent has conversational consequences, and it is worth asking what those consequences are. So, I am going to dig deeper here. To do that, we will want another philosophical concept—the concept of a warranty of truth.[3]

What is a warranty of truth? The philosopher Thomas L. Carson says that it "is a kind of guarantee that what one says is true. It is also a kind of promise that what one says is true" (2006, 293). The promise isn't explicitly stated; it is typically implicit, unlike the warranties on things that we buy. Some philosophers have argued that a person warrants the truth of what she is saying when she makes a statement or assertion in ordinary circumstances, i.e., that this implicit promise is generally present. But like warranties on things we buy, the warranty of truth has exceptions; for example, in some countries, I do not guarantee that what I say is true on the morning of April 1. Carson is writing about lying, not humor. But he argues that humor is one of the circumstances in which the warranty of truth is in abeyance. He argues, "*Convention* dictates that one warrants the truth of one's statements in the absence of special contexts, special signals, or cues to the contrary. In the context of a work of fiction or when saying something in jest, one is not guaranteeing the truth of what one says" (294). Furthermore, "[c]onvention dictates that there are circumstances that remove the default warranty of the truth for our statements. The great majority of the cases in which the warranty of truth does not hold involve storytelling or attempts to be humorous, indeed it is difficult to think of statements that are not warranted as true that do not involve either storytelling or humor" (295).

Where the warranty of truth holds, you can make the implicit promise more explicit by adding things like 'I'm not kidding', or 'no joke'; for example, when Joe Biden was swearing in new appointees a few hours after his inauguration, he said, "I'm not joking when I say this: If you're ever working with me and I hear you treat another with disrespect, talk down to someone, I promise you I will fire you on the spot" (Kacala 2021). Here, Biden means to add additional weight to his words by saying that it is not a joke, making the warranty of truth readily apparent.

While Carson is correct that people often do not warrant the truth of what they say when they speak humorously, he acknowledges that sometimes we express truths humorously. Indeed, someone can make clear that even though they are saying something lightheartedly, with intent to amuse, they are also warranting its truth. The newspaper columnist Dave Barry often does this with the phrase 'I am not making this up'. The truth can be funny; and even if the truth itself is not funny, I can state it in a funny way, as is typical in dark humor.

Does truth-in-jest have a warranty of truth?

One might hope that the concept of a warranty of truth would line up neatly with the distinction between joking in the truth-in-jest sense and joking in the saying-something-false sense—i.e., one might hope that joking in the truth-in-jest sense has a warranty of truth and joking in the saying-something-false sense does not. But it's more complicated than that. Carson suggests that there is a convention that the warranty of truth is typically absent in humor. That may be true. But it is not a universal rule. Rather, when Sybil makes a humorous remark, she can make it clear (e.g., by saying something that she undoubtedly believes, but in an entertaining way) that she is warranting the truth of the remark; or she can make it clear (e.g., by saying something patently false with a humorous tone) that she is definitely not warranting the truth of the remark; or she can say something humorously while leaving it open whether she is or is not warranting the truth of the remark.

This last option—leaving it open whether one is warranting the truth of the remark—admits of degrees. Sybil can leave the issue of warrant open while indicating that she takes the remark as true, or that she wishes Harold to treat it as true. Sometimes, however, speakers take advantage of the ambiguity of humor. Sometimes people use a jocular or humorous tone to disguise their intentions, deliberately making it unclear whether they are joking in the truth-in-jest sense or the saying-something-false sense.

In these cases, a speaker gives herself plausible deniability.[4] Suppose Sybil leaves the issue of warrant open, but she thinks the remark is true; perhaps she is even hoping that Harold will take it as true. Later, she wants to backtrack for some reason—perhaps a conversational partner challenges her, or perhaps what she took to be a private conversation is leaked to the press and is causing a professional scandal for her. She might say—truthfully, but misleadingly—that she was "just joking." How should we interpret what 'just joking' means in more technical terms? First, she means she was joking in the saying-something-false rather than in the truth-in-jest sense. Second, she means there was no warrant of truth—and if she relied on the ambiguity of humor, this is technically true—but furthermore, she denies that she thought it was true or wanted Harold to take it as true—this is where she is lying.

People who wish to derogate other people can exploit the ambiguity of humor. They may say something derogatory that they truly wish to communicate, but say it humorously, thus allowing them to retract it later. Jocular remarks, then, are a useful tool when we want to communicate something outrageous, or inappropriate, or even dangerous because they do not come with a warranty of truth. The absence of a warranty of truth is an important prop for people like Imus who say that a remark was "just a joke."

However, the fact that one does not warrant the truth of a statement is not the same as guaranteeing that it is false, or even guaranteeing that one believes it to be false. Rather, if the truth of a statement is not warranted, one neither guarantees that it is true nor guarantees that it is false. Imus and his ilk are asking us to make a logical mistake. They tell us they were joking, so they were not warranting the truth of the statement—they did not expect us to treat it as true, or to treat it as something that they believed to be true. They want us to conclude that they were expecting us to treat it as false, or as something that they believed to be false. They are asking us to overlook the middle ground—that not warranting the truth of a statement leaves it open as to whether they were joking in the truth-in-jest sense or the saying-something-false sense.

Channeling the common ground

I have already talked about the philosophical concept of the common ground—the assumptions that we all share, and that we assume we all share (see "How amusement affects the common ground" in Chapter 6). The common ground changes as a conversation progresses, and affects what it is appropriate to do next in the conversation. I argued that humor may change the common ground by relaxing some cognitive processes at the expense of others. But humor may also affect the common ground in other ways.

The philosopher Eric Swanson (2022) argues that conversational contributions can make it more likely that the conversation will be channeled in one direction rather than another, and that channeling the common ground has an ethical dimension. Swanson offers the example of a tour guide at Monticello, the estate of former US president Thomas Jefferson. The guide used the active voice for Jefferson's actions, and the passive voice for people who were enslaved by Jefferson—so, for example, he said, "Mr. Jefferson designed these doors" and "The doors were installed originally in 1809," rather than "People enslaved by Mr. Jefferson installed the doors originally in 1809" (174). Swanson argues that using the passive voice for the work of enslaved people makes it less likely that we will talk about them in subsequent parts of the conversation—e.g., it is less natural to ask, "Did they learn their trade from other enslaved people, or from white people?" (174).

Channeling is also evident in Imus's conversation on his talk show. Imus's jocular remark riffs off a previous remark about the National Collegiate Athletic Association women's final by Bernard McGuirk, the executive producer, calling the Rutgers women "hard-core ho's." After Imus's comment, which doubled down on McGuirk by adding racism to the mix, McGuirk continues, drawing an analogy between the match between Tennessee and Rutgers and a rivalry between light-skinned and dark-skinned African American women in the Spike Lee movie *School Daze*, and employing a racial slur used in the movie. Then Sid Rosenberg, a sports announcer, pitches in, comparing the Rutgers women to the Toronto Raptors, a professional—as opposed to college—men's basketball team, who happen to have the name of a bird of prey; perhaps he is suggesting that the Rutgers women are predatory (Turner 2007).

Swanson's concept of channeling is supported by experience. We know that a remark can channel the common ground of a conversation in one way rather than another, and humorous remarks are no exception. Thus, humor can nudge a conversation, and its shared assumptions, toward—or away from—derogation.

The common ground and the ambiguity of humor

Although humor can channel the common ground, we might wonder if humorous remarks enter the common ground; after all, humor comes with no warranty of truth. But there are other contributions to the common ground that do not have a warranty of truth. As I've said, something can be common ground even if the participants do not believe it. This is one way in which the philosophical concept of the common ground diverges from the ordinary concept of the common ground; ordinarily, we think of common ground as beliefs and interests that the participants really have, rather than as something adopted temporarily (see "How amusement affects the common ground" in Chapter 6). On the philosophical conception, the common ground includes things like controversial assumptions that are accepted for the sake of argument or scenarios for which we need to plan—e.g., emergency services planning for a major earthquake on the New Madrid fault might make it common ground that the earthquake is between 7 and 8 on the Richter scale. These elements of the common ground are mutually accepted but not mutually believed. So, the lack of a warranty of truth does not, in itself, mean that humorous remarks can't enter the common ground.

Like controversial assumptions, humorous remarks can enter the common ground temporarily, as ideas that are accepted but not believed, thereafter changing the course of the conversation. However, it may be unclear whether someone who makes a humorous remark accepts what she says in jest—maybe it's joking in the saying-something-false sense; furthermore, it may be unclear whether she believes what she says—it might be intended as truth-in-jest. Thus, the ambiguity of humor leaves the audience on uncertain ground—pun intended—since they are left in doubt as to whether the speaker accepts or believes what she has said, and thus in doubt as to whether she would like them to accept or to believe what is said. Given this doubt, the audience does not know whether the speaker intends the remark to enter the common ground even briefly—in some cases, the speaker may intend to communicate the exact opposite of what she says; and even if it does seem to be a proposed addition to the common ground, the audience may be in doubt as to whether a humorous remark is offered as a temporary or as an enduring element in the common ground.

The linguist Craige Roberts argues that in a fully cooperative conversation, the people who are talking to each other make their intentions publicly evident (2015). However, if they do not make their intentions public, then they do not give enough information to allow for a single interpretation of what they are saying. This leaves other members of the conversation unsure about what was meant. Some people, of course, revel in keeping their intentions hidden, making them unsettling conversational partners.

Nathaniel Henderson, a concrete truck driver, was left in this kind of doubt by a coworker, Reed Moistner, in November 2001. Henderson was the first African American hired by Irving Materials, Inc., and at the time the only African American who worked there. Moistner said that he was going to make sure that he renewed his membership in the Ku Klux Klan. Judge Hamilton, writing for the US District Court for the Southern District of Indiana, says, "[P]laintiff Henderson testified that when Moistner first began to talk about the KKK, Henderson was not sure whether he was joking. Eventually, however, Henderson came to believe that Moistner was 'very serious'" (*Henderson v. Irving Materials, Inc.* 2004). In Henderson's testimony about his response to Moistner's comment that he was going to renew his membership, he said, "And I paused for a little bit, and I said, Were you—Are you really in the Ku Klux Klan, or, Were you really in the Ku Klux Klan? And Willie Taylor [the plant manager] said, What do you mean was? He still is." In terms of the common ground, Henderson wasn't sure whether Moistner wanted to add what he said to the common ground, either as something to be merely accepted, or to be believed, and asked Moistner for clarification. Taylor's reply accepted Moistner's remark into the common ground and confirmed that it should be believed.

Roberts argues that a cooperative speaker makes her intentions obvious to others to narrow things down to a single interpretation. Henderson could not narrow down a single interpretation of Moistner's words. The District Court opinion doesn't tell us what Moistner's tone was—perhaps there was no hint of humor, and it was the shocking content of what Moistner said that left doubt in Henderson's mind. Nevertheless, a humorous tone is one way that a speaker can make her intentions less than fully public, and thus less than fully cooperative.

Humorous remarks are compatible with at least three intentions regarding the common ground: I believe what I am saying, and even though I am not offering a warranty of truth, I am proposing that this be added to the common ground as a permanent addition; or, I don't believe what I am saying, but I am proposing that this be added to the common ground as a temporary addition, something accepted but not believed; or, finally, I do not believe what I am saying, and I am not proposing that this be accepted as part of the common ground at all. Since the joker might have any one of these three in mind for the common ground, saying something as a jocular remark can be a way of testing the waters—or more congruently with the metaphor of common ground, of checking the soil temperature: Is this something that my conversational partners are willing to accept, and thus to add to the common ground? Indeed, the psychologists Donald Saucier, Conor O'Dea, and Megan Strain argue that, because of its ambiguity, "[h]umor allows individuals to 'feel out' their audience" (2016, 77). If the joker receives a negative reaction, they can back off with "I was just kidding." But if the audience laughs at the remark, and goes on in the same vein, the joker doesn't need to say they were just kidding. Of course, there are possibilities for audiences that lie between a very negative reaction and a very positive reaction—an uncomfortable half-smile, for example. I will get back to the significance of an audience's response in Chapters 8 through 11.

Meanwhile, let's return to the examples with which we began this chapter. Fauci tells us, contra the reporter's proposed interpretation, that he was not joking. He genuinely wanted to add to the common ground that he felt very different talking about COVID-19 in the White House Press Room with Biden as president, rather than Trump; or at the very least, he was willing to add it to the common ground. Imus, on the other hand, tells us he *was* joking, thus claiming that he did *not* have the intention to add his remark about the Rutgers women to the common ground—or at least that, if he did, it was a purely temporary addition. But this is a retrospective, and self-serving, report. Imus is using the ambiguity of humor to deny, after the fact, that he intended to add a racist, sexist description of the Rutgers women to the common ground. It's notable that in an interview marking his retirement, Imus said that he regretted "the Rutgers thing." The interviewer asked what Imus regretted about it; Imus replied, "'Cause I knew better. It did change my feeling about making fun of some people who didn't deserve to be made fun of, and didn't have a mechanism to defend themselves" (CBS News 2018).

To sum up, sometimes humorous remarks enter the common ground, as believed or as merely accepted remarks. Sometimes, humorous remarks do not enter the common ground at all. However, it's worth noting that Judge Hamilton ruled that Moistner's remark about the KKK could be considered part of a pattern of racial harassment regardless of whether Moistner was joking, and regardless of whether Henderson thought Moistner was joking. Judge Hamilton writes, "Whether Henderson thought Moistner was joking about being a member of the KKK is also irrelevant. . . . The KKK has a long and bloody history of violence and aggression toward African Americans and others, based on race, religion, ethnicity, and national origin. Moistner's actual membership or actual intent to renew his membership in the KKK is therefore not the point. The hostile atmosphere was created by the contents and implications of the statements" (*Henderson v. Irving Materials, Inc.* 2004).

Conclusion

I began this chapter by asking how a joking remark differs from a serious remark—what effect does joking intent have on a contribution to a conversation? I have argued that joking intent is compatible with saying something you believe to be true, and with saying something you believe to be false. Like non-jocular conversational contributions, jocular remarks can channel a conversation, moving it toward or away from derogation. But whether or not the remark is something the speaker believes to be true, joking intent removes the warranty of truth that is typical of other remarks. In doing so, it creates ambiguity about the speaker's intentions and wishes concerning the common ground, leaving the audience to figure out whether the speaker wants the remark to enter the common ground, and if they do want it to enter the common ground, whether they want to enter it as an idea that is merely accepted, or as an idea that is accepted and believed.

Thus far in this book, I have focused on what the speaker does when they make a scripted joke and when they make a joking remark. I have talked, at times, about the effect of joking, of both kinds, on other people in the conversation—both immediate effects on their cognition and longer-term effects on their thoughts and decisions. But now it is time to talk about what people are doing when they listen to derogatory humor. I turn to this topic in Chapter 8.

8

Listener culpability

Introduction

Debbie Smith worked as an accounts service representative in a small office in Casper, Wyoming. She sued her employer for creating a hostile work environment after a succession of remarks from her supervisor, Curtis Mangus. Judge McKay of the US Court of Appeals for the Tenth Circuit writes, "Because the office was a relatively small, open space without partitions or walls, [Smith's] co-workers could hear Mr. Mangus' remarks and occasionally witness his treatment of [her]. This public setting only increased the humiliation, and, therefore, the severity of the discriminatory conduct" (*Smith v. Northwest Financial Acceptance, Inc.* 1997). Judge Kelly of the Third Circuit cites this ruling in his description of the experience of Charles James Witt, an African American truck driver who sued his employer in part because of racist slurs used at work. In Witt's case, Judge Kelly ruled that there was no "public degradation," as there was for Smith—"Although the dispatcher certainly heard the remark, there is no indication that any of Mr. Witt's fellow drivers heard it" (*Witt v. Roadway Express* 1998).

These court rulings hold that the presence of overhearers makes humiliation public, and thus more severe. But I don't think that is the only reason that the presence of others matters. In previous chapters, I have talked about what derogatory jokes, and derogatory jocular remarks, do—how they communicate derogatory ideas about groups of people, how they insidiously affect our cognitive processes, and how belittling jokes help support injustice. It's more than obvious that people who tell belittling jokes, and make belittling jocular remarks, bear responsibility; the tellers may not be able to articulate the mechanisms by which they are promulgating injustice, and in some cases, may not intend to promote injustice—perhaps they have been misled by Harmless Fun. Nevertheless, they are competent language users and aware of the malicious stereotypes they evoke (although again, they may not fully understand how those stereotypes support unjust disadvantage). I have also said, though, that people who listen to belittling jokes and belittling jocular remarks may have responsibilities, including moral responsibilities. The idea that listeners have responsibilities regarding what others say is a controversial claim, and in this chapter, I will try to convince you of its truth.

What is listening?

When I say that listeners may have moral responsibilities, I don't mean that everyone who *hears* what is said has moral responsibilities. Hearing and listening are not the same. Hearing is a largely automatic process, and speech in particular tends to draw our attention. That's not to say that you hear everything in your auditory environment, or that you hear everything someone says in your vicinity. As you know, you can fail to hear non-speech noises that are always present, like the hum of a fan. And you also know that there are times we can fail to hear speech that would otherwise be audible. There are a couple of ways this can happen. One is known as inattentional deafness. You may have experienced it while absorbed in reading, or while engrossed in a hobby, and you may have observed it when a teenager seems to have no idea that you are talking to them while they are looking at their smartphone. Another is selective hearing, when you hear what just a few people are saying in a noisy environment like a cocktail party or a bistro, and thus fail to hear others. But deliberately tuning out speech, where we are not purposefully attending to something else, is a different matter. It's not that difficult to tune out the conversation at the next table in the coffee shop if I am knitting a complex lace pattern or working on my laptop, but it is more difficult if I am drinking café au lait, thinking of nothing in particular. So, there are circumstances where we just can't help hearing what someone else is saying, even if we would prefer not to hear. We all know, for example, how difficult it is to ignore someone speaking on a cellphone, where we can hear only half a conversation (Emberson et al. 2010).

In my field, the term 'hearer' includes people who do not use auditory capacities for perceiving speech—i.e., to include people who lip-read oral languages and people who use sign languages (see "The terms 'speaker' and 'hearer'" in the Preface). As with oral language, someone who knows sign language may find themselves in circumstances where they cannot help but attend to what someone is saying with sign. And as with oral language, one might see someone's signed utterance without really giving it attention. Since hearing speech, with eyes or with ears, is often unavoidable, I do not think that merely hearing speech gives us special responsibilities because of its belittling content, although hearing may result in other responsibilities—if I hear someone planning a crime, perhaps I should take action to prevent it.

If listeners, but not mere hearers, may have special responsibilities when others say something belittling, what is the difference between listening and hearing? Listening to someone is more than hearing them, and it is also more than intentionally hearing them; Henry Higgins intentionally hears Eliza Doolittle through much of George Bernard Shaw's play *Pygmalion* (and the musical it inspired, *My Fair Lady*), but he is interested in her cockney accent, and doesn't care about what she thinks or what she means (Shaw [1912] 2010; Cukor 1964). So listening to someone is better characterized as intentionally hearing them (with ears or eyes) *and* attempting to understand what they are saying.

I have said that hearing speech is largely automatic, and so is understanding—at least at a minimal level—what someone else is saying, unless they are speaking a language that we do not know well, or using an unfamiliar dialect, or talking in a noisy environment. But if understanding is mostly automatic, then why would I say that listening requires attempting to understand them? The reason is that we can distinguish multiple things that a person is doing when they speak, and we might understand some of these things but not all of them.

The philosopher Susan E. Notess suggests that we distinguish a number of basic tasks of listening (2019). One task is to discern the words that the speaker is using and what they mean; another task is to determine what they want to accomplish by saying that—to take Notess's example, is it a request or a suggestion; a third is to work out any implicatures and make suitable inferences. All of these kinds of understanding have automated aspects that operate below the level of consciousness. But, at least in one's native language, the first of these tasks—interpreting the most basic level of meaning—involves speech processing that we cannot choose to turn on or off. That's not to say that understanding at that level never involves effort. Notess offers the example of listening to a toddler who has idiosyncratic pronunciation and limited vocabulary. With a grownup, you may need to strain to hear, tune out other distractions, guess at mispronounced or muffled words, or interpret a regional accent that is very different from your own; so listening, even at this most basic level, may involve attempting to understand, even though it doesn't always require any effortful processing.

What is it to understand? I don't want to stray from a commonsense definition—to understand is to comprehend what someone means. If Harriet understands Sally, then Harriet is right about what Sally meant. From a philosopher's point of view, this is a rough and ready definition, but for current purposes, it will do.[1]

To summarize, listening to someone is intentionally hearing someone and attempting to understand what they mean, where hearing someone can be auditory or non-auditory, and where understanding what someone means is being correct about what they meant. Both understanding and listening are matters of degree; minimal listening requires intentionally hearing someone and attempting to understand what words they used and what those words mean, whereas maximal listening requires in addition attempting to discern why the listener would say that. As Notess points out, one can listen well without fully understanding someone's meaning. So one does not need to succeed in understanding someone in order to listen to them, but one has to try.

Since there are automated aspects of hearing people speak and of understanding what they say, there are circumstances in which we can't help but hear, and can't help but understand. In circumstances like that, it would be unreasonable to argue that people incur moral responsibilities when they hear a belittling joke; it would be a little like arguing that people incur moral responsibilities when their heart beats. But listening does have an intentional aspect, so the fact that there are automated aspects of hearing and understanding does not rule out the possibility that listeners incur responsibilities when they listen to a belittling joke. Even so, as we shall see in the next section, "Being part of a conversation," I do not think *everyone* who listens incurs responsibilities.

Being part of a conversation

The listeners I have in mind are really a subset of listeners, those who are taking part in a conversation. Idly eavesdropping in a public place may be rude, but those listeners are not responsible for the content of the conversation.

What is it to take part in a conversation? We teach our kids that conversation is a sequence of turns—one person talks, others listen; then someone else talks, and others listen. Linguists document quite a bit of overlapping speech in casual conversation (see, e.g., Levinson and Torreira 2015), so a turn isn't as strict a concept as it is in a game of chess. Regardless, we might think that to take part in a conversation is to be one of the people who is expected to take a turn. In Jane Austen's *Pride and Prejudice*, Colonel Fitzwilliam and Elizabeth Bennet converse with "spirit and flow" in Lady Catherine's drawing room (Austen 2006a, 194). Lady Catherine is not taking part in the conversation; she isn't expected to take a turn, since she has been directing her attention to Mr. Darcy. But the narrator says Lady Catherine does not "scruple"—the clear implication being that she is being rude—to ask what they are talking about; and when Colonel Fitzwilliam tells her they are speaking of music, she says, "Then pray speak aloud. It is of all subjects my delight. I must have my share in the conversation, if you are speaking of music" (194). So Lady Catherine inserts herself into the conversation, insisting that she should have a turn—and as Austen readers will recall, in fact occupying most of the speaking time.

But saying that to take part in a conversation is to be expected to take a turn can't be quite right. Someone can be part of a conversation without being expected to take a turn. Suppose you are having a conversation where one person is extremely shy or socially anxious. You don't expect him to take a turn, although you would be happy if he did; but since you are a kind, thoughtful person, you address your shy acquaintance and make frequent eye contact, making clear that you are including him in the conversation despite the fact you do not expect that he will ever pitch in.

Rather than saying that taking part in a conversation is being expected to take a turn, then, we might say that it is being eligible to take a turn. Suppose I am chatting to a friend at a party, and someone else approaches. The newcomer is not eligible to take a turn, but we might grant them eligibility, and I might indicate that I wish to do so by making physical space for them, looking at them, and addressing them when I'm talking. Alternatively, my friend and I (let's suppose, contrary to fact, that we are impolite and unkind) might not make physical space for the third party, might ignore any contribution that they offer, and might continue to talk about whatever we were talking about before, until the third party feels compelled to drift away again. So eligibility to take a turn is granted—or denied—by other people in the conversation. As the conversation proceeds, those who are already eligible to participate can grant or deny eligibility to others.[2]

There are aspects of eligibility that, for now, I am ignoring. Some people should be granted eligibility, but aren't—think of a wheelchair user who ought to be addressed directly, but instead, the waitperson asks her companion whether she takes milk or sugar in her tea. And there are people like Lady Catherine, who have not been granted eligibility, but pushily take a turn anyway, and may become eligible even though the other participants don't want them to be eligible. But these complications need not worry us here; I'll get back to some of them in a later chapter (see "When challenging is difficult," "When challenging is pointless or dangerous," "When you are the target of belittling speech," and "Social hierarchies and the common ground" in Chapter 11, and the Postscript, "Some practical advice"). Furthermore, there may be people who haven't been granted eligibility by the conversational participants, but are eligible to pitch in at any time because of relationships of authority—like parents who jump in to stop a squabble between their kids. However, I am going to focus on those who are eligible to take a turn because of conversational norms, not just because they are higher in the pecking order.

Being part of a conversation and the common ground

For my purposes, the people who are eligible to take a turn in a conversation matter because those are the people who have influence on the common ground of a conversation—that is, on the ideas we accept for the purposes of the conversation. You may recall that this concept is similar to the everyday concept of common ground, but Stalnaker morphs it a little to help explain how conversations typically develop (see "How amusement affects the common ground" in Chapter 6 and "Channeling the common ground" in Chapter 7). To recap, for Stalnaker, the common ground in a group is the assumptions that the members of the group share and that they assume they all share; these assumptions are presupposed by everyone in the conversation. The common ground of a conversation changes over time, as new presuppositions are added and old ones are dropped. It affects what the participants in a conversation should and should not say, and thus influences how conversations proceed. For example, we should not repeat what is already in the common ground. You may also recall that the everyday concept of the common ground generally involves belief. But in Stalnaker's technical sense, the presuppositions in the common ground are accepted for the purposes of the conversation and do not have to be shared beliefs.

Here, I want to emphasize that constructing and maintaining the common ground is something we do together. Once something is accepted as common ground, even if Harriet didn't propose it as an addition to the common ground, it is now something that she accepts too. Acceptance isn't a permanent state—Harriet isn't committed to it forever. Her acceptance ends if she openly rejects it during the conversation; if it isn't openly rejected, her acceptance may end when the conversation ends, or it may be carried over to another, later conversation.

The common ground evolves during a conversation, as existing presuppositions are dropped and new ones are added; and the people who are eligible to take a turn in the conversation determine, between them, how the common ground changes, by accepting or rejecting a proposed presupposition, or by successfully casting doubt on an existing presupposition. So the common ground is the product of the actions and inactions of everyone who is eligible to take a turn.

The contents of the common ground, then, are a shared responsibility. It is for this reason that some listeners—those who are eligible to take a turn—are culpable for the contents of the common ground, even for things that they did not contribute to the common ground. So if the common ground contains a malicious stereotype or falsehood, then everyone who is eligible to take a turn is partially responsible for the presence of that harmful claim in the common ground, because any of them could initiate—or could have initiated—an attempt to banish it from the common ground. This is why people who are part of a conversation can incur moral responsibilities when someone else makes a belittling remark or joke.

There is no hidden common ground

We don't have shared culpability for absolutely everything that we jointly manage. Suppose, for example, that Raphael and Mark are the fiscal managers in their department, and jointly manage the department's accounts. Mark embezzles department money, skillfully hiding his tracks from Raphael. Even though Raphael and Mark are joint managers, Mark, but not Raphael, is culpable for the theft. So why do I think we have shared responsibility for the common ground? The answer is that Mark successfully hid his financial malfeasance, but there is no way to hide the fact that something is common ground—there is nothing that is in the common ground that is invisible to someone in the conversation, in the way that Mark's wrongdoing is invisible to Raphael. Since the common ground is what everyone accepts and what everyone believes everyone else accepts, when something is common ground it is apparent to everyone that it is common ground.

To see why there is no invisible common ground, let's think through how someone can be mistaken about the common ground. To pick an arbitrary example, suppose the claim that some roses are yellow is in the common ground. That's to say, everyone accepts that some roses are yellow, and everyone believes that everyone accepts that some roses are yellow, and everyone believes that everyone believes, etc. Could someone who is part of the conversation, say, Elinor, think that it isn't common ground that some roses are yellow? The answer to this question is no. There are only two reasons Elinor might think this. The first is that she doesn't accept that some roses are yellow—in which case it isn't common ground that some roses are yellow. The second is that she believes someone *else* doesn't think it is common ground that some roses are yellow—in which case, again, it isn't common ground that some roses are yellow. So, it is impossible for it to be common ground that some roses are yellow and yet for someone to believe that it is not common ground that some roses are yellow.[3]

Since there is no way that something can be common ground without everyone thinking it is common ground, if there's something belittling in the common ground, everyone will realize it's there. This is why I say there are no hidden facts about what is in the common ground, and so nobody can be let off the hook for something that is in the common ground because they were ignorant of its presence.

Suppose someone tells a racist joke, proffering its generalized conversational implicature for inclusion in the common ground. If nobody who is eligible to take a turn in the conversation objects, the generalized conversational implicature will become common ground. Furthermore, since one cannot think that something is not in the common ground when it is, everyone knows that the racist implicature is now part of the common ground.[4] The common ground is a shared responsibility, as I have argued, and its contents are apparent to everyone; so even though the person who told the joke bears greater responsibility than those who listen to the joke, the listeners, too, bear responsibility for the presence of the racist implicature in the common ground. This explains why I feel guilty if I hear a racist joke or a racist slur at a dinner party, and don't say anything—it is appropriate to feel guilty because racism entered common ground that I, along with others, tended.

That's not to say that everyone other than the speaker bears equal responsibility. There are lots of things that may stand in the way of our shifting the common ground. When I talk about listener culpability, people often mention dinners with extended family, particularly on holidays. If a racist uncle crosses the line at Thanksgiving dinner, there may be entrenched familial values and practices that dictate against any of his nieces or nephews challenging his racist addition to the common ground—family bonds, respect for elders, politeness, and the expectation that a holiday dinner is a time when everyone tries to get along may all stand in the way. In other circumstances, there may be social hierarchies or institutional hierarchies that constrain someone's ability to object (see "When challenging is difficult," "When challenging is pointless or dangerous," "When you are the target of belittling speech," and "Social hierarchies and the common ground" in Chapter 11). Institutional hierarchies, for example, explain why Debbie Smith's coworkers did not challenge Curtis Mangus, even though two of the men who worked with her testified that Mangus's behavior was sexually inappropriate, offensive, and intimidating (*Smith v. Northwest Financial Acceptance, Inc.* 1997).

I also note that many people think that listening to belittling speech isn't morally wrong. Rather, they think, it is failing to object to belittling speech that is morally wrong. So, they would argue that there is no such thing as listener culpability, strictly speaking, although we can be culpable for listening without objecting. Thus, I must provide an argument for thinking that it is listening in itself that carries moral weight, rather than the failure to object. I will do so in "Listening versus failing to challenge" in Chapter 11.

Public humiliation

The Supreme Court of the United States has ruled that the social setting is a highly relevant factor in assessing claims of racial or sexual harassment. Justice Scalia writes:

> A professional football player's working environment is not severely or pervasively abusive, for example, if the coach smacks him on the buttocks as

he heads onto the field—even if the same behavior would reasonably be experienced as abusive by the coach's secretary (male or female) back at the office. The real social impact of workplace behavior often depends on a constellation of surrounding circumstances, expectations, and relationships which are not fully captured by a simple recitation of the words used or the physical acts performed. (*Oncale v. Sundowner Offshore Services, Inc.* 1998)

Attorney Michael J. Frank points out that in Scalia's example, whether the incident is public or private may be one relevant factor in that constellation (2002). With the football coach what happens in private is more severe than what happens in public; and Judge Posner, for the Seventh Circuit of the US Court of Appeals, says, "Remarks innocuous or merely mildly offensive when delivered in a public setting might acquire a sinister cast when delivered in the suggestive isolation of a hotel room" (*Baskerville v. Culligan International Company* 1995).

Yet in other cases, the courts have ruled that the presence of others increases the severity of the harassment. They have emphasized the public nature of the humiliation; being shamed in front of others is worse than being shamed privately (*Smith v. Northwest Financial Acceptance, Inc.* 1997; *Witt v. Roadway Express* 1998). But if I am correct, there is another element to public humiliation (or, perhaps, a deeper explanation for why public shame is worse than private shame): The presence of others may increase the number of people who have joint responsibility for the common ground. Once something has entered the common ground, then all those who are part of the conversation presuppose it, i.e., take it for granted as part of the common ground. The philosophers Rae Langton and Caroline West have argued that part of what makes a presupposition so powerful is that it is not just what one person thinks—it is the "general opinion" (1999, 309–10). In the case of racist additions to the common ground, everyone who is participating in the conversation now presupposes a racist idea. So if more people are taking part in the conversation, more people are participating in the harm. Being bullied by a clique is worse than being bullied by one kid at school, and being beaten up by a gang of thugs is worse than being beaten up by an individual. Similarly, I'd argue, having a racist idea presupposed by multiple people is worse than having it presupposed by one person.

There are other aspects of public humiliation that we need to consider, in particular, the experience of being laughed at by a group. But laughter deserves its own chapter, and I will talk about it in Chapter 10.

Good listeners and ethical listeners

There are circumstances in which we are rightly urged to be good listeners. With the exceptions of Corradi Fiumara (1990) and Notess, philosophers have expressed little interest in the concept of listening, never mind in good listening. Michael P. Nichols and Martha B. Straus, both clinical psychologists, offer the following as guidelines for good listening:

1. Concentrate on the person speaking.
    Set aside distractions.
    Suspend your agenda.
    Interrupt as little as possible. If you do interrupt, it should be to encourage the speaker to say more.
2. Try to grasp what the speaker is trying to express.
    Don't react to just the words—listen for the underlying ideas and feelings.
    Try to put yourself in the other person's shoes.
    Try to understand what the other person is getting at.
3. Let the speaker know that you understand.
    Use silence, reassuring comments, paraphrasing.
    Offer empathic comments that convey you both understand what the person is saying (or trying to say) and the feelings that make this important for you to hear.
    Make opening-up statements (tell me more, what else) versus closing-off statements (I get it; the same thing happened to me). (Nichols and Straus 2021, 171)

Clinical psychologists, of course, are professional listeners. So one hopes that their guidelines are on the right track. It's immediately apparent that when the speakers around us are expressing racist or sexist or othering ideas of any sort, being a good listener and being an ethical listener are not the same thing. The good listener doesn't interrupt and encourages the speaker to say more; but perhaps the ethical listener should interrupt and encourage the speaker to keep it to themselves. The good listener paraphrases the speaker's words and reassures them. But it seems that the ethical listener ought not paraphrase the speaker's words, and ought to encourage them to reassess what they are saying. But how should you do that? I will come back to this question at the end of the book (see the Postscript).

Bystanders

I have argued that everyone who is part of a conversation shares responsibility for the contents of the common ground. If Linda asserts or presupposes or implicates a belittling claim, then Mary must either presuppose the claim herself, or must prevent the entry of that claim into the common ground. But I defined those who are part of a conversation as those who are eligible to take a turn in the conversation. What about bystanders who are not eligible to take a turn in the conversation, but hear what is said, and perhaps even listen to what is said? Are those listeners responsible for pitching in when someone says something belittling to people of color or women or transgender individuals or people with disabilities? The argument I have given does not support the claim that bystanders must intervene. But there may be other reasons for supposing that they should.

The philosopher Ishani Maitra raises this question, basing her example on an incident that she witnessed on a train in New Jersey:

> An Arab woman is on a subway car crowded with people. An older white man walks up to her, and says, "F[uck]in' terrorist, go home. We don't need your kind here." He continues speaking in this manner to the woman, who doesn't respond. He speaks loudly enough that everyone else in the subway car hears his words clearly. All other conversations cease. Many of the passengers turn to look at the speaker, but no one interferes. (Maitra 2012, 115)

Maitra argues that since the other passengers can hear what the man says, and since they are aware that the other passengers can hear him too, "we can think of the passengers as (unwilling) participants in one conversation" (115). She points out that we can be drawn into a conversation even if we do not want to converse. The passengers have not been granted eligibility to take a turn by the hate speaker, and thus are not part of a conversation with him in that sense; but Maitra holds that their mutual awareness is, at the very least, characteristic of a conversation.

Maitra's main concern in her discussion of this example is whether the silence of the other passengers grants authority to the hate speaker, and thus provides a condition that allows him to (wrongly) rank the Arab woman as inferior. The idea that silence can give someone authority may seem unfamiliar, but a scene from the movie *Mean Girls* provides an illustration

(Waters 2004). Regina, the Mean-Girl-in-Chief, is wearing sweatpants on Monday. The arcane rules of her clique—consisting of Regina and her satellites, Gretchen, Karen, and Cady—permit sweatpants only on Fridays. Gretchen is lower in status than Regina, but for reasons we need not get into, she is angry with Regina, and tells her that she can't sit with the group at lunch in the cafeteria, because she is breaking the sweatpants rule. Since Regina is used to getting her way, she challenges Gretchen. Karen speaks up, backing Gretchen; and when Regina looks to Cady for support, Cady is silent. Cady's silence, added to Karen's vocal support, has granted Gretchen authority to order Regina to leave the table. Regina gives in and leaves.

On Maitra's view, just as Cady's silence grants authority to Gretchen, the silence of the passengers on the subway grants authority to the hate speaker. Maitra argues that passengers have "some moral obligation to speak up. To put the point in other (and stronger) terms, if I am right . . . then in staying silent, the other passengers are, to some extent, *complicit* in what the hate speaker does" (2012, 116), even though there might be strong prudential reasons for keeping quiet rather than drawing the hate speaker's abusive attention to themselves. Tina Fey's script for *Mean Girls* has a former friend of Regina's tell Cady: "There are two kinds of evil people in this world. Those who do evil things and those who see evil things and don't try to stop it." On Maitra's account, calling the bystanders on the train evil would be too strong; but Maitra would say that they do more than see evil things and fail to stop them. Their silence also enables the hate speaker by giving him authority.

Like Maitra, the philosopher Rae Langton (2018) argues that hearers and bystanders may have responsibilities regarding the speech of strangers, even in places like a subway car or the stands at a football match. Although her argument is substantially different from Maitra's, both are concerned with whether the silence of bystanders provides the conditions needed for someone to rank someone else as inferior and to legitimate discrimination against them. If Maitra and Langton are correct, bystanders have a responsibility to speak up, even if they are not part of a conversation by the definition I have given.

Conclusion

The experience that motivates this chapter is the feeling of guilt some people have when they hear a belittling joke. I have argued that the feeling of guilt can be appropriate if you are listening to the speaker and you are eligible to take a turn in the conversation, although even then, there may be overriding considerations that absolve you of any responsibility. I will get back to what gets you off the hook in Chapter 11. But of course, guilt is not the only experience you might have when you hear a belittling joke—you might find the joke amusing; and you might find it so funny that you laugh. Chapter 9 focuses on the feeling of amusement: If you are amused by a racist joke, does that mean you are a racist?

9
Finding derogatory jokes amusing

Introduction

Derogatory jokes invite very different reactions from different people. A common response to a belittling joke is "That's not funny." But an equally common rejoinder holds that people who deny the joke is funny have lost their sense of humor. Indeed, we know from personal experience that some people find some belittling jokes amusing, and our experience is verified by social psychology studies where participants are asked to rate the funniness of the jokes used in the research (see "Are belittling jokes harmless fun?" and "Assessing Wrong Audience and Wrong Joker" in Chapter 3). We might wonder, then, what—if anything—distinguishes people who find belittling jokes amusing and those who do not. This question may be particularly pressing for you if you sometimes find belittling jokes amusing; you might worry that your amusement reveals an unwelcome truth about your beliefs and attitudes toward the belittled group. It may also be pressing if people you know, and perhaps love, are amused by belittling jokes.

While this chapter deals with amusement, it does not deal with laughter. Even though amusement can lead to laughter, there are several reasons for talking about them separately. One is inward, the other outward; one is something we feel, the other is something we do; and they differ in how much they are under voluntary control. Furthermore, we can laugh without being amused, and be amused without laughing. I will talk about laughter, as opposed to amusement, in Chapter 10.

In this chapter, I will start with what research in social psychology says about amusement. As we shall see, there is some truth to the popular culture claim Wrong Audience—your social identity affects what derogatory jokes you are likely to find amusing. But regardless of your social identity, finding a derogatory joke about a group amusing is correlated with having derogatory beliefs about that group. Since it's just a correlation, amusement at a derogatory joke does not provide conclusive evidence that you have related derogatory beliefs, but nevertheless, I will argue that in some cases you should investigate your subconscious attitudes and biases. In the central sections of this chapter, I turn to the question of why there is a connection between amusement at derogatory jokes and possession of derogatory beliefs about the targeted group. I argue that amusement is brokered not just by the joke itself; it also depends on the circumstances in which the joke is told, and especially on how we feel about treating a derogatory idea as true in a conversation with these people at this time. Finally, I argue that while some derogatory jokers presuppose derogatory ideas, not all do. As I've said, a central reason for thinking that derogatory jokes convey derogatory ideas by generalized implicature is that there is no better explanation (see Chapter 5, "Conclusion"); so, it's important to rule out other potential explanations.

What kind of person is amused by derogatory jokes?

As we have seen, the popular wisdom that one should choose one's audience for a joke carefully has a crumb of truth along with a generous serving of falsehood. A veridical aspect of the Wrong Audience claim is that the social identity of the audience is crucial; e.g., one should be wary of telling a joke that derogates conservatives in the presence of conservatives (see Chapter 3, "Assessing Wrong Audience and Wrong Joker"). We saw already that telling a derogatory joke about someone's group can make the person wonder if others value them, can reduce feelings of competence and motivation, and can increase anxiety and feelings of social exclusion (Ford et al. 2020). But this aspect of the Wrong Audience claim is also bolstered by a connection between perceived funniness and social identity; the social psychologists Mark A. Ferguson and Thomas E. Ford provide a helpful review of this literature (2008). For example, in a study carried out on the day of the US presidential election in 1964, the psychologist Robert F. Priest (1966) found that Democrats enjoyed jokes that disparaged the Republican candidate, Barry Goldwater, more than jokes disparaging the Democratic candidate, Lyndon Johnson, whereas Republicans enjoyed jokes disparaging Johnson more than jokes disparaging Goldwater. The psychologist Lawrence La Fave (1972) found that Christians enjoyed jokes that disparaged agnostics more than they enjoyed jokes that disparaged Christians. So, a joker might be wary of telling a disparaging joke to a member of the disparaged group because they are less likely to be amused. That is not to say that people never enjoy humor that disparages their own group—sometimes, they do. Ferguson and Ford suggest, though, that how much they enjoy the disparaging humor is related to the degree to which they identify with the disparaged group to which they belong.

However, social identity is not the only factor that is associated with amusement; there is also a correlation between amusement and belief. For example, the psychologists Kathryn Ryan and Jeanne Kanjorski found that in a population of college students, men who enjoyed sexist humor were also more likely to endorse rape myths—such as the false beliefs that most women who are raped are promiscuous, and that women who wear short or tight clothing are "asking for it." Enjoying sexist humor was also associated with "behavioral intentions (i.e., the self-reported likelihood of forcing sex) and behavior (i.e., sexual and physical aggression) in men" (Ryan and Kanjorski 1998, 752). Although Ryan and Kanjorski found this effect particularly in men, in their review paper, Ferguson and Ford say there "is substantial evidence suggesting that, regardless of sex, people enjoy sexist humor insofar as they have negative (sexist) attitudes toward women" (2008, 295)—e.g., women who hold negative sexist attitudes toward women are more likely to enjoy sexist humor than women who do not.

If you find yourself amused by a derogatory joke, then, you have circumstantial evidence that you have negative beliefs about the derogatory group; this is so even if you are a member of the derogated group. Like any circumstantial evidence, this evidence may be misleading. Nevertheless, take your amusement as a clue that further investigation may be required, and that you may need to explore your beliefs about the derogated group more deeply. You may think that you are not racist, sexist, or whatever, and thus that you fall into the group of people who are amused despite having no negative stereotypes or beliefs about the derogated group. But research on prejudice makes clear that we can have implicit biases that operate below the level of consciousness. So, you may need to investigate what lies beneath your conscious commitments, unless you have done the necessary archaeology already.

To be clear, even if you are amused by a derogatory joke, you do not always have to explore your beliefs about the derogated group more deeply. Some negative beliefs about some groups are perfectly reasonable. In my considered opinion, e.g., it is reasonable to have negative beliefs about people who build hotels by the beach without evaluating the environmental impact of the development. So, if I find myself amused by a joke that derogates environmentally reckless hotel developers, I do not need to search my soul.

Some negative beliefs about derogated groups are unfair, however. Hotel developers are not an unjustly disadvantaged group, but it would be unfair to suppose that they do not love their children.

So, when should you explore your beliefs about the derogated group more thoroughly? You should think carefully about whether there is good reason to suppose that the disparaged group is unjustly disadvantaged. Thus, if you are amused by jokes about African Americans, you should explore your beliefs—unless you have already exercised due diligence—keeping in mind that your biases may lie below the level of consciousness. When I say it matters if there is good reason to suppose the group is unjustly disadvantaged, what matters is whether there is objective evidence for supposing that the group is unjustly disadvantaged. Your own pre-conceptions and impulses don't count as 'a good reason' here. Suppose, e.g., that someone is amused by derogatory jokes about people who are transgender. Suppose, too, they think that transgender people are not unjustly disadvantaged. Contrary to their belief, there is ample and widely available evidence that transgender people are unjustly disadvantaged; e.g., transgender people suffer high rates of personal violence and sexual assault (US Department of Justice, Office for Victims of Crime 2014). So, even if the amused person doesn't already believe that transgender people are unjustly disadvantaged, they should consult reliable sources, and think it over with ample time and attention.

Am I morally responsible for being amused?

I have argued that derogatory jokes convey derogatory ideas. Where belittling jokes are concerned, the ideas that are conveyed foster unjust disadvantage. We might think, then, that finding those jokes funny is reprehensible. However, in general, you are not blameworthy for your feelings of amusement, and it is not appropriate to disapprove of others who are amused. Amusement, like breathing, has a substantial involuntary component, and blaming someone for something involuntary doesn't make a whole lot of sense. However, while you can't help but breathe, you can (to some extent) change the way that you breathe—e.g., if you habitually take shallow breaths using the intercostal muscles alone, you might learn to breathe more deeply, using the diaphragm as well. Similarly, we can, over time, change what amuses us. As the philosopher William G. Lycan argues, we can cultivate our sense of humor, so that we are no longer amused by objectionable jokes (2020). Furthermore, as we have seen, there are reasons to make this long-term effort to change your habits; your amusement relaxes your critical cognitive processes, and while we do not always need to have System 2 engaged—subjecting everything to the careful processes of System 2 would be time-consuming and cognitively exhausting—it seems prudent to have System 2 engaged when the welfare of our fellow human beings is at stake.

Awareness of derogatory ideas in a conversation

Social psychology teaches us that amusement at derogatory jokes is correlated with possessing derogatory beliefs and attitudes. It also teaches us that amusement at derogatory jokes is correlated with social identity.[1] The statistical mantra that correlation is not causation applies to both these correlations (see "Are belittling jokes harmless fun?" in Chapter 3). Nevertheless, it's worth thinking about why there might be connections between amusement and belief and between amusement and social identity—are there common causes? Is it a coincidence? Or something else?

I think that the philosopher Merrie Bergmann points us in the right direction. In a discussion of humor about feminists, Bergmann says, "Being aware of a sexist belief is not the same as holding it. Because a feminist is aware of sexist beliefs, she may see why particular episodes are thought to be funny yet nevertheless not find them funny herself" (1986, 74–5).[2] Similarly, the philosopher Ted Cohen comments that ethnic jokes rely on presumptions and "commonplaces" (2001, 73), e.g., about Irish people or English people or Indonesian people. He talks of jokes in general having a "shared background" for the teller and the audience if the joke is to succeed: "you need your audience to know something *in advance of the joke*, and you need them to know it without your telling them" (2001, 28).[3] Bergmann and Cohen disagree on pretty much everything else about derogatory humor, but both argue that the audience needs to be aware of the relevant negative stereotypes and generalizations in order to understand the joke, even though they do not need to believe them. And understanding the joke, of course, is necessary for finding it amusing.

In one sense we are always aware of the negative stereotypes and generalizations that percolate in our society; in this sense, they are background information. In another sense, an encounter with a negative idea can make us immediately aware of it in a particular moment, or in a particular conversation—the idea can move from behind the scenes to center stage in a specific situation. Considering how a person might feel when they are aware of a derogatory idea in this second sense is enlightening. I will argue that those feelings underlie the correlation between holding derogatory beliefs and finding derogatory jokes amusing, and between social identity and finding derogatory jokes amusing.

One might expect that being aware of a negative idea or stereotype that we believe is more comfortable than being aware of a negative idea or stereotype that we do not believe. So, we might conclude that there is a simple explanation for why possessing derogatory beliefs and attitudes is correlated with finding derogatory jokes amusing. If a person already believes an idea that is conveyed by a derogatory joke, there is no conflict between what they believe and the idea that is being made salient by this joke. If a person does not believe an idea that is conveyed by the joke, then there is a conflict between their beliefs and the idea being conveyed by the joke. This conflict may stand in the way of amusement, particularly if the person thinks the negative idea in question is not merely false, but potentially dangerous, to themselves or to others.

However, the simple explanation is a bit too simple. Consider Wrong Joker, the popular claim that who is telling a joke matters, at least from a prudential point of view. I've argued that Wrong Joker is mistaken in many regards, but nevertheless, it reminds us that amusement is not just about the joke itself, but about the context in which the joke is told. I might find the very same joke amusing if it is told by a member of the derogated group, and not amusing if is told by someone else. So, in explaining how belief (and social identity) is correlated with amusement, we can't classify jokes as funny-to-me and not-funny-to-me; we need to classify them as funny-to-me in these circumstances, or as not-funny-to-me in those circumstances.

One part of my thesis falls squarely in the no-duh category: What we believe can make us more comfortable, or less comfortable, when a particular idea is brought to the surface. The second part is a teeny bit less obvious: Regardless of whether someone believes something, they may be uncomfortable if other people are acting as if it is true.

The argument for my thesis draws, again, on Stalnaker's concept of the common ground of a conversation. As you may recall, the common ground is the assumptions that everyone in the conversation accepts and that they believe that everyone else accepts (see "How amusement affects the common ground" in Chapter 6 and "Being part of a conversation and the common ground" in Chapter 8).[4] These assumptions are presuppositions of the conversation. I need to delve deeper into how the common ground works, however. First, I'll say more about accepting and presupposing. Then, I will explore factors that affect our willingness to accept something. Finally, I will argue that both the correlations we have noted are explained by our willingness to presuppose derogatory ideas in the circumstances of a conversation.

What is acceptance?

The shared assumptions that make up the common ground of a conversation change as the conversation continues: New assumptions are added and old assumptions are dropped. You also may recall that to count as common ground, an assumption needs to be accepted by everyone, and everyone needs to believe that everyone accepts it. However, while everyone must accept it, nobody needs to believe it—it could be accepted for the sake of argument, or for the presumption of innocence, for example. So what does Stalnaker mean when he says that someone accepts an idea? For Stalnaker, accepting an idea is *treating it as true*, ignoring the possibility that it is false—or even your firm belief that it is false—for the time being.[5] Thus when we accept a derogatory idea, we treat it as true, at least temporarily. The common ground, then, is what everyone treats as true and what everyone believes everyone else is treating as true, at least for this conversation.[6] For example, suppose the weather forecast says there is an 80% chance of rain during our planned picnic. Even though it may not rain at the time of the picnic, we might treat as true that it will rain during a conversation about alternative plans. If we all treat it as true, and all believe that everyone else is treating it as true, it is common ground that it will rain during the picnic.

Acceptance and presupposition

As we saw in the previous section, acceptance is treating as true; now let's consider what has to happen for an idea that one person accepts to count as a presupposition of a conversation. The presuppositions of a conversation are the assumptions in the common ground. As we ordinarily understand the term 'presupposition', a presupposition is something that is presumed or assumed; it might be assumed tacitly, or it might have been stated as something that will be taken for granted thereafter. Stalnaker's technical concept of a presupposition is closely related to the ordinary concept, but it diverges from the ordinary concept in some ways. In particular, with the ordinary concept of a presupposition, someone can presuppose something even if they think others do not share that presupposition, whereas in Stalnaker's technical sense, if someone presupposes something, they take it for granted that everyone else in the conversation treats it as true, or at the very least, they act as if they take it for granted that everyone will treat it as true, at least for the time being.[7]

Suppose, for simplicity, that just the two of us are having a conversation, and you presuppose that it will rain; maybe you say something like, "I bet it will rain. Let's make a plan." You treat it as true that it will rain. I don't demur, so you believe I treat it as true; maybe I say something like, "Well, there's a picnic shelter at the park." Furthermore—and here's another divergence from ordinary usage—as long as I acquiesce, I now presuppose that it will rain as well. This may seem unintuitive, but it is a consequence of Stalnaker's account. Presupposing is taking something for granted, or acting as if I take something for granted, as common ground, i.e., as something that everyone treats as true, and that everyone believes everyone else treats as true. If I acquiesce, I am treating that it will rain as true, and of course I believe you are treating it as true. Given only the two of us are chatting, that is all it takes for me to presuppose it. If there are more people in the conversation, the same general principle applies, the only wrinkle being that to presuppose that it will rain, I would also need to believe that *they* are treating that it will rain as true. The presuppositions of the conversation—as opposed to a person's presuppositions—are the presuppositions that everyone shares.

Now we know what has to happen for an idea that someone accepts to become a presupposition of a conversation. Next, we need to consider when it is *probable* that an idea that one person in the conversation accepts will become a shared presupposition.

Willingness to accept

The philosophical literature on presupposition spends only a little time on what affects one's willingness to presuppose something.[8] But since presupposing something requires both accepting it oneself and believing that others accept it, we might expect to find that someone's willingness to presuppose something will depend in part on how they feel about accepting it, and in part on how they feel about other people accepting it. And since to accept something is to treat it as true, their willingness to presuppose something will therefore depend in part on how they feel about treating it as true, and in part on how they feel about other people treating it as true. (There may be many other factors affecting one's willingness to presuppose something; but these are the relevant factors for present purposes.)[9]

To see how the way I feel about treating something as true might affect my willingness to presuppose it, consider a non-joking conversation. I might be willing to take part in a conversation that presupposes that a stranger's spouse has left her—e.g., to discuss what she would do if she found herself alone. But I might be less willing to take part in a conversation that presupposes that my spouse has left me. Why would that be? I would be bereft if my spouse left me, and because of this, it may be upsetting for me to treat that he has left me as true, even if I know it isn't true, and even if I am not worried that he will leave me. Consequently, I may refuse to take part in the conversation at all; or I may take part in it reluctantly. The exercise of *treating something as true* has an imaginative element that can be upsetting or unsettling even if I know it's not true.[10] So I may not be willing to take part in a conversation where we presuppose something that would be difficult for me if it were true.

In this example, what I don't want to presuppose is false. But that is not essential to the point. There may be things I know to be true, but even so, I do not want to presuppose them in a conversation—perhaps my emotions about the topic are very raw, and I do not want to enter into those emotions here and now. My class is in 30 minutes, say, and right now, I can't discuss with my dear friend the fact that my spouse left me, because I do not want to show up to teach with a scattered mind and streaky mascara. I'll talk to her about it later. Right now, I will compartmentalize, and pretend it never happened.

How might my feelings about other people treating something as true affect my willingness to presuppose it? Suppose a teenager has a large, red pimple on their forehead. They have covered the pimple as best they can by applying makeup and combing their hair to disguise it. Suppose further that their acne embarrasses them, and they would be uncomfortable if you believed that they had a pimple on their forehead. In this case, it may be important to them that you think they do not have a pimple even though they believe they do. And even if you actually think they have a pimple, they might prefer not to know that you think they have a pimple. So they may not wish you to treat that they have a pimple as true. In this case, even though it's true they have a pimple, and even though they believe they have a pimple, nevertheless they may be unwilling to take their having the pimple for granted as common ground. In a case like this, someone may be unwilling to presuppose something even if they do believe it, because of how they would feel if other people treated it as true. The teenager treats having the pimple as true when they are by themselves, scrutinizing it in the bathroom mirror, and googling to find top-rated concealers; but they do not treat it as true when they are conversing with you.

In this example, I'm assuming what the teenager does not want to presuppose in this conversation is true. But, as with the previous example, its truth or falsity is not essential to the point. Even if they do not have a pimple today, they may be sensitive about their propensity to teenage acne, and they may be reluctant to have you treat as true that they have a pimple. You are embarrassing them.[11]

Why amusement is correlated with social identity

I have argued that both my willingness to treat something as true and my willingness to have you treat it as true are relevant to my comfort with taking something as common ground, regardless of the truth or falsity of the thing to be presupposed. Now we are ready to answer a central question for this chapter: Why is amusement with derogatory jokes correlated with social identity? (I'll get to the correlation between amusement and possessing negative beliefs about the derogated group in "Why amusement is correlated with derogatory belief.") For example, can we explain why Democrats find derogatory jokes about Republicans funnier than Republicans do, while recognizing that a Republican may find a derogatory joke about a Republican funny (Priest 1966)?

There are lots of ways someone can attempt to put an idea in the common ground. They can assert the idea (e.g., 'It will rain during the picnic'); they can introduce it as a supposition (e.g., 'Suppose it rains during the picnic'); they can ask a question (e.g., 'What if it rains during the picnic?'). They can also use conversational implicature; 'Hmm, we will need raincoats and umbrellas at the picnic' doesn't say outright that it will rain, but implicates that it will. I argued in Chapter 5 that derogatory jokes have derogatory ideas as generalized implicatures, and so telling a derogatory joke is one way in which people can propose adding a derogatory idea to the common ground. When someone proposes adding a derogatory idea to the common ground, we are aware of it in the present moment; it shifts from being a background stereotype or belief that plagues our society to something that we are being asked to treat as true here and now.

Given that we are being asked to treat a derogatory idea as true, how is social identity relevant to the probability that someone is amused by a derogatory joke? If I am a Republican, I might be less willing to treat as true that Republicans are, say, victims of misinformation than I am to treat as true that Democrats are victims of misinformation, for the sake of a joking conversation. To treat as true that Republicans are victims of misinformation, after all, would be to treat as true that I, my fellow Republicans, and my political representatives are victims of misinformation; and one might expect that I would be less comfortable treating as true that we Republicans are victims of misinformation than treating as true that someone else, whom I do not support, is a victim of misinformation. My discomfort may be sufficient to inhibit any amusement that I might feel about the same joke with regard to Democrats.

In the example about my spouse leaving me, I argued that I can be reluctant to treat something as true whether I believe it or not. So, this explanation of the effect of social identity can be correct even if I do think many of my fellow Republicans are victims of misinformation. Thus, we can explain why Republicans are less likely than Democrats to find jokes about Republicans funny. More generally, we can explain why there is a connection between social identity and the perception that jokes disparaging one's group are funny; and we can do so without taking the dubious position that having negative beliefs about the disparaged group is a *necessary* condition for finding jokes disparaging the group funny.[12]

Why amusement is correlated with derogatory belief

In the previous section, I explained why we would expect a correlation between social identity and finding a derogatory joke funny. Now let's deal with the connection between derogatory beliefs and amusement at derogatory jokes. To recap, what we need to explain is why people who do not have, say, sexist beliefs are less likely to find sexist jokes funny than people who do have sexist beliefs, while also recognizing that they might find sexist jokes funny sometimes.

I have argued that a sexist joke has a sexist idea as a generalized implicature, and thus that telling a sexist joke asks the audience to treat the sexist idea as true. Just as I might be unwilling to treat as true that my spouse has left me, because treating it as true makes me uncomfortable, I may be unwilling to treat a derogatory idea as true. My discomfort with treating the idea as true can be enough to forestall any amusement at the joke that I might otherwise have felt. And as with the example of my spouse leaving me, it may not matter whether I think the idea is true or false. If I think it is false, my discomfort might be due in part to the conflict between what I believe and what I am being asked to accept, but even if I think it is true, and there is no conflict between what I believe and what I am being asked to accept, I may consider the derogatory idea dangerous or insulting. If it's a derogatory stereotype about my group, perhaps I think it is true in general but not true of me. Regardless of my reasons for not wanting to treat the idea as true, my resistance to treating it as true may stand in the way of my feeling amused by the joke. However, note that if I think the idea is true, one potential spoiler for my feeling amusement is absent; the remaining factor is whether I am also willing to treat the idea as true, here and now, in this conversation. Thus, we might expect that people who have sexist beliefs are more likely to find sexist jokes funny than people who do not have sexist beliefs—there are fewer potential obstacles standing in the way of their amusement.

As I have argued, I might resist presupposing an idea not because of how I feel about treating it as true, but because of how I feel about my conversational partners treating it as true. Recall the pimple on the teenager's forehead; in some circumstances, the teenager may not want others to treat that they have a pimple on their forehead as true. Maybe they really have a pimple, and they hope nobody has noticed; maybe they don't have one, but others pretending they do would be embarrassing. Similarly, I may not want others to treat a disparaging idea as true, whether or not I think it's true.

For example, suppose I think it is true that women are generally more concerned with their appearance than men; I still might not want someone to treat that idea as true in a conversation we are having at a meeting of the American Philosophical Association, because I might think that their treating that idea as true will make them take me less seriously as a philosopher. So, I might be reluctant to engage in a joke that someone tells, if the joke conveys that women are generally more concerned with their appearance than men. My discomfort with their treating that idea as true may stand in the way of my finding the joke amusing. Still, I might find the same joke hilarious in other circumstances.

On the whole, a person is more likely to be comfortable with others treating as true something that she also believes to be true. So, although there will be circumstances where someone may believe that something is true and yet wish others would not treat it as true, that's going to be less common than circumstances where they believe it's true and are willing to have others treat it as true as well. So again, we might expect that people who have sexist beliefs are more likely to find sexist jokes funny.

Telling derogatory jokes and presupposition

I have argued that people who tell derogatory jokes invite their audience to treat a derogatory idea as true. One might wonder, then, whether derogatory jokers presuppose derogatory ideas. This question matters in part because people sometimes communicate something by presupposing it. If derogatory jokers communicate derogatory ideas by presupposing them, there is an alternative to my thesis that derogatory jokers communicate derogatory ideas via generalized implicature.[13] Furthermore, if I want to maintain that my explanation of how derogatory jokers communicate derogatory ideas is the best explanation, I need to show that there is no competing explanation that is just as good as, or better than, mine.

One might expect that presuppositions are always old information, something that everyone already accepts. But Stalnaker argues that in some circumstances, a speaker can use presupposition to tell people something new. Stalnaker offers the example of Alice, who knows that Bob doesn't know she has a sister, and thus knows that the existence of her sister is not part of the common ground of her conversation with Bob (2002, 709). Nevertheless, Alice says, "I can't come to the meeting—I have to pick up my sister at the airport," without adding the information that she has a sister to the common ground first—i.e., she doesn't say, "I have a sister, and I can't come to the meeting because I have to pick her up at the airport." It's more efficient for her to presuppose that she has a sister, with what Stalnaker calls an informative presupposition; furthermore, she can do that because she is confident that once she has mentioned her sister, Bob will accept that she has a sister thereafter.

In this example, Alice communicates new information to Bob by presupposing it. If Carol, who already knows that Alice has a sister, is present too, then Carol learns nothing new from Alice's presupposition; but nevertheless, Alice may make her sister salient to Carol in this conversation. With derogatory jokes, very often the derogatory ideas conveyed are familiar to us; so perhaps derogatory jokers operate in the same way as Alice. Perhaps they make derogatory ideas salient in the conversation by presupposing them; and sometimes, they may "teach" derogatory ideas to others by presupposing them.

However, derogatory jokers do not always presuppose derogatory ideas. Jokers presuppose derogatory ideas when they, themselves, wish to treat the derogatory idea that is implicated by the joke as true for this conversation, and when they think the audience will treat the derogatory idea as true too, at least for the purposes of this conversation. For example, if they think that the audience is *not* a 'Wrong' audience, they do presuppose the idea. Some jokers, however, deliberately tell derogatory jokes to audiences who they know will object, and these jokers do not presuppose derogatory ideas. Let me explain.

Let's call jokers like this contentious jokers, because they tell these jokes in part to invite dispute of the derogatory idea that the joke conveys. The teller knows that the audience will find the derogatory content conveyed by the joke unacceptable, and they tell the joke in order to irk the audience, and to provoke the reaction. For contentious jokers, part of the fun is provoking someone's anger; in colloquial terms, the aim is to get a rise out of them. Coincidentally, in explaining the meaning of 'get a rise out of', the *Cambridge English Dictionary* offers this example: "Steve always manages to get a rise out of me with his racist jokes" ("Get a Rise Out Of" n.d.).

As we know, Stalnaker's technical sense of 'presupposition' differs from the ordinary concept of presupposition in some ways. With the ordinary concept of a presupposition, someone might presuppose something that they think others will dispute, whereas in Stalnaker's technical sense, if someone presupposes something, they either believe everyone else in the conversation accepts it as well, or they believe everyone will accept the assumption, at least for the time being.[14] Even with informative presuppositions, it is crucial that the speaker believes that others will accept the presupposition. If they expect others to dispute the new information, then on Stalnaker's account, it's not a presupposition. For example, if Alice says, "I can't come to the meeting, I have to pick up my panda at the airport," she doesn't presuppose that she has a panda, since she realizes that Bob won't accept that she has one. Bob might think Alice is blowing off the meeting. However, if Alice insists that she has a panda, he will dispute the idea that she has a panda, rather than quietly adding that she has a panda to the common ground. So, in the ordinary sense of 'presuppose', perhaps a contentious joker presupposes a derogatory idea. But he does not presuppose a derogatory idea in Stalnaker's technical sense. He knows full well that not everyone will accept that idea. In fact, his goal is to invite dispute, and he will be disappointed if his audience does not take the bait.[15]

So, while philosophers and linguists sometimes use the concept of a presupposition to explain how people communicate things that they do not explicitly say, that isn't the best explanation of what is happening with derogatory jokes. Contentious jokers, as I have said, do not presuppose the derogatory ideas that their jokes share. In the case of contentious jokers, something else must explain how their derogatory jokes convey derogatory ideas. If we argue that in general, scripted derogatory jokes communicate derogatory ideas because jokers presuppose those ideas, we need a different explanation of what happens with contentious jokers. It's more efficient, and more elegant, to give the same explanation of how scripted derogatory jokes work for both contentious and non-contentious jokers. My explanation—that scripted derogatory jokes communicate derogatory ideas by generalized implicature—works for both kinds of jokers.[16]

Huh, I've never met a contentious joker

Sometimes people tell me that contentious jokers must be few and far between, and as a consequence, explaining how contentious joking works is not much of a problem. These people are typically very privileged—e.g., they are educated, cisgender, White men. If you, too, think that there must be very few contentious jokers, please consult with less privileged friends. You do not have to take my word for it—women, people of color, and people who are not cisgender can tell you all about it. I should say, though, that some highly privileged people encounter contentious jokers as well. Derald Wing Sue, a professor of counseling psychology, discusses the experience of young people who have encountered antiracist ideas, and who are on the path to becoming antiracist themselves. They often find that family and friends resist their new beliefs, and humor is one mechanism of resistance: "During holidays when students spend time off campus with family, some report hearing a racist joke from a favorite aunt or uncle and objecting to it. They report that family members may tease them ('You've changed since going to that Ivy League school. What are they teaching you anyway? What liberal crap is the college filling your head with?'), or they may threaten to disown them from the family because of the disrespect shown" (2015, 162).

Conclusion

In Chapter 8, I talked about the responsibilities of people who listen to derogatory jokes. Here, in Chapter 9, I talked about amusement at derogatory jokes, but I didn't say anything about laughter. In Chapter 10, I turn to the topic of laughter. Is it bad to laugh at a belittling joke? And if so, why is it bad?

10

Laughing at derogatory jokes

Introduction

When Nathaniel Henderson was subjected to racist jokes at the concrete plant where he worked, the plant manager, Willie Taylor, laughed (*Henderson v. Irving Materials, Inc.* 2004); similarly, Troy Swinton's supervisor laughed at Jon Fosdick's jokes (*Swinton v. Potomac Corporation* 2001). Writing for the Ninth Circuit of the US Court of Appeals, Judge McKeown makes an intriguing comment regarding Swinton's supervisor, Pat Stewart: "It could even be said that he participated in [the harassment] himself by laughing along with Fosdick's jokes." Judge McKeown doesn't pursue the point, which she makes while addressing the question of whether management at Potomac Corporation knew about the harassment. But why would she think that laughing could be thought of as participation in harassment? And regardless of what Judge McKeown thought, what should we think about laughing at racist and other belittling jokes?

To be clear, I won't speak to the question of whether laughter could constitute part of a hostile environment from a legal point of view. As the philosopher Kwame Anthony Appiah writes in *The Ethicist* column for the *New York Times Magazine*, "laughter is sometimes a response to shocked embarrassment" (2022a). He might also have pointed out that laughter, like amusement, has an involuntary component. For these reasons, it would be imprudent for the courts to hold people legally responsible for laughing.

However, laughter has social significance in a conversation, and in this chapter, I will argue that laughing plays a role in shaping the common ground of a conversation—that is, in shaping the assumptions that conversationalists share, and in shaping the future direction of the conversation. So, while the law might be wise to lay off laughter, we can nevertheless employ the tools provided by philosophy of language and moral philosophy to assess the significance of laughter. In this chapter, I argue that laughing at a derogatory joke welcomes an idea into the common ground, and thus that it can be appraised from a moral point of view. Laughing at a belittling joke also adds your opinion to the opinion of the joker, and thus increases the probability of others welcoming belittling ideas as well. Toward the end of the chapter, I talk about the psychological pain caused by the laughter of a group in a humiliating situation.

Welcoming ideas into the common ground

I have argued that the common ground of a conversation is something that is jointly tended by everyone who is eligible to take a turn in that conversation. Thus, I argued, when someone else says something belittling, we bear responsibility for its presence in the common ground thereafter (see "Being part of a conversation and the common ground" and "There is no hidden common ground" in Chapter 8). As you may recall, the common ground of a conversation is what everyone treats as true, and what everyone believes everyone treats as true, for the purposes of this conversation.

There are lots of ways to treat something as true, and the way we treat something as true matters. I might treat it as true, but do so reluctantly—"I don't agree, but let's suppose that's true for the sake of argument." Or I might treat it as true enthusiastically—"I absolutely agree," or "That's a great point!," or even "No kidding." And of course, there is a lot of middle ground between the extremes. Silence in the face of an assertion or presupposition generally indicates acceptance into the common ground. But while the examples I gave are verbal expressions of enthusiasm—or lack of enthusiasm—one can indicate one's degree of enthusiasm silently as well. Suppose Sam says something that Henry is willing to treat as true for this conversation, but about which he is dubious; he might be silent but with pursed lips or a raised eyebrow. Alternatively, Sam says something with which Henry heartily agrees, and Henry is silent but smiles or nods emphatically. Henry's degree of enthusiasm is likely to affect the course of the conversation thereafter, and certainly affects whether the idea is carried with them once the conversation is over.

Let's draw an analogy with allowing someone into your home. You might permit entry, but unwillingly, say with a disliked relative or a politician you can't abide; or you might greet a visitor, but in a perfunctory manner— perhaps you are not excited about their presence, but willing to go through the motions; or you can fling the door open, envelop your visitor in a hug, offer tea or wine, give them the best seat, and insist that they should stay for dinner. In short, you can admit someone into your home with a degree of welcome that falls along a scale from grudging to effusive.

The warmth with which you permit a visitor can vary, and similarly, in a conversation, you can admit an idea to the common ground coldly or with genuine warmth. With derogatory jokes and joking remarks, laughter is one way in which you can make a derogatory idea at home in the common ground. Not all laughter is equally welcoming, of course—there's a difference between a nervous giggle and a belly laugh. But just as the warmth of your greeting can affect how a visit proceeds thereafter—e.g., how comfortable the visitor is, how long they stay, and whether they come back in the future—the warmth of your laughter can affect how a conversation proceeds as well. I already discussed Eric Swanson's proposal that the common ground of a conversation can be channeled in one direction or another (see "Channeling the Common Ground" in Chapter 7). In this case, a hearty laugh indicates that you welcome a belittling idea into the common ground, and can encourage others to add more belittling ideas. A chilly reception of a belittling joke, on the other hand, can discourage further contributions of belittling material to the conversation.

At the very least, the laughter of Swinton's supervisor and Henderson's manager welcomed racist humor into the common ground. They should not have done that. But was their behavior merely inappropriate? Or would it be fair to say that the laughter was, at least a little, immoral? I turn to this question in the next section.

The morality of laughter

Sometimes, we appraise the welcome given to a visitor from a moral point of view. For example, suppose a White host gives a chilly welcome to an African American visitor because of racial animus; or that a host gives an extravagant welcome to the perpetrators of war crimes. People also give moral appraisals of others who laugh at derogatory jokes, and seemingly of our own laughter as well—I might apologize for my laughter, saying, "I'm sorry, I shouldn't laugh." Our perception that laughing is subject to moral evaluation is supported by a recent study by researchers in organizational management, who used videos with professional actors depicting an interaction where Jamie tells a joke to Pat (Ong, Yam, and Barnes 2022). In some of the videos, it was an inoffensive joke. In others, the joke was inappropriate; two

of the three offensive jokes used were belittling, and the third was derogatory and particularly shocking because it took the suffering of others, and
particularly of children, lightly. If Jamie told an inoffensive joke, whether Pat
laughed or not made no difference to assessments of Pat's morality. However,
if the joke was derogatory, Pat was rated as less moral if he laughed.

The study by Ong, Yam, and Barnes confirms that people evaluate
laughing at derogatory jokes in moral terms. But that doesn't show that it
is appropriate to give a moral appraisal of laughter; sometimes people treat
something—like rock and roll music—as immoral when it is not, and so the
fact that people are inclined to morally evaluate laughter at derogatory jokes
does not mean that laughing at derogatory jokes is morally wrong.[1] However,
we can supplement fact with arguments for the wrongness of laughing at derogatory jokes. The philosopher William G. Lycan argues that the experience
of amusement is not voluntary, and so not subject to moral evaluation. But
he says that laughter is different: "[L]aughing is sometimes an action, the result of a choice, or at least a reaction the agent might have tried harder to
suppress" (2020, 257). On Lycan's view, laughing rewards and gives a modest
endorsement of the act of joking. So, if telling the joke is wrong, laughing at
it is also wrong—although, on Lycan's view, not *as* wrong, since he believes
that as a general rule, endorsing a wrong act is not as bad as doing it oneself.
Lycan has a get-out clause for people who hear the joke but don't know that
telling the joke is wrong—say the person doesn't really understand the joke,
but laughs because everyone else is laughing.

I agree with Lycan that laughter rewards and endorses derogatory joking.
But I think it does more than that. I have argued that the people who are
eligible to take a turn in a conversation have shared responsibility for the
contents of the common ground. Thus, they have shared responsibility for
the derogatory content conveyed by someone else's derogatory joke. On my
view, laughing embraces derogatory ideas, ushering them into the common
ground. If I laugh, I take on my responsibility for the derogatory content of
the common ground joyfully. If the joke is not just derogatory, but belittling,
not only do I fail to acknowledge the broader significance of the belittling
claim, but I treat the belittling claim cordially, even though it is part of a network of forces that unjustly disadvantages some of my fellow human beings.

In the court cases with which I began this chapter, we saw that Pat Stewart
and Willie Taylor laughed when employees who were under their supervi-
sion were subjected to racist jokes; they gave a warm welcome to belittling
ideas. I don't know why Judge McKeown thought that Stewart's laughter

might be considered as participation in harassment from a legal point of view. But we might argue that Stewart and Taylor participated in harassment from a moral point of view by welcoming belittling ideas into the common ground. Another relevant court case involves an employee yelling an appalling racist slur at Gerald Moore—who is African American—at the plant where he worked as a welder. Moore's supervisor, Tom McCauley, "said nothing and had a 'smirk' on his face and was shaking his head. . . . Plaintiff [Moore] testified that he felt 'badly' about the remark, and expected his supervisor to do or say something, but when McCauley did nothing, plaintiff went back to work" (*Moore v. Kuka Welding Systems* 1999). We might argue that while McCauley did not welcome the slur in the way that Stewart and Taylor welcomed racist jokes, he did do something, rather than nothing—he indicated tolerance. One might smirk and shake one's head to indicate that while someone has crossed a line, in your mind the infraction is hardly serious and in fact is entertaining.

Going along with the crowd

Any teenager knows that there is substantial social pressure to conform with the majority, and of course social pressure isn't confined to adolescence. In a famous experiment in social psychology, Solomon Asch asked a group of approximately eight college students a simple question: Which line on one card was the same length as a line on another card? Only one of the eight was a subject of the experiment; the others had been told in advance to give the wrong answer on some of the trials (1956). Asch found that in a third of the trials, subjects conformed by also giving the wrong answer. In post-test interviews, some said they knew it was wrong, but nevertheless gave the same answer as the rest of the group; some said the answers of others led them to doubt their own perceptions; and remarkably, some believed that they were giving the correct answer. While few of the participants always went along with the crowd, 76% gave the wrong answer on at least one occasion. The remaining 24% never succumbed to pressure from the group, although debriefing interviews suggest some considered going with the majority.

We know from these experiments that the joint opinion of a group, even if it is obviously mistaken, can influence what we say and sometimes what we believe. So, what if someone tells a belittling joke, and others laugh? When someone laughs at the introduction of a new idea to the common ground, they treat the idea not just as something that they are willing to think, but as something that they are happy to think, and happy to have others think as well. When they laugh, a single person's opinion becomes an opinion that is shared by two people, and so they add a little weight to the social pressure on others to share that opinion too. In Asch's experiments, the dominant opinion was asserted by everyone but the subject of the experiment, rather than implicated by one and welcomed by others. Furthermore, some people were not swayed by other people's opinions at all. So, we cannot confidently conclude that if a sufficient number of people laugh at an implicated belittling idea, the beliefs of others will be swayed. But we might reasonably be concerned that if the majority of people in a conversation treat something as true—and do so jovially— they will influence others, smoothing its entry into the common ground.

The laughter of others

In addition to the effects of laughter on the common ground, we should consider the effects of laughter on a person who is being victimized by a belittling joke—such as Swinton or Henderson. Personal experience tells us that the laughter of a group stings more than the laughter of an individual. Once, after I had spoken in favor of a proposal at a meeting, a colleague said to me, "Claire, there are pros, but there are also cons." I replied, "I find that's true of so many things." I swear I meant it self-deprecatingly, not as a witty reply, but for understandable reasons my colleague took me to be conversationally implicating that he was stating the obvious. Regrettably for both of us, others laughed. The offended colleague didn't acknowledge me in the hallway for three or four years thereafter.

There have been a few studies of how other people's laughter affects our experience of humiliating remarks, although to the best of my knowledge there have been no investigations of the effects of others laughing at derogatory jokes. I would guess my colleague experienced the laughter as exclusionary laughter. In a social psychology experiment, Stephanie Klages and James Wirth (2014) asked people to recall a time when laughter made them feel excluded, or laughter made them feel included, or to recall an ordinary Wednesday. As one might expect, laughter that made people feel excluded stank; Klages and Wirth argue that the effects are similar to the effects of other forms of social exclusion, such as being told explicitly that you are not wanted. For example, exclusionary laughter worsened mood and self-esteem, increased aggression, and increased temptation toward anti-social behavior.

Another team of social psychologists found that imagining others laughing changed people's assessment of how humiliated they would feel in a situation, although the effect was dependent on the nature of the insult (Mann et al. 2017). In particular, if someone said something that dismissed a person's autonomy—the originality of their ideas, their open and honest expression of political beliefs, or the firmness of their opinions in the face of opposition from friends—others laughing increased their feelings of humiliation; this was not so if they were accused of lack of respect for an elder with dementia, or of being unkind because they did not leave work early to help an aunt prepare a birthday party, or of being disrespectful because they did not give up a seat on a bus. Mann et al. argue that the first three insults affect more central values than the second three in the culture of the Netherlands, where they conducted the study; since other values are more central in collectivist cultures, they expect that in other cultures different insults would elicit the most intense humiliation.[2]

Extrapolating from Mann et al., we might expect that laughter at jokes about valued aspects of ourselves will be especially humiliating. Attributes like race and gender play central roles in our sense of self, and are often aspects of ourselves that we value. So, when coworkers told a joke about Swinton's race, and others laughed, we might expect that it was a more humiliating experience than if others laughed at a more peripheral aspect of his sense of self. Generally, of course, if you are present when someone tells a belittling joke, you have no direct control over whether others laugh. The best you can do is to control your own laughter, and to be aware that adding your laughter to the laughter of others may intensify public humiliation.

Conclusion

I began exploring the moral responsibilities of listeners in Chapter 8. There, I argued that when we listen to a belittling joke in a conversation, we bear responsibility for the presence of a belittling claim in the common ground. I argued in Chapter 9 that although the feeling of amusement at a belittling joke is largely involuntary, we can cultivate our amusement over time, just as we might improve our posture with practice, or might acquire a taste for tannic wines. Here in Chapter 10, I argue that while laughing has an involuntary component, it is more under our control than amusement, and thus laughing at a belittling joke can have moral significance. In particular, laughing at a belittling joke welcomes a belittling idea into the common ground. Belittling ideas play a role in unjust disadvantage; so, laughing at a belittling joke is like enthusiastically welcoming a perpetrator of injustice. In Chapter 11, it's time to talk about other responses and reactions to belittling jokes.

11

The racist uncle, and other awkward situations

Introduction

Naturally, the Court of Appeals opinion in *Swinton v. Potomac Corporation* (2001) does not discuss how Swinton and his fiancée felt about Thanksgiving dinner with her extended family. But since Swinton's fiancée was Fosdick's niece, I surmise that the couple dreaded holiday gatherings, as well as weddings, funerals, and family reunions.

Swinton's fiancée is far from the only person who has a racist relative. When I talk to people about listener culpability, the conversation often turns to uncomfortable holiday meals with extended family. If a racist uncle says something belittling at the Thanksgiving dinner table, there may be strong social forces that discourage any of the next generation from challenging his racist addition to the common ground—speaking up is taking a more senior member of the family to task, in a setting where family harmony is highly valued. A PhD student in my department, Aaron Sullivan, summed this up by saying that in his family, "[i]t's all about Grandma"; rocking the boat over a racist joke or remark will upset Grandma, and everyone else will be upset with Aaron because he upset Grandma. Family hierarchies may be particularly difficult to navigate, but institutional and social hierarchies stand in the way of confronting racist language in many other settings. What if the joker is your boss? Or the Queen Bee in your high school?

I'm going to pursue two main questions in this chapter. I have argued that listening to belittling speech can be morally wrong. But in some cases, there are substantial costs associated with stopping or leaving a conversation with belittling content, or with challenging the belittling speech. In these cases, it is best from a prudential point of view—and certainly easiest—to let the conversation continue. But what, if anything, absolves a listener from blame? The answer to this first question, however, depends on the answer to the other question, which concerns why Aaron—or anyone in a similar situation—should challenge the belittling speech. What good, if any, is accomplished by speaking up, or by ending the conversation in some other way?

Tackling the latter question takes us back to a significant problem that is still unresolved (see "There is no hidden common ground" in Chapter 8). I have argued that someone can be morally responsible for listening to a belittling joke, although as we will see, there are extenuating circumstances. But lots of people think I'm mistaken about this: They say that the reason that people like Aaron come away from these dinners seething with frustration and guilt is not that they listened; rather, it is that they didn't say anything. Indeed, Aaron and his peers might say, after the fact, "I should have said something." So many people would say that listening to racist language, in itself, is not wrong; it is listening to racist language without challenging it that is sometimes wrong. On the other hand, I would say that listening to racist language is sometimes wrong; challenging it is a corrective measure, which can be used to make reparations for the wrong.

You may think I'm splitting hairs here, and certainly that is an occupational hazard for philosophers. But there are other cases where doing something amends a previous wrong, so the difference between my position and the opposing position is a genuine difference. Suppose someone else puts a box of strawberries under my jacket in my cart at the grocery store, and although I know the strawberries are there, I leave the supermarket without paying for them. Before I get to the car, however, I decide to return to the store and pay for the strawberries. I'm morally responsible for leaving the supermarket without paying, but I can atone for my wrong action by going back to pay for them. Similarly, I can be morally responsible for listening to belittling speech—because in doing so I am admitting belittling ideas to the common ground—and challenging the speech or leaving the conversation is a corrective measure for an error that I have already made.

I don't think it's plausible to say that leaving the supermarket with the strawberries is not wrong in itself, but that failing to return to pay for them is wrong. However, the parallel position regarding derogatory jokes—that listening to belittling speech isn't wrong in itself, but that failing to challenge belittling speech is sometimes wrong—is plausible. In this chapter, I will start by showing why I think the wrong done is not just failing to challenge. This brings into focus why challenging belittling speech matters. Then, I will talk about how the social landscape may affect your duty to intervene in the common ground, and how your social history and social identity may rationally affect your willingness to intervene. Philosophical accounts of cooperative conversations and of the common ground traditionally assume that everyone has equal power over the common ground, but this is far from true. Social and institutional hierarchies allow some people more control over the common ground than others. So sometimes, you are not in a position to challenge a proposed addition to the common ground. Finally, I will talk about what is accomplished by ending the conversation, say, by changing the topic or by walking away.

Listening versus failing to challenge

To remind you, I argued that listeners who are eligible to take a turn in a conversation share responsibility for the presence of a belittling claim in the common ground (see "Being part of a conversation and the common ground" in Chapter 8). I also argued—and this is crucial—that listening is an active process. Listening is more than hearing. Listening to someone is intentionally hearing and attempting to understand what they are saying (see "What is listening?" in Chapter 8). Merely overhearing a conversation on the train does not count as listening, although eavesdropping on a conversation on the train does count as listening, because it is intentional. Of course, eavesdropping has moral aspects of its own—we often consider it wrong to eavesdrop on the conversation of others. But setting that aside, I do not think that an eavesdropper who listens to belittling speech is any more in the wrong than an eavesdropper who listens to any other kind of speech. An eavesdropper is not eligible to take a turn in the conversation, and thus shares no responsibility for the common ground of that conversation. So, even if an eavesdropper listens to belittling speech, I do not think they are any more blameworthy than they would be for listening to non-belittling speech. It is the listeners who are eligible to take a turn in the conversation who share responsibility for the common ground, and so these listeners can bear moral responsibility for listening to belittling speech.

However, you might have little sympathy for the argument that I have summarized here. You might reasonably think that there is never anything bad about *listening* to belittling speech—what is bad, if anything, is listening but *failing to challenge* the belittling speech. In fact, this is what pretty much everyone I have ever talked to about this has said. If Henrietta listens to Samantha in the context of a conversation, and Samantha says something belittling, Henrietta has done nothing wrong. However, if Henrietta doesn't challenge Samantha, then she has failed to do something she should have done. She hasn't *done* something wrong; rather, she has *not done* something she should have done. That's why she can be appropriately blamed, and why she can feel appropriate guilt. From there, one can draw on the substantial philosophical literature about how someone can be morally responsible for an omission to explain why Henrietta is morally responsible for this omission in particular. It's going to be convenient to have a shorthand for comparing this explanation of listener culpability to my explanation; let's call this explanation Culpable Silence, and the explanation that I gave in Chapter 8, Culpable Listening. To really compare the two explanations, we need to give more details about how Culpable Silence could work.

It is intuitive that both actions and omissions can be morally wrong. If Alice threw Carol, who cannot swim, into the ocean, that would be a wrongful action. But it also would be wrong for Benjamin, who is a strong swimmer and is passing by, to not jump in to try to save Carol—that's a wrongful omission. But to explain why Benjamin is at fault, one needs to say more. Why should he have tried to save Carol? One option is to say that his trying to save Carol would have been better than his not trying to save Carol. A little bit of fancy footwork is necessary, since Benjamin might have tried to save Carol without succeeding; for this reason, it's too simple to say that it is better for Benjamin to try to save Carol because the outcome is better if she is saved. The philosopher Carolina Sartorio suggests that Benjamin's trying to save Carol would have *promoted* a good outcome; i.e., either it would have resulted in a good outcome, Carol being saved, or it is the kind of action that might reasonably have been expected to result in a good outcome (see Sartorio 2005). So, if Benjamin does not try to save Carol, he is in the wrong because he has omitted an action that would have promoted a good outcome.

Returning to the case of belittling speech, can we apply the same kind of reasoning to explain why Henrietta should challenge Samantha's belittling speech? To do so, we need to argue that Henrietta's challenging Samantha would have promoted a good outcome, and to do that, we need to specify what the good outcome would be. So why is challenging the teller of a belittling joke better than not challenging them? What good outcome does challenging the joke promote? Let's suppose that there is no member of the targeted group present, so the good outcome Henrietta promotes is not supporting someone who is being victimized. This joke has already been told, so Henrietta challenging Samantha does not prevent this particular telling of the joke, and thus the good outcome she promotes is not the prevention of the telling of this joke on this occasion. Henrietta challenging Samantha might discourage Samantha from telling the joke again on another occasion, and in some cases that may be the good outcome which makes challenging Samantha morally better than not challenging her. But even if Henrietta does not expect her challenge to dissuade Samantha in the future—she knows her well enough to know it will not influence her future behavior—and so she does not reasonably expect that she is promoting a good outcome, intuitively, it seems Henrietta ought to challenge Samantha now. Why would this be?

The only remaining good outcome that Henrietta promotes—or achieves—by challenging Samantha is banishing a belittling claim from the common ground. And if this is the good outcome that Samantha promotes, then Culpable Silence must acknowledge that at least part of Culpable Listening is correct—having belittling claims in the common ground is a bad thing. The remaining difference between Culpable Listening and Culpable Silence, then, is that Culpable Listening says a person does wrong by listening to belittling claims, and atones for that wrong by challenging those claims, whereas Culpable Silence says a person does no wrong by listening to belittling claims, but does wrong by not challenging those claims.

Of course, neither Culpable Silence nor Culpable Listening has to rely on outcomes when evaluating Henrietta's behavior—i.e., we do not have to take a consequentialist approach, which as you may recall, evaluates the morality of an action in terms of its effects (for a recap, see "How can jokes be assessed in moral terms?" in Chapter 3). One alternative is to argue that there are duties associated with conversing. For Culpable Listening, we might argue that in general, we have a responsibility to listen in a conversation, at least to a certain degree. The idea that there is a duty to listen is in line with ordinary expectations for conversationalists—e.g., we might reproach someone for not listening, or apologize for not listening. Furthermore, there are circumstances where we think the ordinary obligation to listen might be suspended—e.g., "He just kept droning on and on, so I stopped listening." Then we might argue in addition that there are circumstances where we *should not* listen when someone else is talking in a conversation. So, we shouldn't listen to belittling speech; and there may be other circumstances where the usual obligation to listen is overridden—e.g., perhaps we ought not listen if someone is spreading dangerous gossip, or revealing a secret that they have no right to share. On the other hand, Culpable Silence might agree that in general, there are obligations to listen. But that obligation is not suspended when others are engaging in belittling speech. Rather, where belittling speech is concerned, our ordinary obligation to listen remains in place, but we have an additional obligation, to challenge the belittling speech.

Thinking in terms of duties rather than in terms of outcomes has other advantages. Remember Benjamin, who didn't try to save Carol from the ocean. We hold him responsible for his omission. But he is not the only one who didn't try to save Carol. Sarah Thomas, the first person to swim across the English Channel four times without stopping, didn't try to save her; neither did the Olympic swimmer Michael Phelps.[1] We hold Benjamin responsible for his omission, but we do not attribute any blame to Thomas or Phelps. So, the promotion of good outcomes is not the only factor that leads us to reproach Benjamin; there must be more to it. Perhaps, for example, Benjamin's proximity to Carol and his knowledge of Carol's plight gave him a duty to save Carol that Thomas and Phelps did not share.

Regardless of whether we appeal to outcomes or to duties, Culpable Silence has more work to do. Imagine that Harry enjoys belittling jokes, but he knows he ought to challenge belittling jokes and claims. Harry is having a conversation with Stephen. Stephen starts to tell a series of belittling jokes. Harry listens to the jokes silently, for as long as Stephen tells them. Then, once Stephen has finished telling the jokes, Harry challenges the belittling claims. According to Culpable Silence, there is nothing amiss with Harry's behavior, because there is nothing wrong with listening to belittling speech; after all, Harry challenged the belittling claims, which is what Culpable Silence requires.[2] But don't you think that Harry behaved badly?

I believe it would have been better for Harry to stop Stephen when he first realizes that Stephen is telling a belittling joke; he shouldn't wait for the punchline, and he shouldn't allow Stephen to continue telling more belittling jokes. Culpable Listening can explain why Harry should stop Stephen as soon as possible—when a person is eligible to take a turn, listening to belittling speech is wrong, and once Harry realizes that he will be listening to belittling speech, he should stop listening. Telling Stephen to knock it off is one way to do that. But I do not think Culpable Silence can explain why Harry should stop Stephen as soon as possible—since Culpable Silence says there is nothing wrong with listening to belittling speech. If there's nothing wrong with listening to belittling speech, why shouldn't Harry listen as long as he likes? So Culpable Listening offers a better explanation than Culpable Silence.

When challenging is difficult

As we have seen, I think that listening to belittling speech is—at least sometimes—wrong. I also think that there are times when we should stop listening to belittling speech. One way to stop listening to belittling speech— at least temporarily—is to challenge what the speaker is saying; I'll discuss other ways of stopping listening later in the chapter. Challenging the speaker, of course, isn't always successful. Some speakers will keep going regardless. However, even if the challenge does not stop the speaker, it has value, because while it does not prevent them from saying awful things, it does prevent those awful things from sticking around in the common ground. You are showing that you do not accept them, and things in the common ground must be accepted by everyone. So, by challenging the belittling claims, you make clear that the belittling claims are not part of the common ground. I'll talk more about effective methods of challenging belittling speech in the Postscript.

The philosopher Rae Langton reminds us that our social position makes a difference to our ability to block the entry of a claim into the common ground. Grandma may call Uncle Racist on his remark, because of her senior position in the family, but nephew Aaron may not; and Grandma won't act, regardless of her views about racism, because she does not want conflict on the holiday. Langton points us also to "asymmetric gender norms about risk-taking, initiative, politeness, and deference, [which] all affect the feasibility and costs of blocking" (2018, 161); so, while Aaron and his cousin Annabel would both violate familial norms if they spoke up, Annabel would in addition violate gender norms.

Aaron, then, is in a bind. If he says nothing, he accepts Uncle Racist's obnoxious views into the common ground, and leaves feeling icky and uncomfortable. But if he challenges Uncle Racist, he faces social sanction from his family. He upsets Grandma, and thereby is subject to anger and criticism from his parents' generation, and perhaps from his own as well. Grandma could challenge Uncle Racist, and since it's all about Grandma, her challenge would make Uncle Racist the object of social sanction. Consequently, Grandma bears greater responsibility than Aaron for the addition of Uncle Racist's remark or implicature to the common ground, and is more culpable than Aaron for the presence of racism in the common ground. Both Aaron and Grandma listened, and both of them allowed a racist remark into the common ground they jointly tend. But Grandma, because of her senior position in the family, can shape the common ground without being sanctioned, whereas Aaron cannot.

Similar dynamics play out at work, where the hierarchy is institutional rather than familial. A student is less well positioned to shift the common ground than an untenured faculty member, who is less well positioned than the department chair. Furthermore, the failure of more powerful members of the conversational group to take action may communicate norms to those who are less powerful—it may communicate, e.g., "We don't call Professor Sexist out when he says that kind of thing." I have already mentioned the case of Gerald Moore, who was subjected to an exceptionally obnoxious racist slur in the presence of his supervisor, Tom McCauley (see "How can jokes be assessed in moral terms?" in Chapter 3). We learn from the opinion that "[Moore] expected his supervisor to do or say something, but when McCauley did nothing, [Moore] went back to work" (*Moore v. Kuka Welding Systems* 1999). Moore expected his supervisor to act because the supervisor is higher in the management chain than Moore, and thus will suffer fewer sanctions if he attempts to shape the common ground. But institutional hierarchy and social hierarchy may both be involved—a popular manager may have greater influence over the common ground than an unpopular manager.[3]

Social hierarchy alone may affect one's degree of culpability. It is much more difficult for a bullied teen, who is already a victim of social exclusion, to speak out, than for one of the popular kids to speak out. It is also more difficult for a newcomer to a social group to object than it is for an established member of the group. A friend told me of being invited to dinner as a new resident in a neighborhood where most of the people had lived there a long time and many had relationships to each other of blood or marriage. One of the other guests used a racist slur. But as a Johnny-come-lately, who was also an outsider in terms of social class, my friend didn't say anything, even though he didn't feel good about not saying anything. Your place in the social hierarchy, then, is one factor in assessing how much you are to blame for the presence of nasty ideas in the common ground. The more secure your social position, the easier it is for you to push back on a proposed addition to the common ground.

When challenging is pointless or dangerous

Your social history and social identity may also be relevant to whether it is rational for you to challenge belittling speech. Suppose, e.g., that you know that any objection you raise will be mocked, overlooked, or ignored. Then you might reasonably smother your objections. In a discussion of how people verbally transmit knowledge, the philosopher Kristie Dotson describes a phenomenon she calls testimonial smothering (2011). As Dotson uses the terms 'testimony' and 'testimonial', they cover sharing knowledge in informal conversations—i.e., the terms are not restricted to formal testimony, given in a setting like a courtroom or a public hearing, or to formal testimonials, such as recommendation letters. In a key example, the journalist Cassandra Byer Harvins is working in a public library, and a White woman asks what she is working on. Harvins responds that she is investigating "raising black sons in this society"; the White woman counters with, "How is that any different from raising white sons?" Both the woman's tone and the content of the question display to Harvins that the White woman "just knows that I am making something out of nothing" (1996, 16); furthermore, the White woman will not find anything Harvins says in reply intelligible because she is perniciously ignorant about race in the United States (Dotson 2011, 249). So, Harvins does not share her knowledge about the distinctive aspects of raising Black sons in the United States—she smothers her testimony.

While Dotson is concerned with the transmission of knowledge, similar considerations apply to challenging belittling speech. Sometimes, people may smother a challenge, because they know that the person who has expressed belittling ideas will be unmoved. Sometimes, they are fearful of the consequences. Consider the court cases we have discussed. When Gerald Moore met with his plant manager, he did not answer a question about who had used "race words" partly because he was afraid of the consequences for him on the shop floor (*Moore v. Kuka Welding Systems* 1999). He had an additional reason for not answering the question: McCauley was at the meeting and already knew who the culprits were. Thus McCauley, who had greater power than Moore, could have told the plant manager without incurring any risk, making the names of the perpetrators common ground. You may also recall that Swinton never asked Fosdick to stop telling racist jokes in his presence because Fosdick carried a pistol (*Swinton v. Potomac Corporation* 2001). So, there are circumstances where the rational course of action is to allow a belittling idea into the common ground, either because you are powerless to prevent it, or because any attempt to prevent it incurs serious risk—inviting mockery, or anger, or even violence. In cases like these, you are not culpable for listening to belittling speech.

When you are the target of belittling speech

Charles Witt overheard a coordinator for Roadway Express saying "F[uck] that n____, he don't have no rights," with regard to Witt's complaints about a trucking assignment. Witt testified that he "just kind of shrugged it off and walked away" (*Witt v. Roadway Express* 1998). The coordinator either didn't know or didn't care that Witt was in earshot; either way, since Witt was not in the conversation, he was not one of the joint managers of the common ground. He didn't seek eligibility to take a turn by inserting himself in the conversation, for unspecified reasons—but we can imagine that among his reasons were prudence, a desire to avoid conflict that might jeopardize his job, and a long history of "shrugging off" similar incidents.

Swinton, however, was in the conversation when Fosdick told racist jokes, as was Moore when his coworker told racist jokes. But Swinton and Moore were the intended targets of the belittling speech. While I have argued that people who listen to belittling speech gain culpability, blaming Swinton and Moore for listening would be at least as foolish and insensitive as blaming someone for being mugged. If Culpable Listening implied that Swinton was blameworthy for listening to Fosdick, or that Moore was blameworthy for listening to his coworker when he used "race words," that would be a reason to suppose that Culpable Listening is incorrect. I have already said that Moore and Swinton are not culpable, because they had reasonable fears about the consequences of challenging the speakers, and because they had little or no influence on the common ground. But there's more to say about why they had no influence on the common ground.

Philosophical theories about the workings of conversation idealize human communication. They generally treat conversations as falling somewhere along a continuum from cooperative to uncooperative, and until quite recently they treat the common ground as monolithic.[4] But any teenager learns that it is more complicated than that. In a multi-person conversation, there can be highly cooperative alliances that do not involve everyone. Those in the alliance might treat someone else as a third wheel, or as a hanger-on, or as a target.

Many of you won't have seen the dark teen comedy *Heathers*, but here are the essentials (Lehmann 1989). The three most popular girls at a high school are all named Heather. Veronica, played by Winona Ryder, hovers on the fringes of the group. The Heathers don't care what anyone else thinks; and even among the Heathers, there is a hierarchy, with one of the Heathers being Queen Bee and the others satellites.[5] In a social circle like this, the Heathers—and particularly the Queen Bee, Heather No. 1—have the power to choose who may contribute to the common ground, and who may police what enters and exits the common ground. In a lunchroom scene, Veronica asks, "Heather, why can't we talk to different kinds of people?" Heather No. 1 replies, "Fuck me gently with a chainsaw! Do I look like Mother Teresa? If I did, I probably wouldn't mind talking to the geek squad." Yet Heather No. 1 has just conducted a poll where she asked questions of a so-called geek—so it is not literally true that she doesn't talk to the geek squad. Rather, she talks to them as a display of social power, and she listens to them only insofar as they provide material for mockery.

In a social hierarchy like this one, the most entitled (the Heathers) affect not only the power dynamics of the common ground—who is likely to attempt to change the common ground—but also determine which people count for the purposes of the common ground. From Heather No. 1's point of view, a teen like Courtney, whom she polls in the lunchroom, isn't anyone—so she isn't one of the people whose acceptance of an idea matters for the common ground at all. On Stalnaker's view, when we are considering whether an idea is in the common ground, we need to think about whether everyone accepts that idea. When Heather No. 1 considers whether everyone accepts an idea, 'everyone' consists of, at most, the other Heathers and Veronica. In fact, Heather No. 1 takes her own acceptance of the idea to be sufficient for its being accepted by everyone in the common ground. If she accepts it, the other Heathers and Veronica had damn well better accept it too, and if they don't, they may be cast into the outer darkness of non-Heathers. Heathers No. 2 and No. 3, however, will look to Heather No. 1 when proposing an entry into the common ground. If Heather No. 1 doesn't accept it, they will not press their case.

In Heathers, the allies are at the top of the pecking order. But there may be alliances among those lower in the pecking order too. Suppose, for example, there are two Black women in a group with White women. One of the White women says something that illustrates a basic lack of understanding of the world from a Black woman's point of view—e.g., "I don't know why some women spend so much time and money on their hair. I get mine cut every six months and throw it in a messy bun when I don't want to wash it." The Black women may catch each other's eyes, in mutual understanding that a hair routine like this is not a realistic option for them; for many workplaces, they need a complicated, expensive, and time-consuming regimen for their hair

(Koval and Rosette 2021; Congress.gov 2022). Their shared understanding does not enter the common ground that is shared by everyone in the conversation, but that does not make it unimportant to them, or to their future contributions to this conversation.

Wherever people fall in the pecking order, allies in a conversation may share assumptions that are not shared with others, resulting in multiple common grounds that overlap in some ways and conflict in others. Sometimes, the existence of multiple common grounds may be more or less invisible. Once, I was with my dear friend Karen when I was warmly greeted by a middle-aged White man at a meeting of the American Philosophical Association. I responded appropriately, even though I had no idea who he was—I have issues with facial recognition. Karen could tell I was bluffing, but I hope that the friendly man could not. So, my ally Karen and I shared a common ground that we attempted to keep invisible to him; this hidden common ground included the idea "Claire does not know who this man is, but doesn't want to admit it."

However, sometimes the existence of more than one common ground is apparent to everyone. Belittling speech can serve to openly cement alliances and to victimize others; belittling jokes can have the same role, but in the guise of humor. In Swinton's workplace conversation with Fosdick, there is a conversational group, and an accompanying common ground, that includes Swinton—this is the common ground that is recognized in idealized theories of conversation. But there is also a common ground that is managed by a powerful subset of the people present, where Fosdick takes a role like that of Heather No. 1 and Swinton is excluded like Courtney in the lunchroom. Fosdick's jokes deepen his alliances with everyone but Swinton. The supervisor, Pat Stewart, is in this powerful alliance, and indicates his allegiance with laughter. If Swinton challenged Fosdick, it would have no effect on what the people in the powerful alliance think, or on how they proceed, because while Swinton may be eligible to take a turn in the larger conversational group, he does not have the power to channel the common ground circumscribed by Fosdick and shared by the alliance—a second common ground that is not recognized by idealized theories.[6] While this second common ground is accepted by a smaller number of the people who are present—i.e., it doesn't matter whether Swinton accepts the ideas that compose it—it has greater significance in dictating the dynamics of the conversation as a whole than the idealized common ground.

With regard to shaping the common ground defined by Fosdick, Swinton's position is a little like that of an eavesdropper, with the cruel twist that this eavesdropper is a pivotal member of Fosdick's intended audience. But just as the eavesdropper is not culpable for the presence of belittling speech in a conversation he listens to, Swinton is not culpable for the presence of belittling speech in the common ground that is controlled by Fosdick; Fosdick has not granted Swinton eligibility to take a turn with regard to that common ground, so nothing Swinton says will have any effect on it. For this reason, Swinton bears no responsibility for its contents. He is not a culpable listener.

Between a rock and a hard place

People like Swinton and Moore are not just in a bind, but in a double bind. They have no good choices. They can put up with belittling humor, and belittling language more generally, but this involves swallowing insult, with an accompanying loss of dignity and a growing anger. Furthermore, their putting up with the humor can be held against them at a later date, as evidence that the belittling speech was not unwelcome. For example, Judge Kelly of the Third Circuit Court of Appeals later ruled that Witt's self-contained reaction—shrugging it off and walking away—showed that he did not perceive the use of an egregious slur as severe harassment; but this ruling overlooks the fact that it would be exhausting for Black men to confront every act of racial hostility that they encounter, and if they did, they would unfairly be judged as oversensitive, difficult, and prickly. On the other hand, challenging the jokers involves substantial risk, as we have seen. In the end, as you know, both Swinton and Moore quit their jobs because their situations were untenable.

The philosopher Marilyn Frye has argued that the experience of oppressed people is characterized partly by repeated, systematic, double binds (1983). Everyone, no matter how privileged, faces a double bind once in a while. But Frye and others have argued that for members of oppressed groups, the double binds occur because of their group membership, and they occur frequently, in effect fencing people in. Frye uses the analogy of a birdcage to illustrate the point—a single wire does not cage a bird, because the bird can fly around it, whereas multiple wires, arranged just so, trap the bird. I contend that being subjected to belittling speech is an example of an oppressive double bind. It is part of a system of unjust disadvantage.

Social hierarchies and the common ground

Among philosophers of language, it is a familiar idea that a person's social position affects what they can accomplish when they say something. The philosopher J. L. Austin was particularly attuned to the ways in which some speakers can do special things with speech because of their social role. For example, a speaker needs to occupy a particular social position in order to christen a ship or to make a promise; I can't christen the ship if I am a "low type" passing by, and I can't promise on someone else's behalf (Austin 1975, 23; 1979, 239).[7] But the thesis I have begun to describe above—that the social power of a participant in the conversation may affect their ability to adjust the common ground itself—requires more attention.[8]

Sometimes, a power relationship is explicitly invoked to dismiss a conversational contribution; an op-ed in the New York Times about communication between nurses and doctors provides illustrations: "A nurse I know, attempting to clarify an order, was told, 'When you have "M.D." after your name, then you can talk to me.' A doctor dismissed another's complaint by simply saying, 'I'm important'" (Brown 2011). But there need not be an explicit reference to the discrepancy in power for there to be a discrepancy in the ability of the conversational partners to challenge an assertion. Furthermore, a discrepancy in social power that affects one's ability to challenge and thus one's ability to shift the common ground need not be codified in the way that the discrepancy in power of a boss and an employee, or of an emperor and a courtier, is codified. A discrepancy in power might instead come from unspoken social hierarchies that affect a speaker's ability to change the common ground.

Here is an example from the blog What Is It Like to Be a Woman in Philosophy?:

The final straw came in a graduate seminar, when, during the course of discussion, I made what seemed to be a germane and illuminating point. No one responded to it, so I thought perhaps it was not as illuminating as I had thought. About five minutes later, still discussing the same issue, a male grad student made the same point, literally almost word for word what I had said. The professor and other grad students responded very positively, and thought it was a very illuminating point. They congratulated him on his insight into the matter. This happened multiple times during that seminar, and made me realize that regardless of how good I was at the field, it didn't matter, as I was not going to be listened to.

The grad student who reiterated my comment almost word for word seemed to realize that he was repeating my point, and looked rather uncomfortable with the resulting attention. He did not, however, say anything like "As X already mentioned. . . ." (Jender 2010)

This is one of a number of similar examples posted on this blog, and familiar from everyday experience.[9] The two students make the same point; when the author makes the point, nobody responds—it does not enter the common ground. When the male student makes the same point, it does enter the common ground; indeed, his contribution (which repeats hers) is hailed as insightful and illuminating. This is not what Stalnaker's model of conversation predicts. On his model, it is infelicitous to make an assertion that has already been made; and even if the common ground is not affected by an assertion, the fact that the woman made the point should be what he calls a 'manifest event', as evident to those present as all the lights in the room suddenly going out. Thus, we can see that Stalnaker's model needs to be refined to reflect the effect of social hierarchy.[10]

I suggested above that sometimes a listener is not blameworthy for failing to challenge a belittling joke or other piece of belittling speech; discrepancies in social power may provide extenuating circumstances. A listener may have less authority than the speaker, because she is lower in the hierarchy (e.g., she is a nurse in conversation with the 'important' doctor); or she may find that her contributions are often ignored, and for good reason believe, as the author of the blog post does, that she is "not going to be listened to." If the reasons for failing to challenge the belittling speech are sufficiently great, then it may be asking too much of a listener to challenge the speech, and someone who listens in silence may not be blameworthy for failing to make a challenge.[11]

Changing the topic or walking away

I have argued that sometimes one should stop listening to a conversation; but I have also argued that sometimes challenging the speaker is too much to ask of a listener, because of the risks incurred or because the speaker doesn't have the social standing needed to change the common ground. I have also argued that challenging a speaker is important because while it doesn't necessarily stop the speaker from going on in the same vein, it does oust belittling claims from the common ground. We can stop listening by other means, however. Swinton glared and walked away, clearly indicating his disgust, and removing himself from the conversation. We can change the topic, or turn to someone else and begin a separate conversation, or just tune out.

The philosopher H. P. Grice provides an example of the efficacy of a change of topic: "At a genteel tea party, [Anna] says *Mrs. [Xavier] is an old bag.* There is a moment of appalled silence, and then [Bernadette] says *The weather has been quite delightful this summer, hasn't it?*" (adapted from Grice 1989, 35). Grice argues that Bernadette's intervention is an example of a particularized conversational implicature, with the implicature being "that [Anna]'s remark should not be discussed and, perhaps more specifically, that [Anna] has committed a social gaffe" (35).[12] But Bernadette's topic change also spares Bernadette, and others, from continuing to listen to disrespectful speech about Mrs. Xavier. Bernadette's topic change, however, does not necessarily involve expelling the claim that Mrs. Xavier is an old bag from the common ground. For example, it might be clear that Bernadette also finds Mrs. Xavier disagreeable—maybe she has said so already—but dislikes the term 'old bag' because it is ageist and misogynist.[13] So, assuming that Bernadette is not rejecting the claim that Mrs. Xavier is an old bag from the common ground, does Bernadette accomplish anything by changing the topic?

The assumptions that are in the common ground of a conversation are the shared presuppositions of the people in the conversation; they are background information, taken for granted by the participants. As I have argued, there can be people who are, in some sense, part of a conversation, but have no control over one of the common grounds that govern that conversation— Courtney has no control over Heather's common ground in the lunchroom, and Swinton has no control over Fosdick's common ground at work. Let's restrict the discussion for the time being, however, to participants who have control over the common ground. If someone challenges something that a speaker says, it does not remain part of the common ground. But if nobody challenges it, then everyone is treating it as true, and since everyone also believes that everyone is treating it as true, everyone presupposes it. So, if I am listening to a speaker who says something belittling, and nobody challenges it, I presuppose it myself. I presuppose it myself even if I am inwardly squirming because I don't believe the belittling claim, or because it makes me uncomfortable. On Stalnaker's view, presupposing is to do with one's outward conversational behavior, not with one's beliefs.

At the tea party, nobody challenged Anna's assertion that Mrs. Xavier is an old bag, so Bernadette's change of topic leaves Bernadette, and everyone else, presupposing that Mrs. Xavier is an old bag. However, Bernadette has stopped Anna from proceeding to derogate Mrs. Xavier (assuming that the topic change is successful), so she has saved herself, and everyone else, from presupposing yet more negative descriptions of Mrs. Xavier. Furthermore, Bernadette has channeled the conversation away from further derogation of Mrs. Xavier. So, while the presupposition that Mrs. Xavier is an old bag is still in the common ground—since nobody rejected it—it may become irrelevant to the future course of the conversation.[14]

It's worth noting too that in failing to challenge Anna's assertion about Mrs. Xavier, Bernadette is *allowing* or *permitting* Anna to presuppose that Mrs. Xavier is an old bag. Stalnaker tells us, "What is most distinctive about [speaker presupposition] is that it is a social or public attitude: one presupposes [something] only if one presupposes that others presuppose it as well" (2002, 701). For example, if Anna presupposes that Mrs. Xavier is disagreeable, then she presupposes that others presuppose that Mrs. Xavier is disagreeable as well. If Carol challenges Anna's claim about Mrs. Xavier, then Anna can no longer presuppose that Carol presupposes that Mrs. Xavier is disagreeable (at least, not if she is rational); so, Anna herself can no longer presuppose that Mrs. Xavier is disagreeable. To be clear, Anna may still believe that Mrs. Xavier is disagreeable, but she cannot continue to believe that everyone in the conversation treats 'Mrs. Xavier is disagreeable' as true. Carol's challenge to the belittling presupposition, then, can prevent Anna from presupposing it too. On the other hand, if nobody challenges Anna, then everyone allows her to presuppose that Mrs. Xavier is disagreeable.

So, when I am in a conversation where someone presupposes something belittling, I am not just a bystander who witnesses her making a presupposition. What I do provides conditions that are necessary for her presupposition. If I fail to challenge her, my feeling of having done something wrong may stem partly from my having contributed to the conditions needed for her to presuppose something belittling. On the assumption that people ought not presuppose belittling ideas, I am enabling her to do wrong.

Continuing to listen to a conversation that contains belittling speech, then, enables others to presuppose belittling ideas. Although I have argued that Culpable Listening explains our feelings of guilt better than Culpable

Silence, Culpable Silence is correct that challenging belittling speech is the best way to expel belittling claims from the common ground, assuming that you have sufficient social standing to mount a challenge. Changing the topic is better than doing nothing, however, because while it leaves the belittling claim in the common ground, if the topic change is successful we do not have to continue doing the wrong of listening to belittling speech. Changing the topic, however, also requires a degree of social standing, as my children have yet to learn—their efforts to stop the grownups from talking about grownup concerns are frequent but lack authority.

If you cannot challenge belittling speech, and you cannot change the topic, you may choose to leave the conversation. Perhaps you can walk away as Swinton and Witt did. At a dinner party, you might turn to talk to someone else; at a less regimented social gathering, you might excuse yourself to go to the bathroom or to get another drink; on the plane, you might put in your earbuds and pretend to go sleep. These are all ways of stopping listening to belittling speech, thus saving yourself from being culpable of listening to yet more belittling speech. They also save you from continuing to provide the necessary conditions for someone to presuppose belittling ideas. A person may have the right to speak freely, and thus the right to say belittling things; but that does not imply that anyone has an obligation to listen. The lack of an audience has no apparent effect on the preachers who show up on campus to rail against what they see as appalling social ills, like women wearing leggings, but the average person will stop talking if nobody listens.

Conclusion

In summary, you can be culpable for listening to belittling speech; recall Harry, who listens to as many of Stephen's belittling jokes as he likes. His later challenge ejects the conveyed belittling claims from the common ground, but he still did wrong by listening in the first place. Some people in a conversation are more blameworthy than others for listening to belittling speech, however, because challenging presents fewer costs to them; e.g., Grandma is more culpable for the presence of belittling speech at her Thanksgiving dinner table than Aaron. Further, sometimes it is rational to smother a challenge; it was rational for Cassandra Byer Harvins to disengage, rather than challenge, when the White woman in the library asked how raising Black sons was any different from raising White sons. Finally, a single conversation can have multiple, overlapping common grounds, some of which are more significant than others. There are people, like Courtney in the lunchroom, or Swinton at work, who are members of one of those multiple common grounds but not of others. Courtney is not culpable for the common ground that is governed by Heather No. 1 and shared by the Heathers and Veronica; Swinton is not culpable for the common ground that is governed by Fosdick and shared with Swinton's supervisor. But even when you are, technically, a member of the relevant common ground, discrepancies in social power, including unspoken discrepancies, can provide extenuating circumstances in which you are not blameworthy for listening to belittling speech.

Leaving a conversation or changing the topic are valuable, too; they help you avoid listening to further belittling speech, and prevent the speaker from presupposing belittling ideas. When you cannot reasonably challenge the speaker, the next best thing is to stop listening by one of these methods. But as with challenging, these methods are more available to those with greater social leverage.

This chapter focused on how power dynamics matter in a conversation. In the final chapter, I will turn to how humor can reinforce or undermine hierarchies of power in society as a whole.

12

Joking and power

Introduction

As you know, my usage of 'belittling' and 'disparaging' is not standard. Much of this book has focused on belittling humor—i.e., on jokes and joking remarks that convey negative stereotypes or claims that support or have supported unjust disadvantage, thus diminishing people in power or status. I have said very little about derogatory humor that is disparaging but not belittling—humor that merely lowers people in opinion, and does not support unjust disadvantage. Examples include jokes about privileged groups such as lawyers or about groups that have a social identity but are neither privileged nor disadvantaged, like quilters. The difference between disparaging and belittling humor has much to do with power. Belittling humor is a way of establishing and maintaining social hierarchies. Disparaging humor about the powerful, on the other hand, can be a way of undermining social hierarchies.

This final chapter has three main goals, all of which concern the relationship between humor and power. The first is to explain how belittling jokes support existing power structures. The second is to sketch how disparaging jokes can undermine existing power structures. The third is to say a little about the parallel between my account of belittling jokes and accounts of other kinds of belittling speech—such as pornographic speech and hate speech—offered by philosophers like Rae Langton (1993) and Ishani Maitra (2012). Langton, Maitra, and others hold that speech like this subordinates others. So, one might wonder whether belittling jokes can be considered subordinating speech.

How belittling jokes support unjust disadvantage

In this book, I have outlined a mechanism by which belittling ideas are communicated, and the empirical facts illustrate that, sometimes, communicating ideas by this mechanism makes a concrete difference for specific individuals. But these jokes are belittling even when an instance of telling the joke has no concrete negative effects on anyone in particular on that occasion. It remains belittling because it communicates ideology that plays a crucial role in unjust disadvantage. I will explain.

Suppose that a stream of disparaging jokes about a politician leads to his losing his bid for re-election; he is a White male, and like former US president Bill Clinton, is disparaged for the care he takes with his hair. Let's also assume that, as an elected representative, he had power and status that he has now lost. Why would I not say that the politician has been belittled by the jokes? After all, he has been lowered in power and status. The reason I would not say that he (or anyone else) has been belittled by the jokes is that the jokes do not communicate negative ideas that support unjust disadvantage for people who share his social identity.

Suppose instead that the politician is a Black woman; like Stacey Abrams, who ran for governor in Georgia, she has been derogated for her hair, which is not chemically altered or straightened and is considered "unprofessional." Let's also assume that, as an elected representative, our imaginary politician had power and status, and since she loses her bid for re-election, she loses power and status. I would say that this woman has been belittled by jokes about her hair. But it is not the loss of her status as an elected representative that makes the jokes belittling. They would be belittling even if she had been re-elected, or elected to a higher office. They are belittling because the ideas about Black women's hair that they rely on are a factor in unjust disadvantage for people who share her social identity.

Black women face discrimination in many workplaces for having natural hair, e.g., in the corporate world and in law offices. Chastity Jones had a job offer as a customer service representative rescinded because she refused to cut her dreadlocks (*EEOC v. Catastrophe Management Solutions* 2016). White women are not expected to change their hair texture for work, so Black women face additional burdens because of societal pressure to chemically alter their hair. It takes substantial time, which is a problem for many women (for an overview, see Banks 2000, 151–53), and the chemicals involved may increase the risk of breast cancer (Eberle et al. 2020). Furthermore, straightening hair is expensive, and Black women make on average 63 cents on the dollar compared to non-Hispanic White men (Roux 2021), so this societal expectation places a financial burden on an underpaid group. Expectations about Black women and their hair have much greater nuance than I have described here, as Ingrid Banks, a social scientist, documents in her book, *Hair Matters: Beauty, Power, and Black Women's Consciousness* (2000). But even a simplistic account illustrates that negative ideas about Black women's natural hair are part of an ideology that supports and maintains unjust disadvantage for Black women.

Ideology cannot continue to support unjust disadvantage if it is not communicated. As racism has become more frowned upon, openly expressing negative ideas and stereotypes about Black people has become subject to social sanction, at least in some social circles. But humor—because of the popular wisdom that surrounds it—remains a way of communicating negative ideology. A journalist writing in the *Los Angeles Times*, Charles Fleming, describes how "lessons in bigotry and prejudice were delivered via punchlines to jokes" in his childhood (2020). He tells us, "No one ever said, 'These people are like this.' But within the jokes was a catalog of assumptions."

Fleming's childhood was in the 1950s and 1960s; but humor continues to communicate negative stereotypes among young people today. An adolescent who identified as Black and as Native American in a study in 2016 said, "Once I get to know you or whatever and then I'll, I'll [*sic*] say little jokes too. Yeah of course I will. I'll say jokes too like, 'You loud Dominican you' to my friend 'cause she is SO loud. And then there's that stereotype that they're loud so I'll joke about it'" (Douglass et al. 2016, 74). This study, by a team of researchers in education and psychology, was focused on how friends interact around race and ethnicity in adolescence. They found that adolescents have a complex relationship with ethnic and racial teasing in their friend groups; they consider it harmless, but for targeted individuals, especially those who were already prone to anxiety, it increases anxiety for a few days. The authors say "the friendly settings in which [racial and ethnic teasing] are occurring and the use of humor may allow adolescents to superficially deflect the meaning, but leave them wondering about the underlying intention and meaning of such interactions" (79).

Focusing on localized effects of jokes—like increased social anxiety, changes in beliefs and attitudes, and changes in behavior—establishes that specific joke-tellings and joking remarks can have consequences. But while these localized effects give ample reason to avoid telling belittling jokes and making belittling remarks, my primary reason for saying that jokes and remarks are belittling is not that they sometimes have negative consequences for some people. Rather, my primary reason for saying that jokes and remarks are belittling is that the ideas they convey play a role in supporting unjust disadvantage. Chris Rock's joking remark about Jada Pinkett Smith's hair at the 2022 Oscars ceremony was belittling because it mocked a Black woman for her hair (and because it mocked a medical condition); Pinkett Smith was upset, but that is not the only reason that Rock should not have made that remark (Tsioulcas 2022).

People who study social injustice often emphasize its systemic nature. Multiple, interlocking social structures and restrictions work together to limit a group, so that members of the group remain unjustly disadvantaged. Ideology about the group is one aspect of social disadvantage; negative ideas and stereotypes (such as the idea that natural Black hair is unprofessional) shore up, directly or indirectly, broader social practices and institutions. So belittling humor supports existing power structures by communicating and reinforcing ideology, and it does so in a particularly insidious way, both because humor is shielded by the popular wisdom that it is Harmless Fun, and because humor discourages the use of slow, careful, System 2 cognitive processes and encourages the use of faster and less reliable System 1 processes.

In addition, there are specific instances where belittling humor has a negative effect on its victims or on other people's attitudes and actions regarding the victimized group, so, sometimes it is one of the things that together with others makes up a system of disadvantage. In a system of disadvantage, some of the restrictions and slights experienced by the members of the group are major; others may seem insignificant when viewed in isolation. But even minor inconveniences can accumulate and interconnect to result in substantial disadvantage.

Disparaging humor

As I have said, disparaging humor—as opposed to belittling humor—includes jokes about groups that have a social identity, but are neither privileged nor disadvantaged—like sports enthusiasts or quilters. There's a lot of myth surrounding quilting and its thrifty origins, but most contemporary quilters buy new fabric that is specially designed for the purpose, and spend much more to make a quilt than it would cost to buy bedding at a store. Certainly—and I speak as a devoted quilter myself—cutting up new fabric into little pieces and sewing it back together is a somewhat laughable hobby. But quilters are not, as a group, unjustly disadvantaged, and so humor about quilters is disparaging but not belittling. Thus, disparaging humor about quilters neither supports an existing power structure nor undermines it.

Disparaging humor against powerful people, however, can contribute to undermining existing power structures. People who are relatively disadvantaged can wield humor against people who are powerful. It works for many of the same reasons that belittling humor works. Disparaging jokes about the powerful—about their $400 haircuts or their extensive collection of shoes—convey negative ideas and stereotypes, but indirectly, allowing the joker to undermine the powerful without openly stating those negative ideas. Humor, in general, discourages our critical faculties, allowing more intuitive processes to drive our cognitive processes. Disparaging humor, like belittling humor, goes undercover as harmless fun, so complaints from the butt of the joke can be readily dismissed as oversensitivity. Disparaging joking remarks can disguise the speaker's intent—are they saying something false with intent to amuse, or are they speaking what they see as the truth in jest? For all these reasons, humor offers people a way to adjust perceptions of those in power without suffering the consequences of conveying the same negative ideas by more straightforward means.

However, because of the power differential, for the most part I do not think that telling disparaging jokes is morally wrong. In some cases—where they occur in an authoritarian regime, for example—they may be a force for good. They might develop esprit de corps, or provide a way for people to express ideas that they are not permitted to express openly. There are some circumstances where you shouldn't tell a disparaging joke, however. For example, suppose that in the United States, there is a Republican president, a Republican Senate, and a Republican House of Representatives. You still shouldn't tell jokes about Republicans to your brother's new girlfriend, who is a Republican member of Congress, at her first barbecue with your extended family. As you may recall, the Wrong Audience claim has a smattering of truth—telling a joke like this will increase the girlfriend's feelings of social exclusion (Ford et al. 2020).

It's also worth remembering that some jokes about powerful people are belittling. These are the jokes that reinforce unjust disadvantage for members of their group as a whole. Jokes about Barack Obama's race, or Donald Trump's weight, fall in this category.

Constitution and causes of harm

Dave of Northampton, Massachusetts, wrote to *The Ethicist* column in the *New York Times* to ask about a friend whose winter holiday decorations include a figurine of Santa in Blackface with a slice of watermelon. Dave's friend thinks the figurine does no harm, because no Black person will see it. In reply, the philosopher Kwame Anthony Appiah (2022b) says the friend is mistaken: "For one thing, if the image reflects the way he and his wife think of Black people, as objects of humorous contempt, they are (in my view) wronging Black people, regardless of who learns about it. People can be defamed, furthermore, even if it never becomes known to them or causes them disadvantage. So, you're appalled and offended for good reason."

Appiah argues that the owner of the figurine wrongs Black people. Should we say, in parallel, that telling a belittling joke wrongs the victimized group, even if as a matter of fact, that joke-telling has no direct effects on anyone's life? To take a fanciful example, let's suppose Stephanie tells a racist joke to her friend Harry, and immediately afterward they are both victims of a zombie invasion. The joke counts as a belittling joke, on my view, because it conveys ideology that plays a role in broader systems of unjust disadvantage, even though that specific joke-telling has no further societal effects. But could we also say that Stephanie belittles Black people in telling that joke, just as Appiah thinks the figurine owner wrongs Black people? To address this question, we need to take one more dive into philosophy of language.

The philosopher J. L. Austin persuasively argued that people can perform actions by speaking in certain circumstances. Examples include the act of voting and the act of getting engaged to be married; by saying "Aye" in certain circumstances you can vote on a motion at a meeting, and by saying "Yes" when someone asks you to marry them, you can become engaged (Austin 1975). Any time someone speaks, they perform actions like moving parts of their body to produce meaningful sounds or signs. But the acts that most interested Austin—ordering, promising, betting, consenting, christening, conceding, and so on—are actions of social significance far beyond producing meaningful speech. They change our commitments to each other, and they change facts about the social world. Austin called them speech acts.

Austin distinguished three types of speech act, all of which can be performed at the same time by saying a single thing. There is nothing weird about the idea that one bodily movement can be multiple actions: Flicking a switch can also be turning on a light and also be scaring away a burglar

(Davidson 1963). So, what kinds of act can be performed in speaking, on Austin's view?

Suppose a dear friend says, "I promise you I will come to stay next weekend." She performs a *locutionary* act, because she says something meaningful, referring to herself, you, and the following weekend. In general, to perform a locutionary act is to say something that has a meaning, as opposed to a baby babbling, or to gibberish. She also performs an *illocutionary* act, the act of promising; she commits herself to coming to stay. Illocutionary acts change social facts and commitments—think of nominating, apologizing, welcoming, or marrying. And she may perform a *perlocutionary* act, but which perlocutionary act depends on other factors—perhaps she pleases you because it will be fun to stay up late, drink wine, and talk endlessly with her; perhaps she dismays you, because even though you love her you dislike having people stay the night at your house, disrupting your sleep and expecting you to chat in the morning before you've had your coffee; perhaps she motivates you to spring-clean, because your guest room is an unholy mess and you will have to get it in order before her arrival.

Austin's work has been enormously influential on how philosophers understand belittling speech. The philosopher Rae Langton deploys Austin's framework to argue that some kinds of speech subordinate other people. She asks us to consider a lawmaker in South Africa enacting the legislation of apartheid. He says, "Blacks are not permitted to vote" (Langton 1993, 302). Langton argues that speech acts like this "*rank* blacks as having inferior worth. They *legitimate* discriminatory behavior on the part of whites. And finally, they *deprive* blacks of some important powers: for example, the power to go to certain areas and the power to vote" (303). Ranking, legitimating, and depriving of power are illocutionary acts. Furthermore, in this case the ranking is unfair, what is legitimated is malign discrimination, and the deprivation of powers is unjust. If "to subordinate someone is to put them in a position of inferiority or loss of power, or to belittle[1] or denigrate them," then this speech is an act of subordination (303).[2] Since it is an illocutionary act, it constitutes, rather than merely causes, subordination; however, it may also cause subordination, as a perlocutionary effect.

Voting at a meeting and enacting legislation are both illocutionary acts in an institutional framework, where the speakers are endowed with authority. But lots of speech acts—promising, betting, getting engaged, warning, advising, and many more—don't require a formal framework. Langton and others have argued that there are informal kinds of speech, such as hate speech, pornography, and racial slurs, that constitute subordination. So, we might wonder whether telling a belittling joke also constitutes an act of subordination.[3] If it does, then Stephanie would belittle people by telling the joke to Harry, despite the arrival of the zombies.

However, it is not obvious that we can directly apply an argument like Langton's to belittling jokes. Austin himself explicitly excluded jokes from his analysis of speech acts. So, we must ask why Austin excluded jokes, and if those reasons are sufficiently strong that we should rule out the idea that telling a joke or making a joking remark can be a speech act of subordination.

Jokes and speech acts

Austin excluded jokes from his project partly for practical reasons; the scope of his project is vast already, and needs to be limited somehow. Indeed, he begins the second of a series of lectures given at Harvard in 1955 with the words: "We were to consider, you will remember, some cases and senses (only some, Heaven help us!) in which to *say* something is to *do* something" (Austin 1975, 12). But why draw the limit here, as opposed to elsewhere? He says "there is another whole range of questions about 'how we are using language' or 'what we are doing in saying something' *which may be, and intuitively seem to be, entirely different*—further matters which we are not trenching upon. For example, there are insinuating (and other non-literal uses of language), *joking (and other non-serious uses of language)*, and swearing and showing off (which are perhaps expressive uses of language)" (122, italics mine). So, his principled reasons for excluding insinuating, joking, swearing, and showing off are somewhat tentative. Elsewhere, he tells us that he is not confident that insinuating and swearing with words like "damn" are "as remote" from the speech acts that concern him as "joking or writing poetry" (105).[4] But despite Austin's hesitancy, what he says raises concerns about the viability of the thesis that joking speech can subordinate, since he thinks joking is even more remote from his core examples of speech acts than other things he excludes.

Although poems and plays fall outside Austin's scope, it would be a mistake to conclude that they are uninformative, or that they are never capable of performing actions that change our relationships with each other. Poems and plays can tell us things about our world, or at the very least, about someone's view of our world. A poem can declare one's love—arguably an illocutionary act. Jane Austen's Elizabeth Bennet says that if one's love for someone is not "a fine, stout, healthy love," but is "only a slight, thin sort of inclination, I am convinced that one good sonnet will starve it entirely away" (2006a, 49)—this, because of its causal aspect, would be a perlocutionary act. Austin himself uses a joking invocation of the divine when he says "Heaven help us!" at Harvard, to tell his audience that considering *every* case and sense in which to say something is to do something would be an overwhelming task.

Jokes, like poems and plays, can communicate information; and perhaps some of them can be used to perform illocutionary acts. It is more than plausible that fiction can be belittling; e.g., I would argue that the novel *Gone with the Wind* belittles African Americans with its stereotypical depictions of enslaved people, as does the movie made from it (Fleming 1940; Mitchell 1936). Austin excludes plays, poetry, and jokes from his opus because unlike his core examples, the way they behave is not governed by convention and procedure. Furthermore, he has enough work to be going on with.[5]

Since Austin gives us very little argument, we don't know for sure why he excluded joking.[6] In addition, whatever his reasons for excluding joking, he might have been mistaken. The vision of a philosopher who introduces a wholly new concept, like that of the speech act, may be insightful in some ways and misguided in others. So, in answering the question of whether telling a belittling joke is an illocutionary act, of belittling or subordinating, there are at least two directions open to us. We could say, well, Austin says jokes aren't speech acts, and leave it at that. Or we could say, it is unclear whether jokes can be speech acts; Austin gives us an opinion, but little argument, so we must figure it out for ourselves.

It's obvious that joking is a locutionary act. In the next section, I will argue that joking is also a perlocutionary act. In the section after that, I will argue for a modest conclusion: Austin gives us no reason for thinking that joking cannot be an illocutionary act.

Joking and perlocutionary acts

Joking—whether derogatory or not—can have perlocutionary effects. Think of non-belittling jokes for a moment. A joke can lighten the mood, defuse tension, and create bonds of intimacy, as self-help guides tell us (Robinson, Segal, and Smith 2020). Turning to derogatory jokes, the empirical literature documents any number of perlocutionary effects—effects on our cognition (Bartolo et al. 2021; Chan et al. 2016); effects on our self-perception

(Ford et al. 2020); effects on our attitudes, beliefs, and decisions (Ford et al. 2014; Ford 2000). The law also documents perlocutionary effects of belittling jokes, on people like Troy Swinton and Gerald Moore (*Swinton v. Potomac Corporation* 2001; *Moore v. Kuka Welding Systems* 1999). If to belittle is to lower in power or status with ideas that play a role in unjust disadvantage, then there is no reason to deny that telling a belittling joke or making a belittling jocular remark can be belittling someone as a perlocutionary act. This, in itself, is a sufficient reason for avoiding telling belittling jokes and making belittling jocular remarks.

However, when Stephanie tells a belittling joke to Harry immediately prior to the zombie invasion, there is no time for perlocutionary effects. So, as long as Harry himself is not a victim of belittling perlocutionary effects in that moment, Stephanie has not performed a perlocutionary act of belittling— but only because subsequent events mean her joke has no consequences.

Joking and illocutionary acts

Can telling a joke or making a jocular remark be an illocutionary act of belittling? A compelling answer to this question is beyond my scope here, since it would require evaluating the claim that informal speech can constitute an illocutionary act of subordination, as well as extending Austin's analysis far beyond its original scope. For expediency, I will not address the claim that informal speech, like hate speech and slurs, can constitute subordination. This claim has been vigorously defended by others, such as the philosopher Mary Kate McGowan (2019), although it remains controversial. Rather, I am going to argue for a more modest claim; despite Austin's misgivings, he does not give us a reason for saying that jocular remarks and scripted jokes cannot constitute illocutionary acts. So, if informal speech like hate speech and slurs can constitute subordination, then so can belittling humor.

With regard to whether joking can be an illocutionary act, we can extract two different arguments from the meager textual evidence that Austin provides. One is that joking is not a *type* of illocutionary act—i.e., joking does not fall in the same category as betting or christening or marrying. I think this is partly what Austin is saying in the passage I quoted above, the one that begins "There is another whole range of questions about 'how we are using language'" (1975, 225). He is correct that joking is not a type of illocutionary act. Joking is a much more diverse phenomenon than, say, betting. It does not derive from a relatively simple set of cultural conventions, and it does not have predictable outcomes that are set by community norms. But while it is true that joking is not a type of illocutionary act, it does not follow that one cannot perform an illocutionary act, like betting or appraising, while joking. Bickering and flirting, for example, are also not types of illocutionary act, but we can perform illocutionary acts while bickering or flirting.

The second, and more significant, argument is that if someone utters words that normally would mark a speech act, such as "I order you . . ." while they are joking, in general we would not say that the joker had ordered anyone to do anything. This is the other part of what Austin is saying in the quoted passage, when he describes joking as a "non-serious" use of language. Elsewhere he expands on this point, saying:

> I might mention that . . . we could be issuing any of these utterances, as we can issue an utterance of any kind whatsoever, in the course, for example, of acting a play or making a joke or writing a poem—in which case of course it would not be seriously meant and we shall not be able to say that we seriously performed the act concerned. If the poet says 'Go and catch a falling star' or whatever it may be, he doesn't seriously issue an order. Considerations of this kind apply to any utterance at all, not merely to [illocutionary acts]. (1979, 228)

So, this second argument is that joking will have a fundamental effect on what illocutionary act is performed by an utterance, if any.

Austin is correct that "Go and catch a falling star," as a line in a poem, does not instruct us to catch a meteor.[7] But the poet does communicate by saying it. The poem continues:

> Get with child a mandrake root,
> Tell me where all past years are,
> Or who cleft the devil's foot,
> Teach me to hear mermaids singing,
> Or to keep off envy's stinging.
> (Donne [1633] 2009, 118)

After cataloging these impossible tasks, Donne suggests that finding a woman who is "true, and fair" is also a hopeless quest. So, while he does not order us to catch a meteor, he does communicate that, in his view, women are unfaithful. Now let's set aside plays and poems, and focus on joking remarks in a conversation. Suppose Stephen and Henry have been having an unfruitful conversation. Stephen is frustrated, because he thinks Henry is proposing an impossible course of action. He jokingly says, "Oh, go and catch a falling star." Stephen does not order Henry to catch a falling star. However, while saying 'Go and catch a falling star' would not usually perform the illocutionary act of ending the conversation, in these circumstances, it might.

We can imagine other scenarios. Suppose Sven jokingly says to Harvey, "I promise you I'll be there." Sven has not promised to be there. But from the fact that he has not promised, it does not follow that he has performed no illocutionary act at all. Perhaps he has mocked or insulted Harvey, for example. Or suppose Sebastian jokingly says to Heidi, "I forgive you for using my razor"; he may not have performed the illocutionary act of forgiving, but he may have performed the illocutionary act of accusing Heidi of using his razor. All in all, Austin's well-placed concern that joking *changes* the illocutionary act performed does not show that illocutionary acts *cannot* be performed while joking.

These examples use performative formulas—'I promise you . . .' and 'I forgive you . . .'. But illocutionary acts do not have to use performative formulas. Austin gives the example of warning someone with a sign that says 'dangerous bull,' or even just 'bull'. In some of these cases, we can substitute a performative formula—e.g., 'I warn you that there is a dangerous bull' (1979, 230; 1975, 62). But there are other illocutionary acts, like insulting, where there is no corresponding performative formula—we can't say, 'I insult you.' Austin speculates that this is because "we don't approve of insulting" (1979, 232). Performative formulas make the illocutionary act being performed explicit. But Austin points out at times that we may "trade on" ambiguity or "suffer from or profit by a sort of deliberate ambivalence" (1975, 66, 79); e.g., we might deliberately make it unclear whether or not we are apologizing by saying "I'm sorry," rather than "I apologize." As I have argued, joking remarks can also create ambiguity about our intentions (see "Does truth-in-jest have a warranty of truth?" in Chapter 7). A joking remark, then, could be an illocutionary act, while providing the joker with plausible deniability about their intentions.

Ambiguity about the speaker's intentions is especially valuable when the illocutionary act is something socially sanctioned or illegal.[8] The classic threat in gangster movies, "That's a nice restaurant you have there. It would be a shame if something happened to it," is an illocutionary act of threatening, but yet the gangster can deny that he was threatening anyone or anything. If he denies it, however, I think we would all agree that he still threatened someone; the denial is a lie. I contend that derogatory jocular remarks also have value to those who wish to derogate while retaining plausible deniability about what they intended. The retreat to "Oh, it's just a joke, I didn't mean anything by it" is readily available.

So, Austin provides no substantial reason for thinking jocular remarks cannot be illocutionary acts, and thus he provides no substantial reason for thinking that jocular remarks cannot constitute the illocutionary act of belittling. With belittling joking remarks, as I have defined them, the belittling language is out there in the open. If the speaker did not have joking intent, and we take for granted that informal speech can belittle, they would count as illocutionary acts of belittling. But I don't want to say that if the speaker really, genuinely intended the belittling remark as a joke, they do not perform the illocutionary act of belittling. Illocutionary acts do not have to be intentional. At that meeting long ago, I unintentionally insulted my colleague. Paddington Bear unintentionally bids at an auction in *Paddington Helps Out* (Bond 1961).[9] With belittling jocular remarks, a speaker might not intend to belittle anyone; but because of the belittling language they used, they belittle other people regardless of their intentions. So, if a speaker uses a belittling jocular remark, and then denies that they meant it, it could be true that they didn't intend to be belittling (although often, that too will be a self-serving lie); but their intentions are not relevant to whether or not they performed the illocutionary act of belittling by making that remark.

Let's turn now to scripted jokes. With scripted jokes, the belittling content is usually not in the open—it's not part of the literal meaning of the uttered words. I have argued that belittling scripted jokes convey belittling ideas as generalized implicatures. I would further argue this is the primary purpose of belittling scripted jokes—it is what they are for. They covertly communicate ideology that supports unjust disadvantage. I am taking for granted that if someone openly stated that same ideology, it could be an illocutionary act of belittling. So, if someone implicates that ideology, are they performing an illocutionary act of belittling? There's no principled reason to suppose that illocutionary acts cannot be implicatures. For example, the philosopher John Searle argues that "Can you pass the salt?" is an *indirect* illocutionary act. It is phrased as a question about one's salt-passing capacities, but in fact it is the illocutionary act of requesting the salt; and we know that it is a request because, given the circumstances, the question implicates that the speaker is requesting the salt (Searle 1965).[10] Similarly, a belittling scripted joke can serve as an indirect illocutionary act of belittling.

As with belittling joking remarks, there may be times when a speaker does not intend to belittle someone with a scripted belittling joke. But their intentions do not determine whether or not it was an illocutionary act of belittling. Scripted jokes convey belittling ideas by generalized implicature, regardless of the speaker's intent.[11] So, taking for granted that openly stating the conveyed idea can count as an illocutionary act of belittling, telling a scripted belittling joke can also count as an illocutionary act of belittling, even if the teller does not understand what he is doing—perhaps because he is taken in by Harmless Fun, or perhaps because he does not understand the significance of the conveyed ideology for unjust disadvantage more broadly.

So, when Stephanie tells a racist joke to Harry just prior to the zombie invasion, she has performed the illocutionary act of belittling—at least she has if informal speech can belittle and subordinate. If she had made a bet with Harry, or given him an order, those acts are not undone by the zombie invasion, even though neither she nor Harry will ever have to pay up on the bet, and though Harry will not carry out the order. The lack of consequences makes no difference to whether she has performed an illocutionary act in these cases. Similarly, the arrival of the zombies is irrelevant to whether she commits the illocutionary act of belittling.

Conclusion

Given the role of humor in supporting unjust disadvantage, we should not dismiss belittling humor as Harmless Fun. It's not harmless; and there's nothing fun about unjust disadvantage. If the argument of this book has convinced you, you will not be inclined to tell belittling jokes or make belittling jocular remarks; when making a derogatory joke or remark, you will think about whether it is really only disparaging or whether it is also belittling. But if you are not a hermit, there is a reasonable chance that you will be involved in conversations that include belittling humor. What should you do then? The postscript gives a little practical advice.

Postscript

Some practical advice

Suppose you want to be an ethical listener, rather than a good listener, and you find yourself listening to belittling speech. How might you interrupt? How might you encourage the speaker to reassess? I am going to focus on effective methods in this postscript, rather than on deeper ethical questions. The insight I will offer is not my own. Instead, I will turn to our buddies the social psychologists.

Studies of confrontation suggest that people don't confront racist and sexist speech as often as they would like. The social psychologists Julie A. Woodzicka and Marianne LaFrance (2001) found that out of fifty women who were asked a sexually harassing question in a job interview (such as "Do you think it is important for women to wear bras to work?"), 52% answered the question without confronting it in any way, whereas only 32% of women who were asked to imagine their response in such a situation said that is what they would do. None of the participants refused to answer, although 68% of those asked to imagine their response said they would refuse. Other studies have confirmed that there is a significant gap between what we imagine we will do and what we actually do when faced with racist or sexist speech (Kawakami, Karmali, and Vaccarino 2019).

As discussed in Chapter 11, there may be substantial risks for those who confront belittling speech, such as personal violence or loss of a needed job. I will assume here that the risks are ones you are willing and able to accept.

Concerns about being liked and being respected dissuade many people from confrontation. The social psychologists Margo Monteith, Mason Burns, and Laura Hildebrand conclude in their survey of the literature that there is no way to confront others about racist or sexist speech without risking one's likeability (2019). However, if you are concerned about whether others will continue to like you, and still want to confront what someone said, your best bet is to be assertive but not hostile. You should avoid, e.g., explicitly labeling a person or behavior as racist or sexist, and instead narrow your focus; Monteith, Burns, and Hildebrand suggest you might say something like "That joke isn't funny; it's not fair to gay people" (231). I have argued, as you know, that a belittling joke might be funny, but getting into the philosophical details in a moment like this isn't your best bet. If you're a stickler for the truth, you might say something like "That joke isn't fair to gay people, and I know fairness is important to you and me."

Being liked and respected by other people, however, is perhaps less important than liking and respecting yourself. There are psychological costs if you do not challenge bigotry and prejudice. Research on this topic has documented that targets of discrimination who confront the discriminatory behavior have greater feelings of well-being, less psychological distress, reduced rumination, and even lower blood pressure (Chaney, Young, and Sanchez 2015). Furthermore, there is evidence that failing to confront sexist speech increases one's tolerance of sexual harassment—perhaps because of cognitive dissonance (Mallett, Ford, and Woodzicka 2021). There has been less study of the personal benefits of confrontation on people who are not targeted, such as White people who confront racism and straight people who confront homophobia. It's clear, though, that such people are more effective in changing the minds and hearts of those who have expressed prejudice, and that they face less backlash than targets who confront (Czopp and Monteith 2003; Gulker, Mark, and Monteith 2013; Rasinski and Czopp 2010).

Let's suppose, then, that you don't care about whether others continue to like you or respect you as much as they did before; your goal is to salvage your own self-respect and to moderate prejudiced attitudes and behavior in your community. Another factor that might be restricting your ability to confront racist or sexist speech is lack of practice. I can't say I am enthusiastic about training sessions that include role-playing—quite the reverse—but I should change my attitude, since some studies suggest that role-playing improves one's ability to intervene (Lawson, McDonough, and Bodle 2010).

All right, so you will practice—but what should you say? You should appeal to the perpetrator's image of themselves as someone who cares about fairness and equality; but you should not begin by assuring the person that they are not racist or sexist. Work by the social psychologists Stefanie Simon and Laurie O'Brien (2015) suggests that if the perpetrator is given to believe that they are not sexist, they respond less well to confrontation—perhaps because they think they have no work to do to improve. So, you should not say: "I know you aren't racist, but that joke is unfair to Black people." Perhaps instead you might say: "I think of you as someone who tries to be fair. But that joke is unfair to Black people." Or: "I'm surprised to hear you say that because I know you try to be fair. That joke is unfair to Black people."

It's good to provide motivation for change to the perpetrator. This can be internal motivation, appealing to the perpetrator's own desire to be a person who stands up for social justice, or external, appealing to the societal consequences for the perpetrator in a culture that values social justice. External motivation, however, is more likely to be perceived as hostile, so it's not the best choice if remaining well-liked is important to you (Monteith, Burns, and Hildebrand 2019, 236). In an unsurprising finding, Burns and Monteith (2019) showed that appealing to ideals of egalitarianism and fairness is more effective if the perpetrator actually cares about egalitarianism and fairness; if they don't care, appealing to societal consequences for the perpetrator is more effective. So, know thine enemy. If Uncle Racist has tendencies toward White supremacy, you cannot effectively challenge his racist speech by pointing out his commitment to egalitarianism. But you might get him to express his ideas less openly by reinforcing societal norms that condemn racism.

It is also helpful to allow the perpetrator an opportunity for self-affirmation before taking them to task about their offensive utterance (Stone et al. 2011). At Thanksgiving dinner, you could try asking Uncle Racist about ways in which he is creative before circling back to and challenging the offensive remark. Even if it seems you have had no effect on Uncle Racist, you might prefer trying this rather than seething inwardly over your pumpkin pie and outwardly to your spouse in the car on the way home.

Calling people on racist speech often is effective (Czopp 2019; Czopp and Monteith 2003; Czopp, Monteith, and Mark 2006). Those who care about equality have feelings of self-recrimination and cognitive dissonance, and seek to change. Those who don't care about equality often do care about how others perceive them, and may moderate their behavior in the future. Furthermore, even if you do not affect the attitudes and behaviors of a joker, you may have effects on the people who witness your behavior (Rasinski and Czopp 2010).

When people confront sexist speech, they are less likely to get a positive response than when they confront racist speech (Czopp and Monteith 2003; Gulker, Mark, and Monteith 2013). However, you can increase the effectiveness of confronting sexist speech by giving believable evidence of sexism to the confronted person (Parker et al. 2018). For example, if someone relied on a sexist stereotype, such as 'nurses are women,' pointing that out seems to increase the efficacy of an intervention (Monteith, Burns, and Hildebrand 2019).

It's crucial to note that confrontations are most effective when they come from people who are not members of the targeted group; targeted group members are more likely to be seen as whiny and over-sensitive (Gulker, Mark, and Monteith 2013). So, privileged people of the world have a reason to speak up when they hear belittling speech, rather than looking to a targeted person for a reaction or leaving them to fend for themselves.

Notes

Chapter 1

1. I will use the term 'idea' in a non-technical sense, to mean a claim or proposition.
2. The term was coined by Moya Bailey (2010), writing as moyazb, to "describe the particular brand of hatred directed at black women in American visual & popular culture." The concept was further developed by Bailey and the blogger Trudy (Bailey and Trudy 2018).
3. Imus used words that mean that the women on the team were nappy-headed ho's; in my opinion, he presented it as something he believed and that others should believe too, despite his protestations that it was 'meant to be amusing'. I will argue in Chapter 7 that one can assert something with intent to amuse.
4. Attardo (1993) addresses the question, but not at length. Carroll suggests in passing that racist jokes have racist ideas as conversational implicatures (2020, 545).
5. Noel Carroll's definition of 'joke' is along the same lines. He says: "Jokes are structures of verbal discourse—generally riddles or narratives—ending in punch lines. In contrast to informal verbal humor—such as bantering, riffing, or associative punning—a joke is an integral unit of discourse with a marked beginning and an end. If it is a riddle, it begins with a question and ends with a punch line; if it is a narrative, it has a beginning, which establishes characters and context, and it proceeds to a delimited complication, and then it culminates, again in the form of a punch line" (2001, 323). Carroll's distinction between jokes and informal humor is not the same as my distinction between jokes and jocular remarks. Jocular remarks are a kind of informal humor, but the class of informal humor that Carroll describes includes things that I would not count as jocular remarks. Thanks to Luvell Anderson for pointing out the similarity.
6. There are also jocular questions, imperatives, etc., and these, too, can be derogatory. From a theoretical point of view, these grammatical forms present additional complications, beyond those presented by derogatory jocular remarks. But for reasons of space, I will not talk about these other forms in this book.
7. I'm using the term 'standard meaning' loosely, as an umbrella term to cover the kind of meaning one might find in a descriptive rather than prescriptive dictionary.
8. Of course, there are competing views about whether slurs operate pragmatically or semantically; I intend the term 'standard meaning' to cover both these possibilities. My thinking here is that a specific linguistic item triggers the derogatory content, because of its standard use.
9. For example, Rae Langton has argued that pragmatic models like those of Stalnaker and of David Lewis can be extended "beyond belief"—so that we can think of speech

as resulting not just in shared beliefs but also shared desires and emotions. Hate speech might encourage us to share an attitude of hatred or repulsion toward the targeted group; pornography might encourage us to find something or some scenario sexy (2012). Jason Stanley also holds that emotion has a crucial role in the efficacy of supporting propaganda, which works "indirectly by seeking to overload various affective capacities, such as nostalgia, sentiment, or fear" (2016, 53). As Stanley understands supporting propaganda, it moves us by playing on our emotions rather than by employing rational processes to achieve its ends.

10. The mechanism that I am proposing is not the same as the one Langton proposes for hate speech and pornography or that Stanley proposes for propaganda. Langton suggests that hate speech and pornography invite and create emotions and desires. Stanley suggests that propaganda first affects our emotions, but that those emotional effects may lead to the "discovery of reasons, reasons that in turn will support the political ideal in a characteristically rational way" (2016, 53).

Chapter 2

1. It is based on the Cambridge English Corpus.

2. Kleiman, who died in 2019, was a professor of public policy, but this is a post on a topic outside his academic expertise, on a blog with a broad audience, so I treat it as a popular, rather than a scholarly, source.

3. An anonymous reviewer for Oxford University Press notes that Geoff Nunberg (2018) argues that a main function of slurs is to facilitate group cohesion. Similar claims have been made in social psychology about jokes; e.g., Thomae and Pina (2015) argue that sexist humor facilitates group cohesion for men.

4. Bolinger separates out several different things someone might mean when they say that a slur is offensive. When we say that a use of a slur was offensive, we might mean that offense was morally warranted, even if nobody was offended—perhaps someone used an exceptionally racist slur at a meeting of a White supremacist group. Alternatively, we might mean that someone was offended, even if offense was not morally warranted—e.g., someone misheard a word and thinks a slur was used when it wasn't. Finally, we might mean that it was rational for someone to take offense (Bolinger 2017, 441). What morally warrants offense is, of course, a difficult question; Bolinger argues that speaker intent is one consideration.

5. I found this article through a citation in Davidson (1987).

6. Obviously, more argument would be needed to draw this conclusion with any confidence; even if deprecating others is impolite because it is immoral, we would need to know if the immorality in question involves harm.

7. One source here is Sandy Goldberg.

8. This is not the broad-brush and unappetizing assumption that other-deprecation is *always* harmless. I will argue in Chapter 11 that while other-deprecation is sometimes harmful, it is not always harmful; e.g., jokes that are disparaging but not

demeaning—such as jokes about dictators—may cause no harm, and in fact, do some good.

Chapter 3

1. See also Luvell Anderson's (2023) helpful discussion of the importance of thinking of jokes in an "utterance-specific way" (371).
2. There are some fascinating studies about the relationship between the possession of virtues and benign and corrective humor, such as mocking pomposity (e.g., Ruch and Heintz 2016). The methodology could be—but as far as I know, hasn't been—applied to derogatory humor.
3. The same was true of people who scored high on the Modern Racism Scale; the idea of the Modern Racism Scale is that few people continue to espouse the kind of racism that classifies Black people as inferior, and that racism has morphed into the belief that there is no longer discrimination against Black people in the United States, and consequently that Black people are too demanding in their push for equal rights, and that Black people get undeserved special treatment from media and from government (Hodson, Rush, and MacInnis 2010).
4. There's also some evidence—although in my opinion, it is not compelling—that telling derogatory jokes about an out-group increases group cohesion for the in-group. See Abrams, Bippus, and McGaughey (2015) and Thomae and Pina (2015).
5. Thomas and Esses (2004) evaluated men only; Greenwood and Isbell (2002) evaluate both men and women. A complicating factor in the Greenwood and Isbell study is that although those who were high in hostile sexism found the jokes more amusing than those who were low in hostile sexism, men who were high in benevolent sexism found the jokes more amusing than both women who were high in benevolent sexism, and nonsexist men. So the relationship between kind of sexism and degree of amusement is not entirely straightforward.
6. Thomas E. Ford, personal communication. Ford suggests that it is the adoption of the non-critical mindset, rather than perceptions of funniness themselves, that does the causal work.

Chapter 4

1. See, e.g., Schmidt (2014).
2. I will not develop a view about non-assertoric forms, like jocular questions, and jocular orders.
3. I'm using the term 'standard meaning' loosely, to encompass both semantic and pragmatic meaning that is regularly associated with a particular linguistic token; so, the standard meaning of a slur can include pragmatic aspects.

4. I first found this joke on Facebook, but the post has subsequently been deleted.

5. See, e.g., Frye (1983), Young (1990), Haslanger (2004), and Cudd (2006). Haslanger argues that a prohibition on same-sex marriage, in the absence of any other oppressive social structures, may be oppressive to gay people (2004, 106).

6. It is less clear why one would hesitate to say that short people are oppressed. One might say they are not a group in the correct sense—e.g., short people do not have a shared culture, history, or identity; or one might say that the disadvantage is not embedded in social structures, but rather stems from implicit bias and perhaps aspects of the built environment, which is engineered to the needs of taller people. However, if you think short people are oppressed, please substitute an example of a social group that you think is unjustly disadvantaged but not oppressed. My thanks to Louise Antony for discussion on this point.

Chapter 5

1. The derogatory ideas conveyed by derogatory jokes are also nondetachable, as they should be if they are generalized conversational implicatures—we don't have to repeat the joke word-for-word to get across the same derogatory idea.

2. Attardo (1993) takes a similar route, arguing that usually jokes do not have implicatures, but that derogatory jokes can have derogatory claims as particularized implicatures when the audience takes them seriously.

3. Grice's necessary and sufficient conditions for a conversational implicature make room for an account of this kind, since all three make reference to the speaker in some way—the Cooperative condition concerns whether or not the speaker is to be presumed to be cooperative, the Requirement condition concerns what the speaker must be assumed to think or to be aware of, and the Mutual Knowledge condition concerns the speaker's expectations of the audience. Jennifer Saul argues that in addition to conversational implicatures, there are utterer-implicatures and audience-implicatures, and her framework would allow for an explanation of Wrong Joker (2002).

4. Alternatively, one might argue that there are derogatory implicatures in both cases, but not the same ones, and other factors explain why the popular wisdom gets the facts wrong about which is worse. Again, since the Cooperative, Requirement, and Mutual Knowledge conditions all refer to the speaker, there is room for this kind of explanation.

5. In short, I take an abductive approach to implicature. Audiences begin with what it is probable the speaker thinks and add in information about what he says. Calculating implicatures is an abductive process (often, but not always, subconscious), leading us to what we think is the best explanation of why the speaker said what they did and accordingly to the attribution of implicatures. When a speaker cancels an implicature, and does not give a satisfactory alternative explanation for saying what they did, they have not provided a better explanation of why they said what they did than the explanation we have already. So, they give us insufficient reason to suppose that we were wrong about the initial attribution of implicatures. Rather, we assume the cancelation

is disingenuous. Stalnaker makes a similar distinction between a successful or credible cancelation, and an unsuccessful cancelation (2014, 101n29).

6. This example is not reprinted in *Studies in the Way of Words*; Grice says that the section of the paper "is omitted, since the material which it presents is substantially the same as that discussed in Essay 2, under the title 'Logic and Conversation'" (1989, 229).

7. You may be concerned about another potential objection to my view, namely that the standard examples of generalized implicatures are of single words or phrases. There are no standard examples involving extended pieces of speech, like jokes. So, my account extends the concept of a generalized implicature to a new category.

As Grice defines a generalized implicature, it is an implicature or type of implicature that is normally carried by a form of words. On the contrary, a particularized implicature "is carried by saying that p on a particular occasion in virtue of special features of the context, cases in which there is no room for the idea that an implicature of this sort is normally carried by saying that p" (1989, 37). I was initially drawn to the idea that derogatory jokes have derogatory ideas as particularized implicatures. But Jonathan Cohen pointed out to me that we need no conversational context to identify the implicature that is typically carried by a derogatory joke—so if it is an implicature at all, it is not a particularized implicature. If we think of the difference between generalized and particularized implicatures to be that generalized implicatures are very commonly present when you say that p, but particularized implicatures are not present when you say that p except in special circumstances, then of the two, saying that derogatory jokes generally implicate derogatory ideas is the better explanation.

My explanation expands the typical set of generalized conversational implicatures to include implicatures that are not triggered by word choice, Horn scales, and the like. But that is not a fatal objection. It is conventional implicatures that are supposed to be triggered by word choice.

However, there is another approach I could take, which is to say that derogatory jokes implicate derogatory ideas only against a cultural background. The cultural background is always there in our culture, and so always part of the special features of the conversational context in our culture. So, I could say that these really are particularized implicatures, but that the contextual features needed are generally present in a specific cultural context rather than absent, which is why they might look (to us) like generalized implicatures.

Wayne Davis cites a real-life example that he takes to illustrate an entirely different point. A boy says, "Bosy's mother is a little sick" (1998, 8). In our culture, we would take that to implicate that the mother who is sick is not the speaker's mother. But in this culture, saying 'my mother' would draw inappropriate attention to the speaker: It is the speaker's mother who is sick, and in this culture, what he says does not implicate that the person who is sick is someone else's mother. With this case, we could think of 'Bosy's mother' generally implicating that it is not the speaker's mother in our culture, but not in his culture. Alternatively, we could think of the implicature that 'Bosy's mother' as an implicature that is particularized to our culture.

Derogatory jokes are culturally specific, so it would be reasonable to say that they are particularized implicatures, but that the features of the context that matter are typically present in our culture. On a view like this, the categories of generalized and particularized implicatures are not clearly distinct; the difference between a generalized and a particularized implicature would be a matter of degree. See also Blome-Tillmann, who argues that there is "no deep metaphysical distinction" between generalized and particularized implicatures; the difference "concerns the relative frequency with which a conversational implicature occurs in everyday contexts" (2013, 178).

Chapter 6

1. I should note that the dual-process model is not universally accepted; see, e.g., Melnikoff and Bargh (2018).

Chapter 7

1. The *Collins COBUILD Advanced English Dictionary* distinguishes two senses of 'to joke' as an intransitive verb—to "tell funny stories or say amusing things" or "tell someone something that is not true in order to amuse yourself" ("Joke" n.d.-b). The entry in the *Cambridge English Dictionary* for the verb 'to joke' also distinguishes two senses in which it is used. One is "to say funny things." The second tells us, "If you think that someone is joking, you think that they do not really mean what they say" ("Joke" n.d.-a). Some dictionaries do not distinguish these senses. The *Oxford English Dictionary Online* notes that the entry for 'to joke' has not been updated for the third edition, and the main sense given for 'to joke' is "to make jokes, to jest" with no qualifications about the truth or falsity of what is said. The second sense defines 'you are (*or* have got to be) joking, etc.', which are "phrases indicative of incredulity" ("Joke, v." 2022). There is also a draft addition proposed in 1997, "to utter as a joke, or in a joking manner. Frequently with direct speech or clause as object." Of course, there is a philosophical issue lurking here about the potential mismatch between what you believe to be true (or false) and what is true (or false). The crucial thing, it seems to me, is what the speaker believes to be true or false—so the second sense in the *Collins COBUILD Dictionary* might be amended to "to tell someone something that you believe to be not true in order to amuse." However, for present purposes, I am going to gloss over the issue.

2. See again the *Oxford English Dictionary*'s comments about incredulity, in note 1.

3. For simplicity here, I am writing in terms of a warranty of truth. But the idea that there is a warranty of truth is not essential to my view. An invitation to trust, for example, would work too.

4. Elisabeth Camp (2018) argues that insinuation also has the property of plausible deniability. See "Using implicatures to mislead and insinuate" in Chapter 5.

Chapter 8

1. Suppose Sally says, "The cat peed on the rug." Then we might say that Harriet understands Sally if and only if Sally meant that the cat peed on the rug and Harriet believes that Sally meant that the cat peed on the rug. This definition, while it may be on the right track, is hard to cash out. Let's take Grice's necessary and sufficient conditions for meaning something to be broadly correct, overlooking the familiar objections and refinements from people like Avramides (1989), Searle (1965), and Ziff (1967). By uttering x, a speaker S meant that p if and only if:

   (1) S uttered x intending that their audience A form the belief that p and
   (2) S further intended that A recognize S's intention that A form the belief that p and
   (3) S still further intended that A form the belief that p at least partly on the basis of recognizing S's intention that A form the belief that p.

   Note that one can understand someone without being the intended audience. A first pass might define understanding like this:

   A hearer H understands S if and only if S means that p by x and H believes that S means that p by x.

   But if believing that S means that p by x involves believing conditions (1) through (3), the first pass cannot be correct. Let's suppose that Alex is Sally's intended audience. Sally's meaning that the cat peed on the rug requires that Sally intends that *Alex* form the belief that the cat peed on the rug. But Harriet could understand Sally without knowing that Alex is the intended audience. So Harriet can understand Sally without believing that Sally had the intention that Alex form the belief that the cat peed on the rug, i.e., without believing condition (1). Similar considerations apply with regard to conditions (2) and (3). So it would be preferable to define understanding like this:

   H understands S if and only if (S means p by x to A, and H believes that there is a y such that S means p by x to y).

   On such an account, H could understand S without knowing the referent of all S's indexicals and without grasping all of S's conversational implicatures. But many more details would need to be worked out.

2. One might worry that if eligibility to take a turn is granted by other people in the conversation, I am on the verge of circularity—who granted eligibility to those other people in the conversation? But let's not worry too much. Conversations are begun when someone ventures to address someone else or a group of others (Goldberg 2020; Kukla and Lance 2009). The venturer thus invites the addressees to take a turn, making them eligible; and one of the addressees may respond, either making the venturer eligible to take another turn, or cutting them off to end the nascent conversation.

3. On the other hand, it is possible for someone to wrongly believe that something is common ground when it is not.

4. What if there is someone in the conversation who does not understand the joke? In that case, the implicature doesn't actually become common ground. If it's not obvious to others that the person does not understand, though, others may think it is common ground—and thus should act as if it is. If it is obvious to others that the person does not understand, may others shrug it off? After all, it's not common ground. The answer here is no. Although Stalnaker does not, as far as I know, address this issue, there are plenty of situations where there are subgroups in a conversation for whom something is common ground even if it is not common ground for the entire group. For example, parents often arrange for something to be common ground for the grownups but not for the kids—e.g., by spelling out I-C-E C-R-E-A-M rather than saying it. Grice says that in examples like this, a parent may implicate that the information should not be communicated to the child (1989, 36). In such a case, the members of the subgroup still have responsibility for what is common ground between them, even if it isn't common ground for the entire group (see "When you are the target of belittling speech" in Chapter 11 for more discussion).

Chapter 9

1. It's worth noting that the empirical work settles a dispute in the philosophy of humor. On the one hand, it shows that LaFollette and Shanks are mistaken in thinking that it is necessary to have disparaging beliefs to enjoy disparaging jokes. They have argued that what one finds humorous depends on one's beliefs, and that it is the beliefs and attitudes underlying belittling jokes that make them morally offensive (1993, 337).On the other hand, empirical work also makes it clear that Ted Cohen goes too far in the other direction when he conjectures that there is no connection between belittling jokes and negative beliefs: "Do those who respond to these jokes either believe in advance or come to believe nonsense about Mexican maids, Polish scientists, and black men? I doubt this. And I doubt that one could show any connection between traffic in such jokes and negative beliefs about these groups of people. Even if there is such a connection, I have myself been amused by all three jokes, and I do not myself believe any of those generalizations about the relevant characters, and yet these jokes disturb me" (2001, 78). Cohen is correct, however, that one can find a sexist joke funny without believing the sexist stereotypes on which the joke relies; one can find a joke humorous and believe your amusement to be inappropriate, which is one of the things that can make a belittling joke disquieting.

2. Jeanette Bicknell also argues that "being aware of offensive beliefs or stereotypes is not the same as holding them. It seems possible to laugh at Polish jokes, blonde jokes, or Newfie jokes without harboring any negative beliefs about Poles, blondes, or Newfies" (2007).

3. The presumptions and commonplaces are very often false, and thus cannot be known by the audience; Cohen means the audience must know that the presumptions and commonplaces exist.

4. For ease of presentation, I am oversimplifying here, by leaving out the beliefs that everyone believes that everyone accepts, etc.

5. More precisely, acceptance is an attitude toward a proposition rather than an attitude toward an idea; as always in this book, I am using the term 'idea' here in a loose, non-technical sense.

6. As before (see note 4), I am oversimplifying here.

7. This follows from the definition of acceptance along with Stalnaker's account of presupposition. Presupposing that φ is taking it for granted, or acting as if one takes it for granted, as common ground. Furthermore, it is common ground that φ in a group if all members *accept* (for the purpose of the conversation) that φ, and all *believe* that all accept that φ, and all *believe* that all *believe* that all accept that φ, etc. (2002, 716). First, substitute the definition of common ground in the definition of presupposing that φ: Presupposing that φ is taking it for granted, or acting as if one takes it for granted, that all members accept (for the purposes of the conversation) that φ, that all believe that all accept that φ, and all believe that all believe that all accept that φ, etc. Then, substitute for acceptance: Presupposing that φ is taking it for granted, or acting as if one takes it for granted, that all members treat as true (for the purposes of the conversation) that φ, that all believe that all treat as true that φ, and all believe that all believe that all treat as true that φ, etc.

8. Kai von Fintel comments on two factors that may affect one's willingness to presuppose something. He focuses here on informative presupposition, but the point applies to non-informative presupposition too: "Informative use of presupposition may be successful in two particular kinds of circumstances: (i) the listeners may be genuinely agnostic as to the truth of the relevant proposition, assume that the speaker knows about its truth and trust the speaker not to speak inappropriately or falsely; (ii) the listeners may not want to challenge the speaker about the presupposed proposition, because it is irrelevant to their concerns and because the smoothness of the conversation is important enough to them to warrant a little leeway" (2008, 145).

9. For example, if a colleague at a meeting wants to consider a counterfactual situation that I find far-fetched, I may be unwilling to go along with his presuppositions not because of how I feel about treating them as true, or because of how I feel about him treating them as true, but because I want the meeting to draw to a close.

10. Mary Kate McGowan suggested to me that my willingness to treat something as true may sometimes depend on the stakes of its being true.

11. This example focuses on something negative that the teenager does not wish others to treat as true. But there are cases where we do not want others to treat as true something that is positive—perhaps the teenager won a prize at school, but wishes his family would pretend he had not in this conversation, because he does not want to be the center of attention, or because his parents dwelling on his academic success will undermine his reputation as a cool kid with his friend group.

12. See note 1.

13. It's worth noting that although neither Bergmann nor Cohen uses the term 'presupposition' in Stalnaker's technical sense, they both endorse a view on which derogatory jokers presuppose derogatory ideas. Neither takes a position on whether derogatory

jokers convey derogatory ideas via presupposition. See Bergmann (1986), particularly page 74, and Cohen (2001), particularly pages 28, 32, and 72. See also Noel Carroll's (2000) characterization of Cohen's position.

14. Note that Stalnaker says, "What is most distinctive about this propositional attitude [presupposition] is that it is a social or public attitude: one presupposes that φ only if one presupposes that others presuppose it as well" (2002, 701).

15. Relatedly, Stalnaker discusses a case from Kripke (2009, 369n3): "[A] French monarchist might belligerently say to a republican, 'No matter what you republicans say, I met the king of France last week.'" Obviously the monarchist knows that his conversational partners won't accept that there is a king of France. Stalnaker's discussion of the example is not definitive, but he asks, "Why should one think that presupposition, in any sense, is involved in this case?" (2014, 66).

16. This is a much abbreviated version of a more detailed argument that is of little interest outside academic philosophy, and thus will be published elsewhere.

Chapter 10

1. My thanks to Andrew Mills for suggesting rock and roll as an example.
2. It's also worth taking a look at Otten et al. (2017), who accompanied written insults with a picture of a crowd and a sound clip of multiple people laughing as the stimulus, and measured neural processing with electrodes attached to the skulls of participants as the response. They compared responses to the insult accompanied with the picture and immediately followed by the sound clip versus an insult alone, and found physiological differences. However, the study does not compare responses to the insult with the picture of the crowd and the sound clip of laughing versus the insult with the picture of the crowd but no auditory laughter. So, it does not directly confirm the hypothesis that a laughing crowd evokes different neural processing than a crowd that does not laugh.

Chapter 11

1. See, e.g., Beebee (2004) and McGrath (2005).
2. You might think that Harry's error is in enjoying the jokes; but as I argued, he has little voluntary control over his amusement (see "Am I morally responsible for being amused?" in Chapter 9).
3. See Willsey (2021).
4. Discussions of dogwhistles are a notable exception—since a dogwhistle is meant to communicate with some members of the conversation and not with others. See Saul (2018) and Camp (2018).

5. For more about social structures in school settings, see Wiseman (2016).

6. The common ground that does not include Swinton is a subset of the common ground that includes him. In other instances, the common grounds may overlap with each other.

7. Note also that in his discussion of accommodation, Lewis discusses a case where the master, but not the slave, has the ability to shift the boundaries of what is permissible by declaring it permissible (1979). To keep things less complicated in the main text, I am focusing on the speaker's ability to affect the common ground, but similar issues arise with a speaker's ability to affect the conversational scoreboard.

8. Mary Kate McGowan argues that there are conversational exercitives—speech acts that change the bounds of what is permissible in a conversation. Thinking of one's ability to perform a conversational exercitive might provide a useful way to think about how differences in social power might affect one's ability to adjust a conversational scoreboard (2019).

9. See also entries posted on July 27, 2011; June 9, 2011; April 22, 2011; and others (*What Is It Like to Be a Woman in Philosophy?*).

10. For further discussion, see Horisk (2021). Social power also affects one's ability to make informative presuppositions, but the argument for that thesis will have to wait for another occasion.

11. I do not mean to suggest that these are the only kinds of extenuating circumstance when it comes to listener culpability. There may also be competing moral demands to take into consideration; one example that has come up repeatedly in conversation is the case where the joke teller is a very elderly relative, where there are requirements of respect for the relative.

12. On views like Stalnaker's (2002) and Goldberg's (2020), silence indicates acceptance of something into the common ground. But in this case, the "appalled" silence does not indicate acceptance.

13. To be clear, depending on the circumstances, Bernadette's topic change could count as non-acceptance of the claim that Mrs. Xavier is an old bag, and thus be sufficient for excluding the claim that Mrs. Xavier is an old bag from the common ground.

14. Alternatively, one might argue that Bernadette's topic change is a way of not treating Anna's assertion as true. I'm sympathetic to this claim, but it strays further from existing accounts of the common ground than the position I describe in the main text.

Chapter 12

1. Obviously, Langton is not using 'belittle' in the technical sense that I have given it.

2. Langton here follows MacKinnon (1988, 176); MacKinnon cites Andrea Dworkin (1985), although MacKinnon's definition of subordination differs from Dworkin's account.

3. A full answer to this question would involve much more argumentative complexity and technical language than is appropriate for this book; the answer I give here is, of necessity, sketchy. For example, we should consider whether the example of belittling jokes raises special concerns about the authority problem (Maitra 2012).

4. Recent work in philosophy by Elisabeth Camp (2018) suggests that insinuation may be more theoretically tractable than Austin thought.

5. Austin also points to practical, rather than principled, concerns: "As utterances our performatives are also heir to certain other kinds of ill which infect all utterances. And these likewise, *though again they might be brought into a more general account*, we are deliberately at present excluding. I mean, for example, the following: a performative utterance will, for example, be in a peculiar way hollow or void if said by an actor on the stage, or if introduced in a poem, or spoken in soliloquy. This applies in a similar manner to any and every utterance—a sea-change in special circumstances. Language in such circumstances is in special ways—intelligibly—used not seriously, but in ways parasitic upon its normal use—ways which fall under the doctrine of the etiolations of language. All this we are excluding from consideration" (1975, 21–22, italics mine).

6. I refer the interested reader to the discussion in Austin (1975, 103–5). Austin's main concerns about insinuation and swearing seem to be that they do not involve conventions in the same way as illocutionary acts, and that there is no role for a performative formula like 'I insinuate that'.

7. My discussion here is indebted to Maximillian de Gaynesford (2009, 2011).

8. Relatedly, Camp argues that insinuation is valuable when the content to be communicated is risky in some way for the speaker. For example, a driver stopped for speeding might say, "I'm in a bit of a hurry. Is there any way we can settle this right now?" to propose a bribe without saying so outright (Camp 2018, 43).

9. I recognize that some views rule out the possibility of unintentional illocutionary acts; and also that on some views, insulting is not an illocutionary act (Harris, Fogal, and Moss 2018; Green 2021). If insulting is not an illocutionary act, the existence of unintentional insults does not support my claim that there are unintentional illocutionary acts. But betting is a core example of an illocutionary act, and it is undeniable that there are unintentional bets. So, like Langton (2018) and Kukla (2014), I think there are unintentional illocutionary acts. Thanks to an anonymous reviewer for flagging this issue.

10. Of course, Searle's analysis of 'Can you pass the salt' in particular, and of indirect speech acts in general, has been challenged. However, the controversy does not challenge the claim that, in principle, an illocutionary act can be an implicature.

11. A reviewer for Oxford University Press argues that there are no unintentional implicatures, since they are part of speaker meaning, and speaker meaning must be intentional. This position is open to debate, even for particularized implicatures; for discussion, see Saul (2002), especially section 3. With regard to generalized implicatures, it's highly plausible that there are generalized implicatures that are not meant by the speaker; see Davis's description of sentence implicature (1998, 2019).

Note that Grice himself says, "Since, to assume the presence of a conversational im-plicature, we have to assume that at least the Cooperative Principle is being observed, and since it is possible to opt out of the observation of this principle, it follows *that a generalized conversational implicature can be canceled in a particular case. It may be explicitly canceled, by the addition of a clause that states or implies that the speaker has opted out, or it may be contextually canceled, if the form of utterance that usually carries it is used in a context that makes it clear that the speaker is opting out*" (1989, 39, emphasis mine). Grice's comment here is not conclusive, but on one interpretation, generalized implicatures are present unless canceled, either explicitly or by context.

References

Abrams, Jessica R., Amy M. Bippus, and Karen J. McGaughey. 2015. "Gender Disparaging Jokes: An Investigation of Sexist-Nonstereotypical Jokes on Funniness, Typicality, and the Moderating Role of Ingroup Identification." *Humor* 28 (2): 311–26. http://dx.doi.org/10.1515/humor-2015-0019.

Anderson, Luvell. 2023. "Why So Serious? An Inquiry on Racist Jokes." *Journal of Social Philosophy* 54 (3): 370–84. https://doi.org/10.1111/josp.12384.

Anderson, Luvell, and Ernie Lepore. 2013. "Slurring Words." *Noûs* 47 (1): 25–48. https://doi.org/10.1111/j.1468-0068.2010.00820.x.

"Ann Coulter Criticizes Brian Williams, MSNBC Hosts: 'Knock It Off With The I'm Offended Routine . . . You're Horrible People, Liberals,'" *Huffington Post* March 22, 2012. http://www.huffingtonpost.com/2012/03/22/ann-coulter-brian-williams-msnbc-liberals_n_1372144.html. Accessed October 3, 2020.

Appiah, Kwame Anthony. 2022a. "A Co-Worker Told a Sexist Joke. Should You Be Disciplined for Laughing?" *New York Times Magazine*, January 9. https://www.nytimes.com/2022/01/04/magazine/workplace-sexist-joke-ethics.html.

Appiah, Kwame Anthony. 2022b. "What Should I Do about a Friend's Racist Figurines?" *New York Times Sunday Magazine*, May 22. https://www.nytimes.com/2022/05/20/magazine/ethics-racist-figurines.html.

Asch, Solomon E. 1956. "Studies of Independence and Conformity: I. A Minority of One against a Unanimous Majority." *Psychological Monographs: General and Applied* 70 (9): 1–70. https://doi.org/10.1037/h0093718.

Ashe, Stephen D., Magda Borkowska, and James Nazroo. 2019. "Racism Ruins Lives: An Analysis of the 2016–2017 Trade Union Congress Racism at Work Survey." Centre on Dynamics of Ethnicity, University of Manchester. http://hummedia.manchester.ac.uk/institutes/code/research/projects/racism-at-work/tuc-full-report.pdf.

Atkinson, Rowan. 2018. "Letter to the Editor." *The Times*, August 10.

Attardo, Salvatore. 1993. "Violation of Conversational Maxims and Cooperation: The Case of Jokes." *Journal of Pragmatics* 19 (6): 537–58. https://doi.org/10.1016/0378-2166(93)90111-2.

Attardo, Salvatore. 1994. *Linguistic Theories of Humor*. Berlin: Walter de Gruyter.

Austen, Jane. 2005. *Emma*. Edited by Richard Cronin and Dorothy McMillan. Cambridge Edition of the Works of Jane Austen. Cambridge: Cambridge University Press. https://doi.org/10.1017/9781316676851.

Austen, Jane. 2006a. *Pride and Prejudice*. Edited by Pat Rogers. Cambridge Edition of the Works of Jane Austen. Cambridge: Cambridge University Press.

Austen, Jane. 2006b. *Sense and Sensibility*. Edited by Edward Copeland. Cambridge Edition of the Works of Jane Austen. Cambridge: Cambridge University Press.

Austin, J. L. 1975. *How to Do Things with Words*. 2nd edition. Cambridge, MA: Harvard University Press.

Austin, J. L. 1979. *Philosophical Papers*. Edited by J. O. Urmson and G. J. Warnock. 3rd edition. Oxford: Oxford University Press. https://doi.org/10.1093/0192830 21X.001.0001.

Avramides, Anita. 1989. *Meaning and Mind: An Examination of a Gricean Account of Language*. Cambridge, MA: MIT Press.

Bailey, Moya. 2010. "They Aren't Talking about Me . . . ." *Crunk Feminist Collective* (blog), March 15. http://www.crunkfeministcollective.com/2010/03/14/they-arent-talking-about-me/.

Bailey, Moya, and Trudy. 2018. "On Misogynoir: Citation, Erasure, and Plagiarism." *Feminist Media Studies* 18 (4): 762–68. https://doi.org/10.1080/14680 777.2018.1447395.

Banks, Ingrid. 2000. *Hair Matters: Beauty, Power, and Black Women's Consciousness*. New York: NYU Press.

Baron, Dennis. 2018. "A Brief History of Singular 'They.'" *Oxford English Dictionary*. Accessed September 4, 2018. https://public.oed.com/blog/a-brief-history-of-singular-they/.

Bartolo, Angela, Daniela Ballotta, Luca Nocetti, Patrizia Baraldi, Paolo Frigio Nichelli, and Francesca Benuzzi. 2021. "Uncover the Offensive Side of Disparagement Humor: An FMRI Study." *Frontiers in Psychology* 12: 5268. https://doi.org/10.3389/fpsyg.2021.750597.

Baskerville v. Culligan International Company. 1995, 50 F.3d 428. 7th Cir.

BBC News. 2002. "Why Do People Find Racist Jokes Funny?" May 7. http://news.bbc.co.uk/2/hi/uk_news/1972565.stm.

Beebee, Helen. 2004. "Causing and Nothingness." In *Causation and Counterfactuals*, edited by L. A. Paul, E. J. Hall, and J. Collins, 291–308. Cambridge, MA: MIT Press.

"Belittle, v." n.d. OED Online. Accessed October 19, 2022. https://www.oed.com/view/Entry/17394.

Bella, Timothy. 2021. "Michael Che Shared Cruel Jokes about Simone Biles. He Claims He Was Hacked." *Washington Post*, July 30. https://www.washingtonpost.com/arts-entertainment/2021/07/30/simone-biles-michael-che-jokes/.

Bergmann, M. 1986. "How Many Feminists Does It Take to Make a Joke? Sexist Humor and What's Wrong with It." *Hypatia* 1 (1): 63–82.

Bicknell, J. 2007. "What Is Offensive about Offensive Jokes?" *Philosophy Today* 51 (4): 458–65.

Bigelow, John. n.d. "Comic Relief for the Pathologically Philosophical." Accessed December 28, 2021. http://consc.net/misc/lightbulb.html.

Bless, Herbert, Gerald L. Clore, Norbert Schwarz, Verena Golisano, Christina Rabe, and Marcus Wölk. 1996. "Mood and the Use of Scripts: Does a Happy Mood Really Lead to Mindlessness?" *Journal of Personality and Social Psychology* 71 (4): 665–79. https://doi.org/10.1037/0022-3514.71.4.665.

Blome-Tillmann, Michael. 2013. "Conversational Implicatures (and How to Spot Them)." *Philosophy Compass* 8 (2): 170–85. https://doi.org/10.1111/phc3.12003.

Bolinger, Renée Jorgensen. 2017. "The Pragmatics of Slurs." *Noûs* 51 (3): 439–62. https://doi.org/10.1111/nous.12090.

Bond, Michael. 1961. "Paddington Makes a Bid." *In Paddington Helps Out*, 20–35. Boston: Houghton Mifflin.

Booth, Robert. 2019. "Racism Rising Since Brexit Vote, Nationwide Study Reveals." *The Guardian*, May 20. https://www.theguardian.com/world/2019/may/20/racism-on-the-rise-since-brexit-vote-nationwide-study-reveals.

Boxer, Christie Fitzgerald, and Thomas E. Ford. 2011. "Sexist Humor in the Workplace: A Case of Subtle Harassment." In *Insidious Workplace Behavior*, edited by Jerald Greenberg, 175–205. New York: Routledge. https://doi.org/10.4324/9780203849 439-15.

Brown, Theresa. 2011. "Physician, Heel Thyself." *New York Times*, May 8. https://www.nyti mes.com/2011/05/08/opinion/08Brown.html.

Burns, Mason D., and Margo J. Monteith. 2019. "Confronting Stereotypic Biases: Does Internal versus External Motivational Framing Matter?" *Group Processes & Intergroup Relations* 22 (7): 930–46. https://doi.org/10.1177/1368430218798041.

Calabresi, Massimo. 2010. "Jones' Jewish Joke: No Laughing Matter." *Time*, April 27.

Camp, Elisabeth. 2013. "Slurring Perspectives." *Analytic Philosophy* 54 (3): 330–49. https://doi.org/10.1111/phib.12022.

Camp, Elisabeth. 2018. "Insinuation, Common Ground, and the Conversational Record." In *New Work on Speech Acts*, edited by Daniel Fogal, Daniel W. Harris, and Matt Moss, 40–66. Oxford: Oxford University Press. https://doi.org/10.1093/oso/9780198738 831.003.0002.

Carr, David. 2007a. "Networks Condemn Remarks by Imus." *New York Times*, April 7. https://www.nytimes.com/2007/04/07/arts/television/07imus.html.

Carr, David. 2007b. "With Imus, They Keep Coming Back." *New York Times*, April 9. http://www.nytimes.com/2007/04/09/business/media/09carr.html.

Carroll, N. 2000. "On Ted Cohen: Intimate Laughter." *Philosophy and Literature* 24 (2): 435–50.

Carroll, Noël. 2001. *Beyond Aesthetics: Philosophical Essays*. Cambridge: Cambridge University Press.

Carroll, Noël. 2020. "I'm Only Kidding: On Racist and Ethnic Jokes." *Southern Journal of Philosophy* 58 (4): 534–46. https://doi.org/10.1111/sjp.12391.

Carson, Thomas L. 2006. "The Definition of Lying." *Noûs* 40 (2): 284–306. https://www.jstor.org/stable/3506133.

CBS News. 2018. "Don Imus: The Sun Sets on His Morning Radio Show." March 25. https://www.cbsnews.com/news/don-imus-the-sun-sets-on-his-morning-radio-show/.

Chan, Yu-Chen, Yi-Jun Liao, Cheng-Hao Tu, and Hsueh-Chih Chen. 2016. "Neural Correlates of Hostile Jokes: Cognitive and Motivational Processes in Humor Appreciation." *Frontiers in Human Neuroscience* 10. https://www.frontiersin.org/arti cle/10.3389/fnhum.2016.00527.

Chaney, Kimberly E., Danielle M. Young, and Diana T. Sanchez. 2015. "Confrontation's Health Outcomes and Promotion of Egalitarianism (C-HOPE) Framework." *Translational Issues in Psychological Science* 1 (4): 363–71. https://doi.org/10.1037/tps 0000042.

Cohen, Ted. 2001. *Jokes: Philosophical Thoughts on Joking Matters*. Chicago: University of Chicago Press.

Congress.gov. 2022. "H.R.2116—117th Congress (2021–2022): Creating a Respectful and Open World for Natural Hair Act of 2022." Legislation, March 21. https://www.congr ess.gov/bill/117th-congress/house-bill/2116.

Corradi Fiumara, Gemma. 1990. *The Other Side of Language: A Philosophy of Listening*. Translated by Charles Lambert. London: Routledge.

Cudd, Ann. 2006. *Analyzing Oppression*. New York: Oxford University Press.

Cukor, George, dir. 1964. *My Fair Lady*. Warner Bros. https://www.imdb.com/title/tt0058385/.

Czopp, Alexander M. 2019. "The Consequences of Confronting Prejudice." *In Confronting Prejudice and Discrimination*, edited by Robyn K. Mallett and Margo J. Monteith, 201–21. London and San Diego, CA: Academic Press.

Czopp, Alexander M., and Margo J. Monteith. 2003. "Confronting Prejudice (Literally): Reactions to Confrontations of Racial and Gender Bias." *Personality & Social Psychology Bulletin* 29 (4): 532–44. https://doi.org/10.1177/0146167202250923.

Czopp, Alexander M., Margo J. Monteith, and Aimee Y. Mark. 2006. "Standing Up for a Change: Reducing Bias through Interpersonal Confrontation." *Journal of Personality and Social Psychology* 90: 784–803. https://doi.org/10.1037/0022-3514.90.5.784.

Davidson, Chandler. 1987. "Ethnic Jokes: An Introduction to Race and Nationality." *Teaching Sociology* 15 (3): 296–302.

Davidson, Donald. 1963. "Actions, Reasons, and Causes." *Journal of Philosophy* 60 (23): 685–700. https://doi.org/10.2307/2023177.

Davis, Wayne. 1998. *Implicature: Intention, Convention, and Principle in the Failure of Gricean Theory*. Cambridge: Cambridge University Press.

Davis, Wayne. 2019. "Implicature." In *Stanford Encyclopedia of Philosophy*, edited by Edward N. Zalta. Metaphysics Research Lab, Stanford University, Fall. https://plato.stanford.edu/archives/fall2019/entries/implicature/.

"Disparage, v." n.d. OED Online. Accessed October 19, 2022. https://www.oed.com/view/Entry/54905.

Donne, John. (1633) 2009. "Song." In *The Songs and Sonets of John Donne*. 2nd edition, edited by Theodore Redpath, 118. Cambridge, MA: Harvard University Press.

Dotson, Kristie. 2011. "Tracking Epistemic Violence, Tracking Practices of Silencing." *Hypatia* 26 (2): 236–57. https://doi.org/10.1111/j.1527-2001.2011.01177.x.

Douglass, Sara, Sheena Mirpuri, Devin English, and Tiffany Yip. 2016. "'They Were Just Making Jokes': Ethnic/Racial Teasing and Discrimination among Adolescents." *Cultural Diversity & Ethnic Minority Psychology* 22 (1): 69–82. https://doi.org/10.1037/cdp0000041.

Dworkin, Andrea. 1985. "Against the Male Flood: Censorship, Pornography, and Equality." *Harvard Women's Law Journal* 8: 1. https://heinonline.org/HOL/Page?handle=hein.journals/hwlj8&id=9&div=&collection=.

Eberle, Carolyn E., Dale P. Sandler, Kyla W. Taylor, and Alexandra J. White. 2020. "Hair Dye and Chemical Straightener Use and Breast Cancer Risk in a Large US Population of Black and White Women." *International Journal of Cancer* 147 (2): 383–91. https://doi.org/10.1002/ijc.32738.

EEOC v. Catastrophe Management Solutions. 2016, 852 F. 3d 1018. Court of Appeals, 11th Circuit.

Emberson, Lauren L., Gary Lupyan, Michael H. Goldstein, and Michael J. Spivey. 2010. "Overheard Cell-Phone Conversations: When Less Speech Is More Distracting." *Psychological Science* 21 (10): 1383–88. https://doi.org/10.1177/0956797610382126.

Faber, Judy. 2007. "Rutgers Blasts Imus' 'Despicable' Remarks." CBS News, April 10. https://www.cbsnews.com/news/rutgers-blasts-imus-despicable-remarks/.

Federal News Service. 1998a. "Clinton: 'There Is No Improper Relationship.'" *Washington Post Politics Special Report: Clinton Accused*, January 22. https://www.washingtonpost.com/wp-srv/politics/special/clinton/stories/excerpts012298.htm.

Federal News Service. 1998b. "From the Starr Referral: Clinton's Grand Jury Testimony, Part 4." *Washington Post Special Report: Clinton Accused*. https://www.washingtonpost.com/wp-srv/politics/special/clinton/stories/bctest092198_4.htm.

Feinberg, Joel. 1985. *Offense to Others: The Moral Limits of the Criminal Law*. New York: Oxford University Press.

Ferguson, M. A., and T. E. Ford. 2008. "Disparagement Humor: A Theoretical and Empirical Review of Psychoanalytic, Superiority, and Social Identity Theories." *Humor-International Journal of Humor Research* 21 (3): 283–312. http://dx.doi.org/10.1515/HUMOR.2008.014.

Fleming, Charles. 2020. "Learning Racism on the Playground Was Easy—with Jokes." *Los Angeles Times*, October 12. https://www.latimes.com/opinion/story/2020-10-12/eth nic-jokes-racism-kids-punchlines-humor.

Fleming, Victor, dir. 1940. *Gone with the Wind*. https://www.imdb.com/title/tt0031381/.

Ford, T. E. 2000. "Effects of Sexist Humor on Tolerance of Sexist Events." *Personality and Social Psychology Bulletin* 26 (9): 1094–107.

Ford, T. E., F. J. Johnson, J. Blevins, and C. Zepeda. 1999. "Effects of the Gender of the Joke-Teller upon Perceptions of Offensiveness of Sexist Jokes." Paper presented at the Annual Meeting of the American Sociological Association, Chicago, August 1999.

Ford, Thomas E., Christie F. Boxer, Jacob Armstrong, and Jessica R. Edel. 2008. "More Than 'Just a Joke': The Prejudice-Releasing Function of Sexist Humor." *Personality and Social Psychology Bulletin* 34 (2): 159–70. https://doi.org/10.1177/0146167207310022.

Ford, Thomas E., Hannah S. Buie, Stephanie D. Mason, Andrew R. Olah, Christopher J. Breeden, and Mark A. Ferguson. 2020. "Diminished Self-Concept and Social Exclusion: Disparagement Humor from the Target's Perspective." *Self and Identity: The Journal of the International Society for Self and Identity* 19 (6): 1529–8868. https://doi.org/10.1080/15298868.2019.1653960.

Ford, Thomas E., Julie A. Woodzicka, Shane R. Triplett, Annie O. Kochersberger, and Christopher J. Holden. 2014. "Not All Groups Are Equal: Differential Vulnerability of Social Groups to the Prejudice-Releasing Effects of Disparagement Humor." *Group Processes & Intergroup Relations* 17 (2): 178–99. https://doi.org/10.1177/136843021 3502558.

Frank, Michael J. 2002. "The Social Context Variable in Hostile Environment Litigation." *Notre Dame Law Review* 77 (2): 437–532.

Frye, Marilyn. 1983. *The Politics of Reality: Essays in Feminist Theory*. Trumansburg, NY: Crossing Press.

Gasper, Karen, and Lauren Spencer. 2019. "Affective Ingredients: Recipes for Understanding How Affective States Alter Cognitive Outcomes." In *Handbook of Well-Being*, edited by Ed Diener, Shigehiro Oishi, and Louis Tay, 718–38. Salt Lake City, UT: DEF. nobascholar.com/books/1.

Gaynesford, Maximilian de. 2009. "Incense and Insensibility: Austin on the 'Non-Seriousness' of Poetry." *Ratio* 22 (4): 464–85. https://doi.org/10.1111/j.1467-9329.2009.00445.x.

Gaynesford, Maximilian de. 2011. "How Not to Do Things with Words: J. L. Austin on Poetry." *British Journal of Aesthetics* 51 (1): 31–49. https://doi.org/10.1093/aesthj/ayq045.

"George Carlin Interview: On Comedians Who Pick on the Underdogs." n.d. YouTube, accessed November 16, 2021. https://www.youtube.com/watch?v=F8yV8xUorQ8.

"Get a Rise Out Of." n.d. Cambridge English Dictionary. Accessed May 12, 2022. https://dictionary.cambridge.org/us/dictionary/english/get-a-rise-out-of.

Glick, P., and S. T. Fiske. 1996. "The Ambivalent Sexism Inventory: Differentiating Hostile and Benevolent Sexism." *Journal of Personality and Social Psychology* 70 (3): 491. https://psycnet.apa.org/doi/10.1037/0022-3514.70.3.491.

Goldberg, Sanford C. 2020. *Conversational Pressure: Normativity in Speech Exchanges.* Oxford: Oxford University Press.

Green, Mitchell. 2021. "Speech Acts." In *The Stanford Encyclopedia of Philosophy*, edited by Edward N. Zalta. Metaphysics Research Lab, Stanford University, Fall. https://plato.stanford.edu/archives/fall2021/entries/speech-acts/.

Greenwood, D., and L. M. Isbell. 2002. "Ambivalent Sexism and the Dumb Blonde: Men's and Women's Reactions to Sexist Jokes." *Psychology of Women Quarterly* 26 (4): 341.

Grice, H. P. 1961. "The Causal Theory of Perception." *Proceedings of the Aristotelian Society,* suppl. 35: 121–68.

Grice, H. P. 1989. *Studies in the Way of Words.* Cambridge, MA: Harvard University Press.

Gulker, Jill E., Aimee Y. Mark, and Margo J. Monteith. 2013. "Confronting Prejudice: The Who, What, and Why of Confrontation Effectiveness." *Social Influence* 8 (4): 280–93. https://doi.org/10.1080/15534510.2012.736879.

Hall, Sarah. 2000. "Tory Apologises for Racist Joke." *The Guardian*, December 21. http://www.guardian.co.uk/uk/2000/dec/21/race.conservatives.

"Harmless." n.d. Cambridge English Dictionary. Accessed June 30, 2022. https://dictionary.cambridge.org/us/dictionary/english/harmless.

Harris, Daniel W., Daniel Fogal, and Matt Moss. 2018. "Speech Acts: The Contemporary Theoretical Landscape." In *New Work on Speech Acts*, edited by Daniel Fogal, Daniel W. Harris, and Matt Moss, 1–39. Oxford: Oxford University Press.

Harvins, Cassandra Byers. 1996. "Conversations I Can't Have." *On the Issues: The Progressive Woman's Quarterly*, 5 (2): 15–16.

Haslanger, Sally. 2004. "Oppressions: Racial and Others." In *Racism in Mind*, edited by Michael P. Levine and Tamas Pataki, 97–123. Ithaca, NY: Cornell University Press.

Hedger, Joseph A. 2012. "The Semantics of Racial Slurs: Using Kaplan's Framework to Provide a Theory of the Meaning of Derogatory Epithets." *Linguistic & Philosophical Investigations* 11 (January): 74–84.

Henderson v. Irving Materials, Inc. 2004, 329 F. Supp. 2d 1002. Dist. Court.

Herndon, Ray F. 1990. "Race Tilts the Scales of Justice." *Dallas Times Herald*, August 19.

Hickman, Mary, and Bronwen Walter. 1997. *Discrimination and the Irish Community in Britain: A Report of Research Undertaken for the Commission for Racial Equality.* 2nd edition. London: Commission for Racial Equality.

Hodson, Gordon, Jonathan Rush, and Cara MacInnis. 2010. "A Joke Is Just a Joke (Except When It Isn't): Cavalier Humor Beliefs Facilitate the Expression of Group Dominance Motives." *Journal of Personality and Social Psychology* 99 (4): 660–82. https://doi.org/10.1037/a0019627.

Horisk, Claire. 2021. "Can McGowan Explain Hepeating?" *Res Philosophica* 98 (3): 519–27. https://doi.org/10.11612/resphil.2059.

Hornsby, Jennifer. 2001. "Meaning and Uselessness: How to Think about Derogatory Words." *Midwest Studies in Philosophy* 25 (1): 128–41. https://doi.org/10.1111/1475-4975.00042.

Hughes, Melissa K. 2002. "Through the Looking Glass: Racial Jokes, Social Context, and the Reasonable Person in Hostile Work Environment Analysis." *Southern California Law Review* 76: 1437–82.

Isen, Alice, Thomas Nygren, and F. Ashby. 1988. "Influence of Positive Affect on the Subjective Utility of Gains and Losses: It Is Just Not Worth the Risk." *Journal of Personality and Social Psychology* 55 (December): 710–17. https://doi.org/10.1037//0022-3514.55.5.710.

Jender. 2010. "But the Women Never Say Anything Interesting." *What Is It Like to Be a Woman in Philosophy?* (blog), October 29. https://beingawomaninphilosophy.wordpress.com/2010/10/29/but-the-women-never-say-anything-interesting/.

Jiang, Tonglin, Hao Li, and Yubo Hou. 2019. "Cultural Differences in Humor Perception, Usage, and Implications." *Frontiers in Psychology* 10: 123. https://doi.org/10.3389/fpsyg.2019.00123.

"Joke." n.d.-a. Cambridge English Dictionary. Accessed June 27, 2022. https://dictionary.cambridge.org/us/dictionary/english/joke.

"Joke." n.d.-b. Collins COBUILD Advanced English Dictionary. Accessed June 27, 2022. https://www.collinsdictionary.com/us/dictionary/english/joke.

Jokes of the Day. n.d. "An Irishman and an Englishman Walk into a Bakery." Accessed October 27, 2022. https://jokesoftheday.com/irishman-englishman-walk-bakery/.

"Joke, v." 2022. Oxford English Dictionary Online. http://www.oed.com/view/Entry/101580.

Judge, Timothy A., and Daniel M. Cable. 2004. "The Effect of Physical Height on Workplace Success and Income: Preliminary Test of a Theoretical Model." *Journal of Applied Psychology* 89 (3): 428–41. https://doi.org/10.1037/0021-9010.89.3.428.

Kacala, Alexandra. 2021. "Biden Promises Appointees He Will Fire Them 'on the Spot' If They Disrespect Others." *Today*, January 20, 2021. https://www.today.com/news/biden-promises-appointees-he-will-fire-them-spot-if-they-t206392.

Kahneman, Daniel. 2011. *Thinking, Fast and Slow*. New York: Farrar, Straus and Giroux.

Kawakami, Kerry, Francine Karmali, and Elysia Vaccarino. 2019. "Confronting Intergroup Bias: Predicted and Actual Responses to Racism and Sexism." In *Confronting Prejudice and Discrimination: The Science of Changing Minds and Behaviors*, edited by Robyn K. Mallett and Margo J. Monteith, 3–28. London and San Diego, CA: Academic Press. https://doi.org/10.1016/B978-0-12-814715-3.00001-1.

Klages, Stephanie V., and James H. Wirth. 2014. "Excluded by Laughter: Laughing Until It Hurts Someone Else." *The Journal of Social Psychology* 154 (1): 8–13. https://doi.org/10.1080/00224545.2013.843502.

Kleiman, Mark. 2010. "Concerning Jew-Jokes." The Reality-Based Community: Everyone Is Entitled to His Own Opinion, but Not His Own Facts. April. http://www.samefacts.com/2010/04/humor/concerning-jew-jokes/.   https://web.archive.org/web/20100428055503/https://www.samefacts.com/.

Koval, Christy Zhou, and Ashleigh Shelby Rosette. 2021. "The Natural Hair Bias in Job Recruitment." *Social Psychological and Personality Science* 12 (5): 741–50. https://doi.org/10.1177/1948550620937937.

Kripke, Saul A. 2009. "Presupposition and Anaphora: Remarks on the Formulation of the Projection Problem." *Linguistic Inquiry* 40 (3): 367–86. http://www.jstor.org/stable/40284322.

Kukla, Rebecca. 2014. "Performative Force, Convention, and Discursive Injustice." *Hypatia* 29 (2): 440–57. https://doi.org/10.1111/j.1527-2001.2012.01316.x.

Kukla, Rebecca, and Mark Norris Lance. 2009. *"Yo!" and "Lo!": The Pragmatic Topography of the Space of Reasons.* Cambridge, MA: Harvard University Press.

La Fave, L. 1972. "Humor Judgments as a Function of Reference Groups and Identification Classes." *Psychology of Humor,* edited by Jeffrey H. Goldstein and Paul E. McGhee, 195–210. New York and London: Academic Press.

LaFollette, Hugh, and Niall Shanks. 1993. "Belief and the Basis of Humor." *American Philosophical Quarterly* 30 (4): 329–39.

Langton, Rae. 1993. "Speech Acts and Unspeakable Acts." *Philosophy & Public Affairs* 22 (4): 293–330. http://www.jstor.org/stable/2265469.

Langton, Rae. 2012. "Beyond Belief: Pragmatics in Hate Speech and Pornography." In *Speech and Harm: Controversies over Free Speech,* edited by Ishani Maitra and Mary Kate McGowan, 72–93. Oxford: Oxford University Press.

Langton, Rae. 2018. "Blocking as Counter-Speech." In *New Work on Speech Acts,* edited by Daniel Fogal, Daniel W. Harris, and Matt Moss, 144–64. Oxford: Oxford University Press.

Langton, Rae, and Caroline West. 1999. "Scorekeeping in a Pornographic Language Game." *Australasian Journal of Philosophy* 77 (3): 303–19.

Lawson, Timothy J., Tracy A. McDonough, and James H. Bodle. 2010. "Confronting Prejudiced Comments: Effectiveness of a Role-Playing Exercise." *Teaching of Psychology* 37 (4): 257–61. https://doi.org/10.1080/00986283.2010.510968.

Lehmann, Michael, dir. 1989. *Heathers.* New World Pictures, Cinemarque Entertainment.

Levinson, Stephen C. 1995. "Three Levels of Meaning." In *Grammar and Meaning: Essays in Honour of Sir John Lyons,* edited by F. R. Palmer, 90–115. Cambridge: Cambridge University Press.

Levinson, Stephen C., and Francisco Torreira. 2015. "Timing in Turn-Taking and Its Implications for Processing Models of Language." *Frontiers in Psychology* 6: 731. https://doi.org/10.3389/fpsyg.2015.00731.

Lewis, David. 1979. "Scorekeeping in a Language Game." *Journal of Philosophical Logic* 8 (1): 339–59. https://doi.org/10.1007/BF00258436.

Lycan, William G. 2020. "Humor and Morality." *American Philosophical Quarterly* 57 (3): 253–68. https://doi.org/10.2307/48574437.

MacKinnon, Catharine A. 1988. *Feminism Unmodified: Discourses on Life and Law.* Cambridge, MA: Harvard University Press. https://www.hup.harvard.edu/catalog.php?isbn=9780674298743.

Maher, Bill. 2012. "Please Stop Apologizing." *New York Times,* March 22. http://www.nytimes.com/2012/03/22/opinion/please-stop-apologizing.html?_r=1.

Maitra, Ishani. 2012. "Subordinating Speech." In *Speech and Harm: Controversies over Free Speech,* edited by Ishani Maitra and Mary Kate McGowan, 94–120. Oxford: Oxford University Press.

Mallett, Robyn K., Thomas E. Ford, and Julie A. Woodzicka. 2021. "Ignoring Sexism Increases Women's Tolerance of Sexual Harassment." *Self and Identity* 20 (7): 913–29. https://doi.org/10.1080/15298868.2019.1678519.

Mann, Liesbeth, Allard R. Feddes, Anne Leiser, Bertjan Doosje, and Agneta H. Fischer. 2017. "When Is Humiliation More Intense? The Role of Audience Laughter and Threats to the Self." *Frontiers in Psychology* 8. https://www.frontiersin.org/article/10.3389/fpsyg.2017.00495.

Manne, Kate. 2017. *Down Girl: The Logic of Misogyny.* New York: Oxford University Press.

"Many a True Word Is Spoken in Jest." n.d. Cambridge English Dictionary. Accessed June 23, 2022. https://dictionary.cambridge.org/us/dictionary/english/many-a-true-word-is-spoken-in-jest.

McDowell, Edwin. 1983. "Ethnic Jokebooks Flourish Despite Criticism." *New York Times*, July 30. http://www.nytimes.com/1983/07/30/books/ethnic-jokebooks-flourish-desp ite-criticism.html.

McGowan, Mary Kate. 2019. *Just Words: On Speech and Hidden Harm*. Oxford: Oxford University Press.

McGowan, Michael. 2018. "Trevor Noah Responds to Boycott Calls over Racist Joke about Aboriginal Women." *The Guardian*, July 23. https://www.theguardian.com/cult ure/2018/jul/23/trevor-noah-responds-to-boycott-calls-over-racist-joke-about-abo riginal-women.

McGrath, Sarah. 2005. "Causation by Omission: A Dilemma." *Philosophical Studies: An International Journal for Philosophy in the Analytic Tradition* 123 (1–2): 125–48. https:// www.jstor.org/stable/4321576.

Melnikoff, David E., and John A. Bargh. 2018. "The Mythical Number Two." *Trends in Cognitive Sciences* 22 (4): 280–93. https://doi.org/10.1016/j.tics.2018.02.001.

Mirza, Shazia. 2016. "Why It's OK to Laugh about ISIS." Zócalo Public Square, September 19. https://www.zocalopublicsquare.org/2016/09/19/ok-laugh-isis/ideas/nexus/.

Mitchell, Margaret. 1936. *Gone with the Wind*. New York: Macmillan.

Mobbs, Dean, Michael D. Greicius, Eiman Abdel-Azim, Vinod Menon, and Allan L. Reiss. 2003. "Humor Modulates the Mesolimbic Reward Centers." *Neuron* 40 (5): 1041–48. https://doi.org/10.1016/S0896-6273(03)00751-7.

Monteith, Margo J., Mason D. Burns, and Laura L. Hildebrand. 2019. "Navigating Successful Confrontations: What Should I Say and How Should I Say It?" In *Confronting Prejudice and Discrimination: The Science of Changing Minds and Behaviors*, edited by Robyn K. Mallett and Margo J. Monteith, 225–48. London and San Diego, CA: Academic Press. https://doi.org/10.1016/B978-0-12-814715-3.00006-0.

Moore v. Kuka Welding Systems. 1999, 171 F.3d 1073. 9th Cir.

Moore, Jeff, Eugene Waters, Mary Tilki, and Lisa Clarke. 2012. "Fresh Perspectives: A Needs Analysis of the Irish Community in London." London Irish Centre. https://www. irishinbritain.org/assets/files/publications/fresh-perspectives-final-web.pdf.

Murray, Douglas. 2010. "Why Can't Anyone Take a Joke Any More?" *The Spectator*, August 14. https://www.spectator.co.uk/article/why-can-t-anyone-take-a-joke-any-more/.

Nichols, Michael P., and Martha B. Straus. 2021. *The Lost Art of Listening: How Learning to Listen Can Improve Relationships*. 3rd edition. New York: Guilford Press.

Notess, Susan E. 2019. "Listening to People: Using Social Psychology to Spotlight an Overlooked Virtue." *Philosophy* 94 (4): 621–43. https://doi.org/10.1017/S003181911 8000529.

Nunberg, Geoff. 2018. "The Social Life of Slurs." In *New Work on Speech Acts*, edited by Daniel Fogal, Daniel W. Harris, and Matt Moss, 237–295. New York: Oxford University Press. https://doi.org/10.1093/oso/9780198738831.003.0010.

"Offensive." n.d. Cambridge English Dictionary. Accessed June 30, 2022. https://diction ary.cambridge.org/us/dictionary/english/offensive.

Oncale v. Sundowner Offshore Services, Inc., 1998, 523 US Reports 75.

Ong, Wei Jee, Kai Chi Yam, and Christopher M. Barnes. 2022. "Moral Evaluations of Humor Apply beyond Just Those Telling the Joke." *Social Cognition* 40 (1): 107–26. https://doi.org/10.1521/soco.2022.40.1.107.

Otten, Marte, Liesbeth Mann, Jos J. A. van Berkum, and Kai J. Jonas. 2017. "No Laughing Matter: How the Presence of Laughing Witnesses Changes the Perception of Insults." *Social Neuroscience* 12 (2): 182–93. https://doi.org/10.1080/17470919.2016.1162194.

Parker, Laura R., Margo J. Monteith, Corinne A. Moss-Racusin, and Amanda R. Van Camp. 2018. "Promoting Concern about Gender Bias with Evidence-Based Confrontation." *Journal of Experimental Social Psychology* 74 (January): 8–23. https://doi.org/10.1016/j.jesp.2017.07.009.

Petri, Alexandra. 2012. "In Defense of Foster Friess's Aspirin Joke." *Washington Post*, February 17. http://www.washingtonpost.com/blogs/compost/post/in-defense-of-foster-friesss-aspirin-joke/2012/02/17/gIQA6K7XKR_blog.html.

Plester, Barbara. 2016. *The Complexity of Workplace Humour: Laughter, Jokers and the Dark Side of Humour*. Cham: Springer.

Priest, R. F. 1966. "Election Jokes: The Effects of Reference Group Membership." *Psychological Reports* 18 (2): 600–602. https://doi.org/10.2466/pr0.1966.18.2.600.

Psaki, Jen. 2021. "Press Briefing by Press Secretary Jen Psaki." Press Release. The White House, January 21. https://www.whitehouse.gov/briefing-room/press-briefings/2021/01/21/press-briefing-by-press-secretary-jen-psaki-january-21-2021/.

Rasinski, Heather M., and Alexander M. Czopp. 2010. "The Effect of Target Status on Witnesses' Reactions to Confrontations of Bias." *Basic and Applied Social Psychology* 32 (1): 8–16. https://doi.org/10.1080/01973530903539754.

Roberts, Craige. 2015. "Accommodation in a Language Game." In *A Companion to David Lewis*, edited by Barry Loewer and Jonathan Schaffer, 345–66. Chichester: John Wiley & Sons. https://onlinelibrary.wiley.com/doi/10.1002/9781118398593.ch22.

Robinson, Lawrence, Jeanne Segal, and Melinda Smith. 2020. "Managing Conflict with Humor." Help Guide, December. https://www.helpguide.org/articles/relationships-communication/managing-conflicts-with-humor.htm.

Roux, Mathilde. 2021. "5 Facts about Black Women in the Labor Force." US Department of Labor Blog (blog), August 3. https://blog.dol.gov/2021/08/03/5-facts-about-black-women-in-the-labor-force.

Ruch, Willibald, and Sonja Heintz. 2016. "The Virtue Gap in Humor: Exploring Benevolent and Corrective Humor." *Translational Issues in Psychological Science* 2 (1): 35–45. https://doi.org/10.1037/tps0000063.

Ryan, Kathryn M., and Jeanne Kanjorski. 1998. "The Enjoyment of Sexist Humor, Rape Attitudes, and Relationship Aggression in College Students." *Sex Roles* 38 (9): 743–56. https://doi.org/10.1023/a:1018868913615.

Saucier, Donald A., Conor J. O'Dea, and Megan L. Strain. 2016. "The Bad, the Good, the Misunderstood: The Social Effects of Racial Humor." *Translational Issues in Psychological Science* 2 (1): 75–85. https://doi.org/10.1037/tps0000059.

Sartorio, Carolina. 2005. "A New Asymmetry between Actions and Omissions." *Noûs* 39 (3): 460–82. http://www.jstor.org/stable/3506238.

Saul, Jennifer. 2002. "Speaker Meaning, What Is Said, and What Is Implicated." *Noûs* 36 (2): 228–48. https://doi.org/10.1111/1468-0068.00369.

Saul, Jennifer. 2018. "Dogwhistles, Political Manipulation, and Philosophy of Language." In *New Work on Speech Acts*, edited by Daniel Fogal, Daniel W. Harris, and Matt Moss, 360–83. Oxford: Oxford University Press.

Schmidt, Samuel. 2014. *Seriously Funny: Mexican Political Jokes as Social Resistance.* Tucson: University of Arizona Press.

Searle, John. 1965. "What Is a Speech Act?" In *Philosophy in America*, edited by Max Black, 221–39. Ithaca, NY: Cornell University Press.

Shaw, Bernard. 1907. "John Bull's Other Island." In *John Bull's Other Island and Major Barbara*, 1–126. New York: Trow Press. https://books.google.com/books?id=JTsWA AAAYAAJ.

Shaw, George Bernard. (1916) 2003. *Pygmalion*, edited by Dan H. Laurence. London: Penguin Books.

Simon, Stefanie, and Laurie T. O'Brien. 2015. "Confronting Sexism: Exploring the Effect of Nonsexist Credentials on the Costs of Target Confrontations." *Sex Roles: A Journal of Research* 73 (5–6): 245–57. https://doi.org/10.1007/s11199-015-0513-x.

Smith v. Northwest Financial Acceptance, Inc. 1997, 129 F.3d 1408. 10th Cir.

Stalnaker, Robert. 2002. "Common Ground." *Linguistics and Philosophy* 25 (5): 701–21. https://doi.org/10.1023/A:1020867916902.

Stalnaker, Robert. 2014. *Context.* Oxford: Oxford University Press. https://doi.org/ 10.1093/acprof:oso/9780199645169.001.0001.

Stanley, Jason. 2016. *How Propaganda Works.* Princeton, NJ: Princeton University Press.

Stohr, Karen. 2012. *On Manners: Thinking in Action.* New York: Routledge.

Stone, Jeff, Jessica Whitehead, Toni Schmader, and Elizabeth Focella. 2011. "Thanks for Asking: Self-Affirming Questions Reduce Backlash When Stigmatized Targets Confront Prejudice." *Journal of Experimental Social Psychology* 47 (3): 589–98. https:// doi.org/10.1016/j.jesp.2010.12.016.

Sue, Derald Wing. 2015. *Race Talk and the Conspiracy of Silence: Understanding and Facilitating Difficult Dialogues on Race.* Hoboken, NJ: John Wiley & Sons.

Swanson, Eric. 2022. "Channels for Common Ground." *Philosophy and Phenomenological Research* 104 (1): 171–85. https://doi.org/10.1111/phpr.12741.

Swinton v. Potomac Corporation. 2001, 270 F.3d 794. 9th Cir.

Thomae, Manuela, and Afroditi Pina. 2015. "Sexist Humor and Social Identity: The Role of Sexist Humor in Men's In-Group Cohesion, Sexual Harassment, Rape Proclivity, and Victim Blame." *Humor* 28 (2): 187–204. http://dx.doi.org/10.1515/humor-2015-0023.

Thomas, Caroline, and Victoria Esses. 2004. "Individual Differences in Reactions to Sexist Humor." *Group Processes & Intergroup Relations* 7 (1): 89–100.

Truss, Lynne. 2003. *Eats, Shoots & Leaves: The Zero Tolerance Approach to Punctuation.* London: Profile Books.

Tsioulcas, Anastasia. 2022. "Jada Pinkett Smith's Hair Loss, Noted at the Oscars, Is a Struggle for Many Women." NPR, March 28. https://www.npr.org/2022/03/28/108 9133964/whats-behind-the-slap-will-smith-gave-chris-rock-at-the-oscars.

Turner, Karl. 2007. "Don Imus Transcript." *Cleveland.com*, April 12. https://www.clevel and.com/pdextra/2007/04/don_imus_transcript.html.

Tversky, Amos, and Daniel Kahneman. 1983. "Extensional versus Intuitive Reasoning: The Conjunction Fallacy in Probability Judgment." *Psychological Review* 90 (4): 293–315. https://doi.org/10.1037/0033-295X.90.4.293.

US Department of Justice, Office for Victims of Crime. 2014. "Responding to Transgender Victims of Sexual Assault." June. Accessed April 22, 2022. https://ovc.ojp.gov/sites/g/ files/xyckuh226/files/pubs/forge/sexual_numbers.html.

Von Fintel, K. 2008. "What Is Presupposition Accommodation, Again." *Philosophical Perspectives* 22 (1): 137–70.

Waters, Mark, dir. 2004. *Mean Girls*. Paramount Pictures. https://www.imdb.com/title/tt0377092/.

Watkins, Mel. 1999. *On the Real Side: A History of African American Comedy*. 2nd edition. Chicago: Chicago Review Press.

Watt, Nicholas. 2002. "How a Racist Joke Became No Laughing Matter for Ann Winterton." *The Guardian*, May 6. http://www.guardian.co.uk/uk/2002/may/06/race.conservatives.

Willsey, Alek. 2021. "Authoritatively Speaking: A Speech Pragmatic Analysis of Authority and Power." PhD dissertation, University of Missouri, Columbia. https://doi.org/10.32469/10355/85825.

Wiseman, Rosalind. 2016. *Queen Bees and Wannabes: Helping Your Daughter Survive Cliques, Gossip, Boyfriends, and the New Realities of Girl World*. 3rd edition. New York: Harmony.

Witt v. Roadway Express. 1998, 136 F.3d 1424. 3rd Cir.

Woodzicka, Julie A., and Marianne LaFrance. 2001. "Real versus Imagined Gender Harassment." *Journal of Social Issues* 57 (1): 15–30. https://doi.org/10.1111/0022-4537.00199.

Young, Dannagal Goldthwaite. 2008. "The Privileged Role of the Late-Night Joke: Exploring Humor's Role in Disrupting Argument Scrutiny." *Media Psychology* 11 (1): 119–42. https://doi.org/10.1080/15213260701837073.

Young, Iris Marion. 1990. *Justice and the Politics of Difference*. Princeton, NJ: Princeton University Press.

Ziff, Paul. 1967. "On H. P. Grice's Account of Meaning." *Analysis* 28 (1): 1–8. https://doi.org/10.2307/3327605.

Index

For the benefit of digital users, indexed terms that span two pages (e.g., 52–53) may, on occasion, appear on only one of those pages.